THE ALTITUDE JOURNALS

THE

ALTITUDE

JOURNALS

A SEVEN-YEAR JOURNEY FROM THE LOWEST POINT
IN MY LIFE TO THE HIGHEST POINT ON EARTH

DAVID J. MAURO

PLAID VERMIN
PUBLISHING

Cover design by Michael Nagin.

THE ALTITUDE JOURNALS

A Seven-Year Journey from the Lowest Point in
My Life to the Highest Point on Earth

ISBN   978-1-5445-0049-2 *Paperback*

978-1-5445-0050-8 *Ebook*

978-1-5445-0061-4 *Audiobook*

This book is dedicated to Lin. I have heard it said that love lifts us up. Lin's love lifted me all the way to the top of the planet. I am infinitely grateful to Lin and the forces that brought her into my life; online dating, positivity, and a sympathetic resonance for all things silly.

CONTENTS

PROLOGUE

PEOPLE ASK ME WHY I DID IT. THEY WANT TO KNOW WHY
I chose to risk my life so many times, why, at age forty-four,
after living a comfortable, safe life as a financial planner, I
suddenly declared myself a mountain climber and took on
the highest summit of each continent—the Seven Summits.
Only sixty-five Americans have survived this quest. I am
the sixty-fifth.

I get this "why" question all the time, when I'm speaking at gatherings or just walking down the street. But the
answer is too complicated to even make a run at it. Could I
explain about the Grand Wager without sounding insane?
And what about the mad obsession, the personal demons,
the calling, and the glory that passed through me with the
resonance of pure love as I stood on each summit? Would
anyone understand the essential part that performance
improv played in this quest? I certainly could not mention
the voice. Nope. People who hear voices end up featured

in unflattering headlines. So when people ask me why, I just tell them, "It's a long answer. Maybe someday we can grab a beer and I'll tell you all about it." I never have.

The truth is that most of the time I was on this journey, I did not know why I was doing it. Though I am not a religious person, I am spiritual. I believe life has laid out an incredible path for each of us, and when we quiet our minds, it is revealed one stone at a time. I didn't know where this path was heading and often hoped it would be a beach instead of a frozen peak in air so thin my brain couldn't manage simple math. But it was always another mountain, in some far-off place where getting there was sometimes more dangerous than the climb itself. So I went, even though it made no sense, trusting that some greater purpose was being served and that one day it would all ring true. It has.

Though I now understand the meaning behind this seven-year period of my life, my "why" answer remains long and complicated. Books are a good place for "long and complicated." So, in November 2013, I sat down and began writing. Something very special had taken place in my life, and I felt I owed a debt, a debt that could only be satisfied in sharing my experience. I have changed the names of anyone who appears in this story in a negative light. As well, I have changed the name of any individual for whom I have not been granted permission to use their real name...though they are probably good and decent people.

THIS IS HOW IT STARTS

I was an Olympic hopeful for a short while in my youth. I was going to represent the United States in ax throwing. This notion came to me shortly after throwing an ax at a stump and having it stick. What are the chances of that just happening? I wondered. It had to be skill! I was one of the lucky ones, blessed at birth with projectile Zen. It was 1972, and the summer games were taking place in Munich. Even at the age of ten, I could not help being swept up in the fanfare and national pride as we watched the Olympics on TV. Yes, ax throwing was not a featured sport. But by the time I hit my prime, I reasoned, it probably would be.

I pledged myself to a rigorous training regimen consisting of ax throwing and the consumption of saltine crackers adorned with mayonnaise. But the ax stuck less and less as the day wore on. Eventually, I was missing the stump altogether. I had peaked. Lamenting the short-lived nature of athletic careers, I retired from ax throwing the same day I had taken it up then spent the remainder of that afternoon trying to imagine some other means by which I could represent my country while consuming crackers laden with condiments. What else was a chubby kid to do?

Baseball had not worked out. The sound of the ball cutting through the air as it sped toward me in the batter's box prompted an almost immediate emptying of my bladder. Danny, my older brother by two years, was an excellent baseball player. Fast, fearless, and batting five hundred, he was typically the first selection coaches made when assembling a Little League team. I always felt bad for these coaches when they later wasted an early draft pic on me. They assumed I would have similar abilities to Danny, but soon learned that I just liked wearing the uniform.

I tried out for basketball, soccer, and boys' choir, just looking for somewhere I might fit in, but failed to make the cut in each. Oddly, it is my recollection that slow foot speed was cited in all three cases. So I turned to sports of my own making, contests I always won by virtue of having no competitor. There was a don't-step-on-any-cracks marathon that lasted an entire day, a golf-like game played with a basketball and a bat, and a challenge to see how long I could hold my breath without anyone noticing.

My father had disappeared the year before. One day he packed up his new family, the family he had married into shortly after my mother divorced him in 1968, and moved away. There was no warning or forwarding address, and likewise no child support.

The grocery store had started coming to us soon after my father vanished. Pleasant strangers holding bags of food would show up at our door unannounced. I never saw my mother pay them money, but it seemed like she returned the favor by listening while they talked about God. When we did go to the store, our money looked very different from other people's. It was colorful and crisp. My mother said this was because we were special. I believed her, partly because this also explained why the lady who ran the cash register at the school lunch line just waved me by.

My mother was an attractive woman, so men took notice. But she never brought them around, fearful that we kids might get our hopes up for having a stepfather. She eventually married one suitor, Jack, a good-humored general contractor who loved us and provided me with a model of what it meant to be a good man. By then, I had come to understand the truth of our poverty, but had not stopped believing we were special. Jack coming into our lives was proof of it.

I continued to try my hand at various sports in middle and high school, displaying an explosive mediocrity in track, swimming, tennis, and football. Though no longer chubby, I was not particularly fast, strong, or tall. My football coach put me on the team our varsity squad practiced against. Too injured to play by the time Friday arrived, I was allowed to suit up out of recognition for my personal sacrifice. Again, I found myself engaged in a pursuit for the love of wearing its uniform.

By the time I started college, my biological father, Don, had returned to Washington State from where he had been hiding in Lima, Ohio, all those years. Child support authorities had tracked him down there, and since he was now required to make payments, there was not much sense in hiding. Soon after putting the last of his entitled and orthodonically challenged stepchildren through college,

Don's second wife ran off to Florida with a dentist. The children he raised had no use for him. Alone and lonely, Don reached out to me. Though I still could not forgive my father for his abandonment, some part of me at least wanted to. So, Don and I began a cautious relationship.

I graduated from college, and in 1989 I married Jenny. We had met while working in Alaska during the summers. Jenny and I moved about eighty miles north from Seattle to Bellingham when I was hired by Merrill Lynch. We bought our first home a few years later, a simple log house heated by a woodburning stove. We had chickens and cows and dogs and cats. I hunted and fished. Jenny tended a small vegetable garden. Still in the lean early years of my career, money was tight. But we got by just fine. Our first son, Trevor, was born in March 1992. Then his brother, Chase, came along in November 1993. In summertime, I would drag our boys through the dry grass on a plastic tarp as they laughed and screamed, falling off then diving to get back on their "magic carpet." We were happy.

We traded up to bigger and nicer homes as greater prosperity came to my career, eventually purchasing a waterfront residence on Bellingham's Lake Samish. Our family enjoyed lavish travel, new cars, and all the other trappings of success. Yet something was wrong.

Jenny and I had disagreed, but never cursed at one another. We had argued, but never in front of the boys. We had gone through periods of disillusionment, yet remained faithful. But for all of this civility, it was clear we had fallen out of love. We were growing in different directions and resented each other for their part in this. Several months of marriage counseling failed to make any headway. Then, on September 22, 2006, Jenny told me she was leaving. I felt relieved. Finally, one of us had found the courage to end it. But Jenny retracted her statement the next morning. We did not speak again until two days later, when I announced I was leaving. It felt like we had walked out a door together, and I could not walk back in. I packed a bag and moved in with my sister, Michelle. A few weeks later, on my forty-fourth birthday, I sat on the edge of the futon in her guest room regarding the disaster my life had become. The walls all around me were lined with dolls arranged on multilevel shelves, the excess possessions of Michelle's daughter, Brooke. Some dolls were going to the ball, others the beach. A few celebrated their native heritage. All had stopped in their tracks, I imagined, as the news spread among them of my split with Jenny. None spoke. They did not need to. Their sad judging expressions said what they were thinking. I was a failure at marriage, just like my father.

My clothing was arranged on the floor, folded, and stacked in orderly towers. A photo of my boys lay loosely on the nightstand. The only other possession I had taken with me was my brother's shotgun. It became mine when he died of alcoholism eight years earlier. The whole family had fought like hell to save Danny. There were rehabs and pleas, passing victories and crushing disappointments. I had done all I could for Danny, and it was not enough. I looked at the dolls again. They somehow knew about this too. I had failed to save my only brother.

"Fuck you," I said to the dolls.

Divorce is just the final destination in a long road trip of unbelieving, its route crossing rivers and mountain ranges, zigzagging randomly and pausing for occasional breakdowns. You litter each rest stop with the wrappers of what you once held as truth: love is forever. I can make her happy. She believes in me. I believe in her. I believe in us. And finally, the last wrapper to be cast off: I believe in me.

A cardboard tube, addressed to me, had arrived in the mail that day, a birthday gift from my sister, Noelle, and her husband, Ty, in Anchorage, Alaska.

Ty had worked for several years as an evening news anchor for the ABC affiliate in Anchorage. In 1999, he filmed a documentary detailing his team's attempt to climb Mount McKinley (Denali), the high summit for North America (20,320 feet). He won an Emmy for the piece. Television began transitioning to high definition a few years later, but almost nothing had been filmed in HD. So in the spring of 2006, Ty decided he would produce a follow-up documentary one year hence, again attempting Denali, but this time filming in high definition. He assembled a team of strong climbers, firemen from Kenai,

Alaska. But Ty also wanted a few nonclimbers on the team for the human interest and fresh perspective they would bring to the story line.

About five months prior to Jenny and I separating, Ty called to ask if I would be interested. "I wouldn't even invite you if I didn't think you could do it," he said.

"But I'm not even a mountain climber," I said. "And things are not good between Jenny and me right now. There's no way she would support it."

"Well, just think about it. It's a year away," he said.

I did think about it. Though I never seriously considered joining the climb, it made me feel good that Ty had thought enough of me to offer. During the final tumultuous weeks of my marriage, I hid often within the fantasy of climbing Denali. At one point, I made the mistake of mentioning the invitation to Jenny. In the simplest of language, she confirmed my suspicion she would not support my going, then asked, "Do you really think you could do it?" The doubt in her voice stung, even though there was no reasonable basis for believing I could stand atop Denali.

I removed one end of the cardboard tube and poured out its contents. Two climbing poles fell to the floor. The enclosed note read, "Happy birthday, Super Climber!" In other words, "Your wife holding you back is no longer a problem, so how about it?" I still did not believe I could make it to the top of Denali, but I felt certain my life was at a low enough point that failing would not bother me much. I realize now that a person who believes he has nothing left to lose is a fantastic and dangerous soul. But at that point, I was focused on Ty's belief in me. It felt like the one good thing I could hold onto, and the notion hatched that if I could make it to the pinnacle of North America, I might come to believe in myself again, the way Ty believed in me. By climbing standards, it was probably the worst rationale a person could choose for taking on the continent's most dangerous mountain. But in that moment, I decided I would accept the challenge, and in so doing, set my life on a path through forests and wastelands, over glaciers and clouds, beside cannibals and penguins, and in the company of elephants and gun runners. Over the next seven years, I would speak with the dead, fall in love again, and come to know the greater purpose of my life.

DENALI

REGRET

I CALLED TY THE NEXT DAY AND TOLD HIM I WAS GOING
on the climb. Then I purchased several books about Denali
and was horrified by what I had committed to. There was a
photo of one climber whose beard and face were so caked
with ice that he was breathing through a frozen hole the
size of a half-dollar. Frostbite is common on Denali during
the *warm* part of the year when expeditions attempt the
mountain (May through June). Temperatures at the higher
camps can dip regularly to −30°F. As well, the extensive
glacier travel required on the mountain's lower flanks
exposes climbers to crevasse falls, which take several lives
each year. But the most troubling aspect of what I learned
related to altitude.

Three conditions typically result when a human fails
to properly acclimatize to high altitude. The first is acute

mountain sickness (AMS). An intense headache, nausea, and weakness typify this affliction, sending the clear message that the climber should not yet proceed higher or perhaps should descend. The second condition is high-altitude pulmonary edema (HAPE), where excess fluid accumulates in the lungs, impairing breathing. Lastly, there's high-altitude cerebral edema (HACE), another common side effect where the brain swells with fluid. In the absence of swift treatment, the last two conditions are fatal. Climbers can do many things to improve their prospects of successful acclimation, but in the end, it will all be for naught if they lack the genetic predisposition for the complete respiratory overhaul that high-altitude climbing demands. Curiously, there is no correlation between a person's ability to acclimatize and their age, fitness, or gender. As well, there is no test one can take ahead of time to determine genetic disposition. In short, climbers must go into high altitude to find out if doing so will kill them.

TRAINING

All this overlays the extraordinary physical demands of climbing Denali. The information I found described shouldering seventy-pound pack loads while simultaneously pulling eighty pounds of provisions in a sled uphill. Peak physical condition was strongly suggested. Though I had belonged to an athletic club for some time, my typical workout was designed for basic fitness. I was going to need help.

I hired a local trainer, who assembled a grueling regiment. Over the months that followed, I came to see how preparing for Denali also helped me cope with my divorce. The demands that training placed on my time left little pause for self-pity. But I gradually succumbed to the ceaseless acrimony of the divorce process and slipped into depression, a condition I had battled off and on my entire adult life.

My doctor wrote a prescription for Prozac and suggested I see a therapist.

DOCTOR FERGUSON

I reconnected with Doctor Ferguson, the therapist Jenny and I saw for marriage counseling. He was an easy choice since he already knew my story and I trusted him. I had seen other therapists at various points in my life and found them to be entirely capable. But there was something special about Doctor Ferguson—his granular voice, wise weathered face, and a squeamishness that surfaced from time to time. I liked that about him. It told me he was genuine, even if it also challenged his professionalism.

I was sleeping little—and troubled by bizarre imagery when I did. One such dream occurred the night before my first postseparation visit with Doctor Ferguson.

"Hey! You're a shrink," I blurted out the next day. "Tell me what this dream means."

"Okay, tell me what you got," he responded with a roll of his eyes.

"I am kissing Phyllis Diller. And not just a peck either. Her crazy white hair is teased straight up. Whenever we part, she makes that crazy cackle of a laugh. But we don't part much because we are mashing! And I am *loving it!*"

A look came over Doctor Ferguson's face as though I had just poured vinegar in his mouth. "That's just *wrong*," he stammered. "I don't even want to fucking *hear* that!" I laughed for the first time in weeks. I laughed so hard my eyes teared. The months of struggle, the depression and isolation, the grieving and self-loathing all poured out of me through those tears as laughter turned to sorrow, and we settled in for the long haul of fixing me.

A NEW HOME

I moved out of my sister's guest room in December 2006, renting a nice apartment big enough for my two sons and me. I woke that first morning to a fresh blanket of snow outside. My mattress was still on the floor. Boxes were stacked in each room. My new life was waiting to be unpacked and assembled. I searched out a cup and a packet of instant coffee then settled onto a box next to the window. The snow was still falling, soothing and peaceful, laying an even sheet across the neighborhood.

My mother, Jack, and Michelle arrived to help me settle in. They all wore smiles and did their best to celebrate my new start. After all the boxes had been unpacked and disposed of, my mom began decorating the apartment for

Christmas. She and Jack had brought several items from their own collection, including decorations I had grown up with.

Michelle and I spent many hours planning my new life during my time with her. It was full of possibility. But we agreed the largest challenge would be the off weeks when my boys lived with their mother. The loneliness could be crippling. So, Michelle brought me a companion that first day, a blue betta fish I named Axel. Relentlessly aggressive, Axel would lunge at the glass whenever I touched a finger to it. I liked this about him. His spirit. His attitude. Over time, Axel came to speak through me, often in a caustic tone, liberally dosed with expletives. He disliked politicians, televangelists, and Jenny. Axel was always hatching some plan to seize control of the world. I would come home from work, and he would immediately ask about our coup in Madagascar. "It is ours," I would answer flatly. To this Axel laughed maniacally, making snorting noises through his tiny fish nose.

There was just one place I felt good throughout this period of my life: the stage at Bellingham's Upfront Theatre. I had been a cast member there for two years, performing live improv four shows a week. The demands of improv required me to clear my mind so completely that I could escape the demons of my day-to-day life for the duration of each eighty-minute show. I counted the hours to each show, anxious to step out of who I was and make people laugh.

THE ICE AX IN THE ROOM

I trained hard over the months that followed and felt my body responding. My clothes fit differently. I stood differently. I was carrying heavier loads up the steep Cedar Lakes Trail where I trained. Each workout was the price of calling myself a Denali climber for another day. I felt good whenever I had this thought and did not want to let it slip away by missing a workout. But I kept my dream private for the most part. The few times I mentioned the climb to others, their reaction belied both doubt and concern.

I started dating. It did not go well. It seemed a universal truth among women that a man in the process of divorce was only looking for sex, had little to offer emotionally, and was simply not worth the trouble. Second dates were rare. Truly, I just wanted someone to watch TV with.

The woman who sold me furniture felt differently. My nice apartment and free-flowing wine made up for the risks. It was not love, but we did share some good times. We had been seeing each other exclusively for four months by the time I left for Denali. Like everyone else around me, she shared her concerns as my departure drew near. "I want to be free to see other people while you are away" is how she expressed them.

I tried to talk to my boys about the climb, but it had come to represent something negative in their minds, another sign their dad had gone nuts. They just walked away when I laid the route map down on the table. I could not blame them. They were dealing with a lot of heavy stuff already. My climb was one more thing. So, we did not talk about it. There might have been an ice ax in one corner of the living room, but no one acknowledged it.

RENDEZVOUS

I arrived in Anchorage on May 26, 2007. My sister Noelle picked my massive gear duffels and me up at the airport. We chatted excitedly as she navigated her comfortable pickup truck through downtown Anchorage traffic. I felt nervous, like someone masquerading as something he was not. My kit seemed more like a collection of props than useful tools.

Our team of nine had already been whittled down to seven when the Park Service denied two members' names on our recreational climbing permit. They had failed the vetting process by claiming to be professional guides leading a climb on Denali, though neither was licensed to do so.

Ty emerged from the house and greeted me as I unloaded my duffels from the back of the truck. "Hey there, Super Climber!" He was followed by three big men, each standing about six foot five.

"This is Big Sam," he said. Powerfully built with a baby face, Sam looked like he could not only pick Denali up and move it to one side, but also whistle a happy tune while doing so. Still nervous, I botched the handshake, and Sam's giant paw closed around my entire hand. We both laughed.

"This is Mark," Ty continued. I focused this time, getting the grip right, but my tiny hand was more passenger than pilot.

"And this is Harris," Ty concluded. John Harris and Ty had been climbing partners for several years. They had successfully summited Denali as a two-man team in 2002 and climbed several other daunting peaks throughout the state. As Ty would be preoccupied with the filming of his documentary, Harris would assume the primary role as team leader for our expedition.

"Good to meet you, Dave," John said enthusiastically. He grabbed my hand with a firm wag. All three were firemen and EMTs from Kenai, Alaska. As well, they were experienced in cold weather climbing and capable of carrying massive loads. Ty could not have done better in choosing them for our team. I felt my confidence lift.

Kirk arrived a few hours later. I was pleased to see he was of average height and build. Like me, Kirk was invited on the climb to play the part of rookie in our documentary. His brother was one of the two climbers who had already dropped out, but Kirk, an attorney from Washington, DC, felt obliged to continue on since he had accepted sponsorship monies from various interested parties. Quiet but friendly, Kirk settled in as we practiced rope work in the front yard.

The last team member to arrive was Greg Heister, a television sportscaster from Spokane, Washington. He and Ty became friends years earlier while they both worked at an Anchorage television station. A charismatic figure, Heister was known for using his celebrity to talk his way out of speeding tickets.

Soon after Greg's arrival, it became clear that something was troubling him. He had spent many months training, bought expensive equipment, and cleared his schedule. But Greg and his wife had learned a few days before he left that they had finally conceived after years of difficulty. She had asked him to stay. Greg felt too committed to do so, but the long plane ride had given him time to think. Greg went through the motions with us at first. He bought several hundred dollars worth of provisions, packed individual ration bags, and purchased the plastic sled he would pull up Denali.

But the next day, Greg called Ty aside and informed him of his decision to drop out. He caught the next flight home, leaving his provisions for us to pick through like crows. We had not even left Anchorage, and our nine-man team was now down to six.

FINAL WARNINGS

Denali Base Camp is situated on the Kahiltna Glacier at an elevation of 7,350 feet. The small single-engine planes that take climbers in and out of camp struggle at that altitude when burdened with two passengers and a tail section full of gear. So pilots gain access through One Shot Pass, a low breach in the surrounding mountains. It is a missing picket in the long skyward fence formed by Denali's foothills. So narrow is One Shot Pass that only one plane can attempt it at a time. I rode curled up in the tiny space behind the pilot, gear packed all around me, while Ty filmed through the windshield from the copilot's seat. We bounced and jolted as the engine worked hard. I saw the lush green lowlands fall away as the world beneath soon gave way to ice. Our pilot, a clean-cut middle-aged man in khakis, offered unsolicited counsel as we slowly gained altitude. "Wounds don't heal up high," I heard him say. I had read about this during my preparations, how the body focused on core functions at high altitude, leaving everything else to fend for itself.

We flew past base camp then banked hard to trace the cul-de-sac shape of the valley's terminus. A soft bump came a moment later as our skis settled upon snow. The pilot helped us unload then lifted off, returning to Talkeetna. Once the remaining members of our team had arrived, we all checked in at the ranger hut. Back in Talkeetna, we had been required to attend a preclimb cautionary lecture featuring graphic photos of black toes and frozen bodies hanging from fixed lines. But the Denali Base Camp ranger was more frank still. "Probe the area of your camp thoroughly for hidden crevasses, and don't leave that area without clipping into a rope. Step outside the probed area unroped, go home in a bag," she cautioned.

Ty and Harris chose an area to make camp while the rest

of us ferried provisions on our sleds. I was surprised to see it was midnight by the time we settled into our sleeping bags. Owing to its northern location, the sun never really sets in Alaska during springtime. It just scoots along the horizon and then starts back up again. But any warmth the sun might have offered is lost while it tracks low. The cold of night was present even when the darkness was not. I burrowed into my forty-below sleeping bag, a chill running up my spine. "It was a good first day, Mr. Mauro," I heard Ty say from the confines of his own bag.

"Yeah. Look at me! I'm a Denali climber," I said with mock pride.

"That's right, Super Climber!"

A ROOKIE START

I woke at five to the roar of our white gas stove. Ty was sitting in the tent doorway scooping fresh fallen snow into a pot that sizzled atop the hot blue flame. It was an early start. We would be crossing several miles of trapdoors: thin snow bridges formed by the wind and frozen solid in the biting cold of night. The entire five-and-a-half-mile route would be slashed horizontally with deep crevasses, some of them visible, others disguised as innocuous flat expanses. There would be no way of knowing whether a bridge would hold a climber's weight, so we would travel in roped teams of three, moving constantly, never trusting the ground we stood upon.

I snaked an arm out of my sleeping bag, pulling our thermometer down from the tent ceiling. It was 20°F. Everything inside the tent was frozen—my harness, my outer layers, my bags of food. Already wearing a thin base layer of silk thermals, I decided to add a medium weight layer of insulation before putting on my protective hard-shell pants and jacket. I pulled each item into the warmth of my sleeping bag to thaw it before putting the garment on. Halfway through this process, I heard the rest of the team taking down the other two tents. I panicked, realizing I was holding up the team. I started putting on frozen clothing, which only made me colder, so I added yet another layer of insulation. I choked down a quick bowl of oatmeal as Ty packed the stove away and then began packing up my gear. The other four team members began taking down our tent as I was still scrambling to gather my things. I heard the rainfly being pulled off, then the tent walls went limp as stakes were removed. I started tossing my things out the tent door expecting to be greeted with peevish expressions, but was surprised to find warm smiles instead. They seemed to understand. This was part of having a rookie on the team. They had all been rookies at one time. There was no point in commenting. The team would not be going anywhere until the entire team was ready. The best use of energy was to aid the slow man.

I was grateful for the grace I had been shown but did not wish to test its limits. From that point on, I would prepare for morning before turning in each night, packing everything but my breakfast and keeping the next day's clothing with me in my sleeping bag.

THE COLD WEATHER PROBLEM: HEAT

We set out from Denali Base Camp in snowshoes, each of us pulling a sled and carrying a pack. Like the other rookie, Kirk, I was positioned in the middle of my three-man team, where my responsibilities consisted mainly of not stepping on the rope that connected us. Ty was leading. Sam was the anchor. The air was still, and the soft puff of our snowshoes beat a hopeful rhythm. Both rope teams paused after thirty minutes to remove their heavy down coats then continued on. By the time we stopped to hydrate an hour later, I was already fatigued and struggling to keep up. I couldn't understand this. Yes, the loads were heavy. My sled held almost ninety pounds. And yes, the packs were heavy. Mine was sixty-five pounds. But I had trained for this, packing similar weight while dragging a tire around on the roads of my neighborhood back home. Too soon we were underway again.

I began sweating as I worked harder. I felt my heart rate rise well above the level I could maintain. My energy plummeted just as we stopped for another break. I pulled off my thick wool hat. My hair was completely soaked with sweat. Not noticing the rest of the team had already traded their warm hats for baseball caps, I put it back on.

I drank half of my water supply for the day as I sat on my pack panting. Both Sam and Ty seemed to be doing just fine. I reasoned this was owing to their prior experience. It was going to be harder for me, and that was all there was to it. We continued on.

After just twenty minutes more, I called out to Ty for another rest. We were halfway to camp one, and I was totally exhausted. Sam walked up to where I lay collapsed in the snow. He looked at me and immediately knew I was severely overheated. "You shouldn't be wearing this still," he commented, removing my hat. "Oh gee," he muttered at the sight of my soaked hair. Sam unzipped my hard-shell coat and counted the three layers of insulation I had put on that morning. "You are *way* overdressed," he said with concern.

The sun had risen, with temperatures following suit. Soon the reflective solar heat would turn the Kahiltna Glacier into a convection oven. We had to be off the glacier by then, or team members would start falling through the weakened snow bridges. Sam helped me dress down to just my silk layer and hard shell on top. He then showed me how to partially unzip the legs on my shell pants to create greater ventilation. I felt substantially improved, but my mistakes had taken a toll. By the time we arrived at camp one, I was completely spent. "I'm gassed," I announced emphatically as I threw off my pack. Too tired to even consider helping set up camp, I sat on my sled full of cargo trying to recover.

"Welcome to an easy day on Denali," Ty said. I knew he was right—but also knew I had learned things that would make the next day better.

THE ICE LOUNGE

We rested the next day, enjoying the carved ice amenities left behind by an earlier expedition. A four-foot-deep pit had been dug with snow bench seats against the walls and an ice island center table for cooking. Though sunny, a biting wind had picked up. But the low relief of our subterranean ice lounge offered shelter where we could talk the day away while drinking hot cocoa.

I learned that Sam had felt out of place in college the same way I had felt out of place through much of my life. One day in his freshman year, he realized he wanted to be a fireman. He dropped out that day and enrolled in a technical program that trained firefighters. Coaching basketball was Sam's other passion. A committed family man, he was already missing his wife and three kids on day two of our expedition.

The air was a chill 23°F when we woke the following morning, but I wore only a base layer and hard shell. Once I started working, it would be enough. In the meantime, I wore my down coat over the top of these layers, planning to take it off just before we set out. Harris came over to check on me as I tied into the rope with Sam and Ty. Ebullient as ever, he slapped me on the back and asked if I felt ready for the day. He seemed reassured by my choice to wear lighter layers. "You wanna leave camp cold," John agreed.

Our packs and sleds were burdened with half-loads. We were making a "carry," taking provisions 3,200 feet up Ski Hill to camp two, then returning to camp one. This would be the only way we could progress up the much steeper terrain now before us, moving our camp in two stages: a carry followed by a move. This would also serve the gradual process of altitude acclimation as our bodies compensated for the thinner air.

JOHN HARRIS AND SAM SATOTHITE. PHOTO BY DAVE MAURO.

The carry to camp two was taxing. I could feel the diminished benefit of each breath as the air grew stingy. Sam watched me struggling and noticed I had stopped taking hydration when we paused. Walking up to where I stood, he removed my water bottle from its holster and handed it to me. "Thanks, coach," I said.

By the time we returned to camp one that evening, I was again exhausted. Still, I was not nearly as wiped out as I had been on that first day. My spirits lifted. The journal entry I made read, "Redeemed!" I was still in the hunt. I expected to fail at some point, but did not want it to be here. If I could make it halfway, I reasoned, I would feel good about what I had accomplished as a rookie.

But the carry had gone poorly for Kirk. He struggled, holding his team back and requiring additional rest breaks. I empathized with him completely. "I'm just glad to see I'm not the only mortal on this team," I told Kirk.

A moment later, Harris called out. "There it is, boys!" We all climbed up out of the ice lounge to snatch our first glimpse of Denali's summit, heretofore obscured by cloud cover. Lining up shoulder to shoulder, we stood like children staring into a Christmas tree. Some twelve thousand feet above us, the top of North America soared beautiful and distant. Just the sight of it scared the hell out of me. No way, I thought. We are going all the way up there? I took a moment to examine the face of each team member as they looked skyward. All were painted with pure elation, save one.

Kirk looked completely demoralized and, in that moment, I could read his mind: "If the climb has already been this difficult and the summit is still that far away, there is no way I'm going to make it." A few hours later, as we sat eating our freeze-dried dinners, Kirk tearfully announced he would be leaving the expedition.

All climbers have a bad day now and then. The worst thing you can do is look at the summit on such a day. It is too dominating, too far away. The human tendency to extrapolate recent experience into the future racks up an awesome toll of suffering to come, and that climber is crushed beneath the weight of it. Both Harris and Ty spent time talking with Kirk privately, encouraging him to give it just one more day. But Kirk was resolute.

NO LONGER OPTIONAL

Ty and I woke the next morning with Harris squeezed between us in our two-man tent.

"I sold Kirk to a team of Germans for some tuna fish and chocolate," he joked. Harris had heard a descending team approaching our camp in the middle of the night and asked if Kirk could rope up with them for his return to base camp. They politely agreed then gifted Harris with vacuum-sealed tuna and several large chocolate bars, weight they were glad to shed before heading out across the crevasse field.

"So the thing is this," Harris explained as we passed the chocolate around, "I couldn't send Kirk back without a tent. It might be a few days before he can catch a plane out. So we are down to two tents. He also needed a stove. So it's just our two primaries. No backup." Only four days into the expedition, our margin of safety was gone. Moreover, Kirk's share of the group gear and film equipment would have to be distributed among the remaining five team members.

At this point, I began to feel a shift in how the team viewed my presence. Where before I had been a novel participant with little expectations, my continued participation was now essential since the loss of one more team member would require the entire expedition to go home. This meant my prerogative of declaring a qualified victory somewhere short of the summit had just been taken away. By this time, we had all bonded as partners in a grand adventure, and I did not want to disappoint my teammates. I accepted that I was now going to last out the expedition as far as I possibly could. In that moment, I considered, for the first time, that I might make it to the summit. My throat caught, and tears came as I imagined what that would mean to me. So much was being taken away from me in the process of my divorce. But this, the fact I had stood on the summit of Denali, could never be taken away. It would always be mine, always be with me. It would make me special and, I felt, restore my belief in myself.

We broke camp and packed for the move to camp two. John and Mark were on one rope. Ty, Sam, and I were on the other. It was hard work, but our rest stops lasted a bit longer as Ty now took time to shoot video. "You're doing good, Dave," Sam called out to me during one break.

"I hurt like Willie Nelson at a tax audit," I shot back.

Several teams had begun their expeditions on the Saturday of Memorial Day weekend. Being three days behind them meant taking our choice of preconstructed camps recently vacated as those teams moved higher. We settled into an excellent circumstance at camp two. The prior occupants had not only dug out a flat pit for the tents, but also constructed protective wind walls from blocks of cut snow, saving us many hours of work.

A PLUMBING PROBLEM

The discussion at dinner that night centered on the topic of pee bottles. It is at best uncomfortable, at worst dangerous, for a climber to step outside the shelter of his tent to urinate at night. So, it is common practice to relieve yourself into a plastic one-liter bottle. The bottle is then capped tightly and kept in the climber's sleeping bag to avoid having its contents freeze. In the morning, it is emptied into a designated pee hole. Ladies use a funnel device in conjunction with the pee bottle.

I was having difficulty. Where other team members could just roll to one side and pee into their bottles from the comfort of their sleeping bag, I had to get upright on my knees. This allowed cold air into my bag, the effect of which was to turn off my plumbing. A practical concern, we discussed it in the frank terms that any failed piece of equipment might be scrutinized.

"Try pinching it off," Sam suggested. "You will be able to relax enough to build up some pressure."

"But once I get going, I am afraid I'll overfill. That shuts the flow down again," I said.

"Put on your head lamp," Mark advised.

"Or just keep a finger inside the bottle," Harris said. "But it would be best if you could learn to piss on your side. It takes practice."

As we settled into our sleeping bags that night, Ty, Harris, and I were packed into a two-man tent. It was so tight that two of us had to lie on our sides at all times. I had my back to Harris and was drifting off when he said "Hey, Dave." Looking back to face him, I could see John was smiling. Then I heard the unmistakable sound of his pee bottle filling.

"You're my hero," I said.

DOWNTIME

We rested the next day, and with that much time on my hands, I found myself thinking about my sons. I missed them and wondered if they missed me. Maybe this time apart was welcome to them, a chance for some space from their crazy father and his midlife crisis. Maybe they weren't thinking about me at all. They had their own busy teenage lives and were doing what they could to live normally within the toxicity of divorce. I had done my best to provide a stable, loving home for them to come to during their weeks with me, but it is not in the nature of a child to tell their parent what a wonderful job he is doing. Most of the time, I had no idea how my sons felt about me and never found the courage to ask.

We made a carry the following day to camp three. The 1,800 feet of vertical gain might have been more manageable had most of it not come in the final half-mile. I was breathing hard, sweat pooling on the inside of my sunglasses as I labored, head down. My sled tried to pull me back down the hill with every step I took. Again I reached a point where I knew I would have to call for a rest, singling myself out as the weak link. But for all the disadvantages associated with being the middle person on a rope team, it occurred to me there was one clear positive: the person in the middle controlled all communication. Given the forty-foot distance between roped climbers and the auditory camouflage provided by the wind, it was necessary to relay information by shouting man-to-man.

"Hey, Ty," I shouted up ahead, "Sam needs a rest."

Then I turned back toward Sam. "What's wrong?" he questioned. "Why are we stopped?"

"Ty needs a rest," I answered. In this fashion, I found a means by which I could stand with these remarkable mountaineers. I would introduce fictional vulnerabilities to each whenever I was hungry, thirsty, or cold. I would decide when Ty needed to pee, or Sam wanted to take a photo, and in this fashion the combined needs of my rope mates completely eclipsed my own.

We arrived at camp three at about eleven that morning. After burying our provisions in two deep trenches, the team ate lunch and stretched out in the comfortable sixty-degree temperatures of a sunny day. We were talking about the nature of climbing and climbers when Ty asked me, "Would you do this again just to do what we've done so far?"

"No," I replied.

"Really!"

"You guys are all mountaineers," I explained. "You love just being in the mountains. I haven't had that kind of experience in my life. I'm here for a shot at the summit or to see how close I can get. But without the possibility of the summit, I wouldn't be here."

A BLIND CLIMB

A light snow was falling softly through the featureless whiteout fog that consumed our camp the next morning. These were poor conditions, but we had already seen the route to camp three during our carry there and knew it to be well-marked. Denali expeditions carry a supply of short bamboo wands that are used to identify the trail when visibility becomes problematic. The wands, each adorned with a small colorful flag, are placed periodically along the route by ascending teams, which then gather them up during their descent. We had seen the wands of several expeditions during our carry the prior day and judged them numerous enough to navigate the move to camp three in low visibility. The tents were struck. The sleds were loaded. We ate hot oatmeal, washing it down with plenty of cocoa, then hoisted our massive packs.

I could barely see Ty forty feet ahead of me, but the rhythmic soft puff of his snowshoes confirmed his presence at the lead of our rope. We kept our breaks short, knowing the real work would come in the final half-mile. Longer rests would be needed there.

A cloud of hot breath escaped from Ty with each exhalation, then hung in serial succession with those before it, a contrail of toil. Still discernible by the time I reached them, my own breath echoed Ty's cadence. We paused at the base of the steep section. The whiteout conditions thickened there, enveloping me so completely that I could not see Ty or Sam, each only forty feet away. All was silent. I had heard it said that in the desert, a man can only know God. In as much as that might be true, I thought, in a whiteout a man can only know himself.

All the problems I had run from began parading through my mind. I remembered standing in the checkout line at a grocery store when the woman in front of me, a former friend from my married life, turned and said, "I understand you have been going through some difficult times."

"That would be an accurate statement," I answered. Then I added, "I don't have anything else to say."

Tears ran down her face. "And you don't have to say anything," she said, then gathered up her groceries and ran out of the store. She literally ran. I felt like such a leper. I would eventually learn this woman had chosen to leave her own marriage shortly after that incident. Her reaction had been a symptom of her own personal crisis, not a judgment of mine, but I had been too self-involved to pick up on this.

By the time we pulled into camp three a few hours later, I had sweated through my base layer. Crushed by exhaustion, I sprawled out atop my sled while the other team members merrily put up tents. I was useless, possessing little energy and still less dignity, draped like a starfish over my massive black duffel. But no one said anything to me. There was no chiding or grumbling. They all just went about the duties of building camp. I felt grateful for this, their understanding that the most I could be at that moment was cargo. Feeling I could not keep this up for many more days, I ransacked my mind for a way out. Faked injury? Real injury? Real self-inflicted injury?

That night, as I lay in my sleeping bag, a loud crack startled me awake. The shuddering rumble that followed told me the hillside above us had broken loose in avalanche. We had chosen a campsite on a ridge formation we believed to be safe from avalanches, as the load would split on either side. In any case, there was nothing we could do but lie there and listen. Mountaineers do not like to validate danger, so in times like these, they will cheer as though it is all part of the fun. Maybe it was fun. For them. All I could think about was my boys back home and, for some reason, my pet fish Axel. The rumble passed on one side like a noisy locomotive. It shook us in our tents, leaving me so jacked up with adrenaline that I could not sleep for what seemed like hours.

THE BUSINESS END OF A SHOVEL

Denali is massive enough to generate its own weather systems. This is the chief reason few summer tourists are able to look upon its distant peak. But Denali's proximity to the Bering Sea also makes the mountain a frequent recipient of the horrific storms generated there. One such storm arrived as we woke the next morning at camp three.

Heavy snow began falling, and the temperature dropped as the sun was eclipsed by thick dark clouds. We all jammed into one tent to pass the time playing cards, but after a few hours, it became necessary to shovel out our camp. The snow kept coming harder and harder. It seemed like it was falling faster than we could shovel it. We set up a round-the-clock rotation whereby each man would shovel for two hours. This went on for the next two days and nights.

At first, I dreaded the arrival of my shift. But the body heat generated by hard work came as a welcome change from shivering in our tent. It also kept my mind too busy to dwell on unpleasant things. I had been thinking about all the friends I used to have, friends who had not reached out to me with so much as a phone call through the course of my divorce. Mostly they were guys, cowards the likes of which I had always been when it came to emotional suffering. I remember being afraid that a guy might break down and cry in front of me. I remember being afraid that I wouldn't know what to say. Now I knew that the only thing a guy wants is to speak what's in his heart and have someone say they understand. He doesn't need you to take sides. He doesn't even need you to agree. He just needs you to understand.

That night I had another kissing dream. This time it was Whoopi Goldberg. Though I am not attracted to her in waking hours, in this dream I could not get enough. I told my teammates about this as we ate oatmeal the next morning. They all looked confused and concerned. "I kinda wish you hadn't said any of that," Big Sam said.

We shoveled throughout that day and into the darkness. One of my shifts fell in the middle of the night, wrapping up at four o'clock. I woke Ty to take over then fired up our camp stove to make a meal. As I waited for the snow to become water, and the water to boil, I pawed through the various freeze-dried meals in my provisions duffel. I decided on the chicken and mashed potatoes. But it had been a hard day, and I felt compelled to dress up the meal a bit to treat myself. Digging again, I came upon two small individually wrapped cheddar cheese packets. Both were frozen hard. I wanted to combine them to make cheesy chicken and mashed potatoes, but doubted they would thaw when added to the meal. If I added them to the boiling water, they would cool it to the point of further delaying a meal for which I was already ravenously hungry. Then it occurred to me that I could tuck one cheese packet under each armpit. By the time the water boiled, the cheese would be soft enough to add to the meal. The joy this brought me would have been outsized in any other circumstance. But here, where just getting by was a full-time endeavor, it fit in perfect proportion. My cheesy chicken and mashed potatoes were like sipping fine wine from a tin cup. They made the day worth doing and hinted at a better tomorrow.

WINDY CORNER

The storm let up on the third day, so we set out to make a carry. Motorcycle Hill, so named for its steep pitch resembling the hills used for uphill motorcycle challenges, rises 457 feet right out of camp three. It levels off to form a small bench at the top where climbers often rest. We paused there while Ty filmed another team working its way up the hill. Next came Squirrel Hill, a two hundred–foot rise with a pitch still steeper than Motorcycle Hill. My sled conspired with gravity there to produce such opposition that the thrust of both legs was required to gain ground. I would power upward like a squat lifter then drive my ice ax deep into the hillside to avoid sliding back. It was by far the most difficult challenge we had faced thus far. Even the big men had to work hard. I could hear their grunts and heavy breathing as they toiled against loads larger than my own. We reached the top then crossed a broad expanse of modest incline, which delivered us to the doorstep of Windy Corner.

The route around Windy Corner narrows to a small icy ledge that falls away at a steep slope into a large open crevasse thirty feet away. Our sleds quickly left the ledge, tracking sideways beneath us on their leashes. Their weight on the steep slope pulled hard toward the hungry crevasse below. As we fought the powerful headwind and resisted the sideways tug from our sleds, it became clear that a single misstep would deliver all members of the rope team to the bottom of the crevasse. We stomped hard with our spiked crampons to obtain the best traction possible as the team moved slowly, methodically, step by careful step. Airborne bits of ice stung my face and bounced off my goggles like a hail of BBs. We clung close to the rock wall and grappled for handholds wherever they could be obtained. I watched Ty as he led Sam and me, rehearsing in my head how I would fall with the point of my ice ax down if Ty should stumble. But the hard glossy ice looked wholly impenetrable. I doubted I could arrest my own slide, let alone that of others. I was watching the loose material on Ty's jacket snap franticly in the breeze when suddenly it fell limp. He had exited the gale. A few moments later, I too stepped free of the rip, followed shortly by Sam. On this side of Windy Corner, it was a pleasant sunny day. It was as if Denali had offered up a test to dissuade the meek from venturing higher. Mark and Harris joined us as we exchanged high fives, celebrating our having passed that test.

We dug two deep trenches a few hundred feet up the route and buried our loads to form a cache. It was necessary to bury our cache because ravens—hungry, mischievous, and highly intelligent—will scatter unattended provisions in short order. Capable of thriving at astonishing altitudes, ravens will follow climbers all the way to the summit of Denali, feeding on the trail mix and other food bits left behind at lunch stops. But they are not just casual scavengers. Ravens are industrious and have learned how to dig out a shallow trench and even open the zipper on a duffel. One such pillaged cache lay strewn about like a gutted straw man near the cache we dug, a cautionary tale that told of hardships to come for the team that was counting on it. We marked our cache with a long bamboo wand, then GPS coordinates were also taken before returning to camp three.

We rested the following day, caching our snowshoes and a modest reserve of provisions at camp three. It is standard practice to leave some provisions at each camp as a team advances up the mountain. This creates a margin of safety in the event of a hasty retreat. As well, it lightens the weight carried, if only marginally.

GO, DOGS. GO!

We broke camp the following morning and once again started up Motorcycle Hill with ridiculously heavy loads. With the benefit of acclimation and a few tricks I learned during the carry, I felt more capable than I had a few days prior. We passed our forward cache around noon, continuing up to camp four at Genet Basin.

Climbers refer to camp four as "fourteen," recognizing its elevation at 14,235 feet. It is a broad, deep bench, allowing ample room for many teams to camp well clear of any avalanche danger. Denali continues skyward from there, forming a great U-shaped wall so steep it is unclimbable in all but a few places. Until recently, this was also the ceiling for helicopter rescue. Climbers injured higher than fourteen would have to be lowered down a shear rock face by a massive spool cable located at high camp (17,253 feet).

I was amazed by the number of climbers already camped at fourteen. While the weather below had been intermittently workable, the last two weeks had seen a constant pummeling of the mountain's higher flanks. Some three-dozen teams had thus been held at bay on this snowfield in the sky. Evidence of their restlessness could be observed in the form of igloos and overly elaborate wind wall systems that had been built from ice. A nonstop volleyball game was underway on the south end of camp, while other climbers who had packed up snowboards carved graceful curves down the fall line below the headwall.

Teams from Korea, the United Kingdom, Argentina, and Norway all socialized. Ice climbers dared a steep face to the west of camp. Everything about the scene we walked into reminded me of a favorite childhood book, *Go, Dog. Go!* In the end of that story, the dogs all have a wild party way high up in a tree. This was the climbers' equivalent.

There would be no readymade camp for us to slide into at fourteen. We set up our tents in the lee of another expedition and made plans to build a properly fortified camp the next day. Before turning in that night, I traded a roll of toilet paper (also known as mountain money) for three minutes of time on the satellite phone of another team. Ty used this time to call home to Noelle, reporting on our condition and progress.

THE BIG SLEEP

I woke the next morning feeling good about myself. I had made it to fourteen thousand feet. For many Denali expeditions, this camp is their final goal. These people were serious climbers, and yet I, a pure novice, had made it here too.

We had oatmeal and cocoa for breakfast while examining the ridge high above us at seventeen thousand feet. A long veil of spindrift stretched far out from the ridge, indicating powerful winds at work. There would be no teams moving up that day.

The sound of a helicopter approaching from below

caught our attention. We watched as its rotors lashed hard at the thin air, slowly gaining enough purchase to lift the machine up onto our bench at fourteen. It set down next to the ranger hut but did not power off. Four park rangers crouched low and loaded a stretcher onto the machine, which then lifted off and disappeared quickly into the clouds below. A Swiss climber had died that night. He had taken a prescription sleep aid and never woke up. Narcotics of any sort are a strict no-no at high altitudes. He had obviously not been aware of this.

Many climbers suffer from sleep disturbances at high altitude. The most common among these is Cheyne-Stokes breathing, which causes interrupted sleep. My first experience with Cheyne-Stokes came at camp two. It did not occur again until our first night at fourteen. The fact that my episodes came and went tended to suggest my body was acclimating normally. This was critically important, as I had never been higher than ten thousand feet and did not know if I possessed the physiology required for high-altitude climbing.

We woke that first morning at fourteen camp to a perfect day. Though harsh winds continued to tear at Denali high above us, our sheltered location brought conditions kind enough that coats were optional. Our spirits had recovered with the benefit of ten hours' sleep, and we chatted excitedly about having achieved our first major objective: get to fourteen camp. Aside from retrieving our cache near Windy Corner, there would be no load carrying for at least three days. We had earned a rest.

DONE?

Harris selected a site for the construction of a proper snow camp. While workhorses Sam and Mark dug out a large oval where our tents would be placed, Harris, Ty, and I sawed blocks of ice, placing them to form a protective wind wall. We were happy, joking among one another as we worked. But forty minutes into the project, I started to feel lightheaded. Though I slowed my pace, the lightheadedness turned to dizziness. No one else seemed to be struggling. I did not want to stop and be the weak one again, but my condition worsened so quickly that I just dropped the saw and walked away. I felt like a lead-weighted blanket had suddenly been draped over me. I wanted to surrender to gravity and lay down right where I was.

So this is it, I thought as I walked back to our tent. I've hit my ceiling. I definitely won't be going any higher. I can't. The guys are going to be disappointed. They've worked so hard.

I arrived at the tent, consumed with dread, and fell asleep soon after stretching out on my sleeping bag. I was awakened some time later by Mark, who noticed my absence and became concerned.

"How are you feeling?" he asked.

"Tired. I have a headache," I said.

"Are you nauseous?" he asked, now engaged in his working role of EMT.

"No. Just kinda weak. Man, it really hit me all of the sudden."

"How much liquid have you taken in today?"

I thought about it. Aside from a cup of cocoa with instant coffee mixed in, I had not consumed any liquids. Normally I would drink a liter of Gatorade with breakfast, but had been so excited to be at fourteen camp I had just jumped up and started my day.

"You're dehydrated," Mark pronounced, "and you have an acute case of mountain sickness. Drink this," he said, handing me a liter of energy drink. "Take a couple ibuprofen. I'll be back to check on you."

Mark returned every few hours with another liter of fluid. By late that afternoon, I emerged feeling much improved. In the meantime, the team had built camp, retrieved our cache, and moved everything in except the tent I was sleeping in.

I walked across fourteen camp to empty the contents of my pee bottle at a designated pee hole, and then found myself following another climber on the return. In the fashion of the day, the climber's pants hung loosely at the waist, revealing the cleft of his buttocks. My internal monologue commented, "Damn, boy, you losin' yo pants!" The climber looked back and laughed, then hoisted his pants with one hand. I had actually said the words out loud. This effect, the inability to differentiate between thinking to myself and speaking out loud, continued for me. The guys and I were sitting around drinking hot tea after dinner that evening, and I thought of a comment to contribute, then did so. They all just stared at me and asked why I had said the same sentence twice. Not wishing to concern them, I spoke as little as possible from that point on, assuming some of my thoughts were finding their way out and the net effect would approximate normal. Aside from this cognitive glitch, I was feeling pretty good again and had started thinking I might be able to go higher. There were two days of rest ahead. I would see how I felt after that.

A KOREAN VICTORY

A heavy snow fell the following day. Aside from the occasional climber wandering to the pee hole, the residents of fourteen camp hunkered down in their tents. Then a commotion began to stir at the Korean camp by midday. Their advance team had radioed down. They were descending from high camp. They had summited. This struck many as questionable, as there had been no weather windows in over two weeks. A crowd of climbers gathered around the Korean camp as the descending team appeared on the lower flanks of the headwall. If indeed they had summited, they were going to need some help. Frostbite would almost be a certainty. A few might need to be carried the remaining distance to camp. Mark and Sam started climbing up to meet them while their own team members unfurled a sponsorship banner from outdoor gear manufacturer Mammut and prepared for celebratory photos. Unfamiliar with the text, they held the banner upside down.

I watched as the Koreans grew clearer, their flamboyantly colored climbing suits now visible through the falling snow. Their pace was impressive, their posture solid. I could see them smiling now as they fist pumped the air. Mark and Sam trailed them into camp looking unconvinced. Much celebration ensued among the Koreans while the rest of us stood around, glad for the spectacle that beat sitting in our tents. We would have liked to believe they had made the top of Denali. It would have served as a positive affirmation for the rest of us. But I could read on the faces of those assembled that no one, aside from the Koreans, believed this to be the case. Still, mountain climbing is a pursuit of honor. If someone declares they have summited, then they have summited. It is only in the rarest of circumstances that a climber will challenge the claim of another. We all wandered off to our tents, leaving the Koreans to enjoy their moment.

GOLD RUSH

I woke the next day to the sounds of climbers making ready. The weather up high had finally broken, and the chalkboard outside the ranger hut predicted two days of perfect climbing conditions. A long line of teams soon stretched all the way up to the ridge above the headwall, resembling a photo of the Klondike gold rush. By then, some teams had run out of provisions, or time, or will. They used this same weather window to descend.

We allowed the crowds to thin above us then loaded our packs to make a carry up the headwall. Though my strength had recovered, I was nervous about how I might perform, so I hydrated thoroughly and packed a modest load of perhaps fifty pounds.

Rising 1,400 feet out of fourteen camp, the approach to the headwall is a serious piece of work. Fortunately, the crowds before us had beaten a serviceable path through the deep accumulation of snow. Once again our trailing strategy had served us well. Though the sleds would remain at fourteen, the steep ascent and thin air made for extremely taxing work. I found myself choosing smaller and smaller goals. "Just make it to the headwall" became "Just make it to the next trail wand," which then became "Just do ten more steps." At one point, a thought passed through my head: "If I'm having this much trouble on the approach, how am I ever going to make it up the headwall?" Then I realized this was probably the last question a person asks before quitting.

We stopped for a rest just then. As I sat on my pack, panting so hard my throat felt raw, I asked myself a better question: is this the day the dream dies?

The answer came back immediately: no. I was hurting.

No doubt. But I could hurt worse and keep going. This much I had learned through my training. What about the headwall? I didn't know. It would certainly be much more difficult. But my immediate problem was the approach. There would be plenty of time to worry about the headwall when I got to it.

I looked up the trail, taking aim at the next wand, stood, and shouldered my pack.

We rested at the base of the headwall, which was sufficiently steep that we could lean against it while we stood there sipping energy drinks. The other members of the team talked casually. It seemed clear they had not been tested the way I had. Here at sixteen thousand feet, the oxygen content of each breath was only 56 percent of one taken at sea level. The pause to take a drink required five deep breaths to recover.

The Denali climbing rangers had set a protective fixed line on the headwall to reduce the risk of climber falls. Ty clipped into it with his ascender, a mechanical device that allows the rope to pass in just one direction. He then snapped a carabiner at the end of his safety leash onto the line and began climbing. I waited until he had advanced enough to take up the forty feet of team rope that connected us, then I too clipped in.

I had never used an ascender before, so Harris gave me a brief demonstration. It is unforgivable for a climber to arrive at Denali's headwall having never used an ascender.

If I had seriously thought I might make it this far, I might have sought out training in advance. But I hadn't—and I didn't.

I kicked into the ice face with the forward teeth of my crampons and swung my ice ax high. Since I could use my upper body as well as my legs, the climbing seemed less difficult at first. But soon my calves fatigued from supporting so much weight on the toe points. My legs shook spasmodically. Seeing this, Harris shouted to me from the lead of his rope below.

"Hey, D. You can't toe point this whole face. Duckfoot your feet out to the sides and stand on the whole foot."

I did so and found myself again able to proceed.

The fixed line was secured to the headwall by deep anchors, which required the team to pause intermittently while each climber unclipped from protection and rejoined the line above the anchor. When one of us came to an anchor, he would shout out, "Anchor!" The team would then pause until he shouted, "Clear!" I came to see these pauses as saviors. The ten seconds that others took stretched into thirty whenever I passed an anchor, which was just long enough to quiet the burning in my muscles.

"You're doing great," Sam shouted from below.

"You're a madman, D," Harris added.

By the time the headwall crested, I had been torn down to thinking of nothing more than the next hopeful step. Even as the face flattened out on top, I chose to crawl on all fours. I collapsed on one side next to Ty as he coiled our rope at his feet and lay there panting with my pack still on. I thought of my boys and wondered what they were doing at that moment, if they missed me, and if they would be proud knowing how far I had gotten.

We lunched on beef jerky and trail mix, then cached our loads in a pit we dug at the top of the headwall. By four, we were back down in a sparsely populated fourteen camp, celebrating our successful carry. "I could eat the leg off a frozen dog," I said to Ty as we gathered for dinner. Indeed, I consumed two complete dinner packets—portions designed for four people.

An intoxicating satisfaction came over me as I settled into my sleeping bag.

Yes, the carry was incredibly difficult, I thought. But I did it! I tasted sixteen thousand feet! Tomorrow is a rest day. By the time I have to face the headwall again, my body will be acclimated. I'll be stronger. High camp is only a thousand feet above the headwall. Once we get there, we are done packing weight uphill! The summit push only requires us to carry a backup set of clothes. Is it really possible? Could I stand on the summit of Denali?

I pictured that moment.

No, I thought, pushing the image away. It's too soon for that. There's far too much work ahead. Just leave it be. Your next summit is high camp.

A BOLD NEW PLAN

We slept ten satisfying hours, waking to another perfect day at fourteen camp. I stopped by the ranger hut that morning to check the weather forecast on my way to the pee hole. Another two days of excellent weather had been added. My team members whooped with joy when I shared this news with them at breakfast.

Around noon, a climber from another team eased into our camp pulling a sled full of food rations. His team was heading down and wanted to offload as much weight as possible. We picked through the provisions, claiming a few vacuum-sealed packets of smoked salmon. I asked how their climb had gone and was surprised when he said they had summited.

"Yeah, we did it in one shot," he added. "We left here early yesterday with just our summit gear, stopped for lunch at high camp, then pushed on to the top. We made the summit in the middle of the night, then started back down."

"You didn't build a camp at seventeen?" I asked.

"No. Fuck that," he said as though this was something only marginal climbers did.

The problem was that this climber seemed believable. He looked like he had been climbing for twenty-four hours. He sounded capable. And the truth is some part of us *wanted* to believe him, the part that was missing our families, was tired of sleeping on ice, and just wanted to go home. I could sense each of us measuring ourselves up against this man and, with the exception of me, concluding, "If he can do it, I can do it!"

Talk began as soon as the climber walked away. Instead of making a move to high camp, as planned the next day, we should go fast and light, hit it in one shot like this guy had done. Bold. Aggressive. The good weather was not forecast to last long enough for us to summit after taking the typical rest day at high camp, as per standard practice. This would solve that problem. I said nothing as the discussion then turned to what a strong team we were and how we had passed other teams on every leg of the climb. All of this was true, but doing so had nearly been the end of me many times. Then we voted.

We had pumped ourselves into a state of shear euphoria. The outcome felt like a foregone conclusion. In short order, Harris, Sam, and Mark all voted to change our plan and attempt a one-shot summit bid. Ty was next, but, sensing my hesitation, he walked the line between yes and no. Then it came to me.

I could see the excitement in their faces. We were leaving for the summit tomorrow! They had all been so good to me. I wanted to give this to them. There was no doubt in my mind they could do it. Yet there was no part of my mind that believed I could.

"I have no reasonable basis for believing I can do it," I said.

Their expressions melted.

For the next few minutes, Harris, Sam, and Mark tried to convince me I could make it. They told me how well I had done, how much help I would get from the team, and so on.

"If I completely gas out above seventeen, we won't even have a camp to fall back on," I challenged. A few of the Denali fatalities I had read about were owed to this very circumstance. They continued to argue the point for a moment more. Then Ty spoke up in my defense.

"Hey, I know we're all ready to go home, and it would be great to be able to say we had summited from fourteen, but I think we gotta put the ego aside here." Harris bristled at this and, for the first time, a tension arose between him and Ty. Though we had not agreed to stay with our original plan, it now seemed clear there was not sufficient support to pursue the one-shot attempt. Ty and Harris argued openly as the rest of us stood by watching, then we all parted in separate directions, pissed off and spilling with resentment.

Ty and Harris were holding a private conference off to one side of camp when I returned. I climbed into the tent we shared and began journaling. "We are moving to seventeen tomorrow," Ty announced as he joined me a few moments later. Nothing more needed to be said. For the time, at least, he and Harris had cobbled us back together, and we were sticking with our original plan. We gathered for dinner that night and pretended as though nothing had happened. But I could feel Mark was cool to me and imagined what he might have to say if this prolonged approach failed to produce a summit.

MOVE TO HIGH CAMP

I rose early the next morning and set out to check the weather forecast on the board outside the ranger hut. It promised just two more days of climbable weather. The team discussed this at breakfast. We would move to high camp at 17,200 feet that day, then rest the next day. We would just have to hope for a third good day after that. If the weather was not friendly for a summit push, we could wait it out at seventeen for a few days. Much past that, we would be too weakened to climb higher. In a worst-case scenario, we might find ourselves trapped at high camp by a storm. Frostbite or worse were distinct possibilities under those circumstances.

My earlier decision to carry a modest load to our cache above the headwall brought the consequence of shouldering a ridiculous weight for the move on this day. All the tension straps of my expedition pack had to be released to accommodate the volume of compression sacks containing my gear. My bedding was strapped to the outside of the pack. My share of group gear was strapped atop that. I estimated the total load to be eighty pounds. My teammates carried packs that were heavier still.

We rested after thirty minutes of climbing. I was glad for the break, already feeling my heart rate hit its red line.

The steep approach to the headwall rises 1,021 feet out of fourteen camp. With the loads we carried, that alone would feel like a full day's work. I called for another rest forty-five minutes later and threw off my pack. As I sat on it, panting between sips of Gatorade, I glanced downhill at Sam, Mark, and Harris. They stood in place with their packs still on. I took this to be a message of some sort. Then Mark, who must have thought he was far enough away that I would not hear him, exclaimed "C'mon! Fuck!"

I confronted Mark once the team came together at the base of the headwall.

"Have you felt pushed to your limit any day of this climb?" I asked him.

"No."

"Well I have felt pushed to my limit *every* day of this climb! And what I don't need is you poppin' off with 'C'mon! Fuck!' while I am doing the best I can! You got that?"

Mark looked surprised. "Hey. No one is criticizing you," he said.

I stared at him, thinking, "No one but you!" I could have said more, but my point had been made. It was time to let it go and press on.

If the headwall was any easier the second time around, I could not sense it. Again, I survived for the pause that came with each anchor passing, feeling dizzy and desperate as I lingered there. Sam and Harris shouted encouragements to me from below as my shoulders cursed me from within. At some point, the next anchor became too great a goal, so I counted steps instead. Just five more steps, I thought. The 960-foot rise of steep ice seemed to reach into Alaska's sky ad infinitum.

The mountain consumed what was left of me as we clawed higher. The cold air burned in my lungs, while sweat ran freely down my face. But a primal urge had been awakened. This was no longer a mere climb, but a battle. Time seemed to slip away as my focus was reduced to singular motions. Swing. Breathe. Step. Pull. Swing. Breathe. Step. Pull. Then I looked up and saw the hillcrest thirty feet above me.

Again I crawled on all fours to the place where Ty stood coiling our rope at his feet. He then belayed in the line beneath me as Sam approached. I lay on my side breathing hard for twenty minutes. By the time I stood, Mark and Harris had arrived, and the team was busy eating energy bars and hydrating. They had all watched me lying there, spent. They had heard me snap at Mark. I felt broken, both physically and mentally, and assumed they were of the same opinion about me. No one spoke of it though. I drank some Gatorade and tried to assemble the words I would speak in telling the guys I was done.

The thought of the summit crept in, and again I reminded myself of the vast reward that awaited me there. I would believe in myself again. But the potency of this drug had been drained away with my strength. I felt helpless, weak, and defeated in a manner that had characterized my life over the last year. Like a shadow of myself that I could chase but never catch, personal demons had robbed my life of meaning and satisfaction while eluding my ability to understand them. They were with me in that moment, and I knew they would stay a few steps out of reach, above me, always looking down at me, if I continued to climb upward. But now I wanted to confront them, finally battle them, and suffer whatever that brought. They were running out of room as I chased them up Denali, ever closer to the summit. They could taunt me and run away laughing only so many more times. But it was a certainty I would have them within arm's reach at some point if I only kept climbing.

We finished lunch then shouldered our packs to continue on. My right crampon came loose almost immediately after we started underway. I tried to replace it, but Ty, around a corner at the lead, sensed tension on the rope and fought back hard, assuming someone was falling. He pulled me off my feet every time I tried to replace the metal apparatus. I was flailing, squandering what strength I had left. Sam scrambled up to help me, while Harris climbed around the large rock formation above us to call off Ty's efforts. I felt completely spent again, lying there on the ice while Sam attached the crampon. Once finished, he smiled at me and said, "You're doing good."

I tried to stand, but could not. The struggle had taken too much out of my legs. The team gathered around me, lying helpless in the snow.

"I'm sorry guys," I began. "But I am just gassed, and with these heavy loads, I can't hack it."

"Do you think you can make it to high camp if we lighten your pack?" Harris asked.

"I don't know," I answered. "I can try."

Mark and Ty dug up the cache we had left at the top of the headwall a few days earlier, while Harris sorted through my pack. Anything essential to going higher was retained; all else was added to the cache and buried. Harris gave each team member a piece of my gear then helped me shoulder my reconfigured pack. It was half the weight of a few minutes earlier.

"Can you carry that?" Harris asked hopefully. I said I could, then the team again started up the narrow ridge leading to high camp.

We arrived an hour later, stopping at the first camp we came to at seventeen. I dropped my pack and sat on it, breathing hard. Ty chatted with the team at that camp, asking about the conditions up high and how many teams had summited that day. Then he, Harris, Sam, and Mark continued on to find a vacant spot on the crowded shelf. I remained, an uninvited guest, resting on my pack in the other team's camp.

We retreated to our tents early that evening as the sun dipped then disappeared around the west flank of Denali. The temperature quickly dropped to –30°F, so our team meeting, shouted back and forth through thin tent walls, was conducted with each member burrowed deep inside his down sleeping bag.

"So, here's the thing," Harris began. "The weather forecast still says tomorrow is a good day. But there hasn't been any update for the day after. It could be good, or it could be the start of bad stuff. How are you feelin', D?"

"Whooped," I shouted back.

"Yeah. I know it was a rough day, but you did good. Do you think there's any chance you would be up for a summit push tomorrow?"

The thought of resting the entire next day had been a big part of what kept me going.

"Don't we need to go fetch our cache tomorrow?" I asked, hoping to deflect attention from myself.

"Not for a summit push," Harris answered. "Most of that cache is extra food, batteries, and fuel. We can always get it the next day if we summit then weather holds us here."

I thought about it for a moment. "I don't know," I said.

"From here up, we don't pack any weight," Harris offered, "just your lunch and heavy down gear."

No one else spoke. It was just Harris shouting to me

from the tent he shared with Sam and Mark, with me shouting back from the tent I shared with Ty.

"I guess I will have to see how I feel in the morning," I answered.

"Okay. Sounds good, D. We'll check back then," Harris ended.

We were silent for several moments while each team member mulled the possibilities. Then I rolled over to face Ty and asked, "Do you think I can do it?"

Ty could have said yes, and I would have believed him. He could have said no, and I likewise would have accepted his judgment. But Ty said neither. I now see that as a gift. Any summit push entails great effort and great risk. A climber may own success or he may own failure, but the least he is owed is full ownership.

YES

Long tendrils of icy hoarfrost hung from the ceiling of our tent the next morning. I examined them through the small opening in my sleeping bag, from which I had been breathing for the last ten hours. The morning light cast a warm yellow glow upon the tendrils as it passed through the thin lining of our tent. I increased the opening enough to stick my head out. There was a faint layer of ice upon our sleeping bags and everything else around us. It was six in the morning, and high camp was held in a sub-zero stasis.

Incredibly, I had not experienced any Cheyne-Stokes

breathing that night. I sat up in my sleeping bag, releasing a quiet ice storm of frost as I bumped my head against the ceiling. Ty stirred, then sat up next to me.

"Good morning, Super Climber," he said.

"Morning," I responded.

Then Harris shouted over to me. "What do you say, D? How are you feelin'?"

I had been preparing for this question since waking, running through a checklist of how my body felt.

"Let's go up," I shouted back. Cheers erupted from Harris, Sam, and Mark. Sam would later tell me this was the most exciting moment of the climb for him. Ty reached over and slapped me on the back. This was it. We would take our shot.

The first part of the climb was Denali Pass, a thousand-foot gain traversing up and out of the half bowl above high camp. Deceptively steep, many teams choose to forgo the time and bother of using the fixed-line protection installed by the rangers. As a result, Denali Pass claims more fatalities than any other part of the mountain. Several Asian teams have tumbled down one particularly steep section of Denali Pass. In a term lacking both sensitivity and political correctness, that section had come to be called The Orient Express.

I felt good as we started up the pass. The sky was clear, and the windless air seemed to suggest Denali was holding its breath just for us. We used the fixed-line protection, pausing at anchor points as each man passed. It took time, but I was glad to be starting off at an easy pace. Two hours later, the team crested Denali Pass to a small flat area where we rested briefly.

The next section consisted of a steep series of steps, each about thirty feet tall. The riser of each step was spaced such that each man on the rope had to climb in unison and then rest on the small flat ledge at the top before taking on the next step. Even with the light load, I felt myself working very hard. It was eleven when we arrived at a thin ridge looking down on the entire West Buttress Route our team had spent days climbing. We ate lunch there while Ty shot video footage under perfect conditions. We were giddy with excitement, joking with one another, but careful to not speak the words that would declare victory. Things were going very well, and the team was looking strong. But there was more hill above us, and the air was getting thinner.

The team moved slower as we continued higher up a demanding slope of switchbacks. Even Big Sam called for a rest break. We were feeling it. Silence replaced the talkiness typical of our stops.

We crested twenty thousand feet at one o'clock, looking out across a vast flat expanse known as the Football Field. A three hundred–foot rise on the far side, Pig Hill, connected to a ridge leading to the final steps of Denali's summit. I could see it all laid out before us, but now I was visited by the debt of that skipped rest day.

I became aware of music coming from the far left side of the Football Field. It was a live concert. The Allman Brothers were playing "Statesboro Blues" to a cheering audience. I made a conscious effort to not look in that direction, fearful that my auditory hallucination might include a visual accompaniment.

Halfway across the flat expanse, I became aware of someone walking beside me. I looked over, expecting to see Sam, but it was my brother, Danny, who had died eight years earlier. He was walking in tennis shoes, smoking a cigarette, and wearing his favorite old coat.

"Hey," he said to me with a smile.

"Hey."

"I think you're gonna make it," Danny said.

"Oh! That would be *so* great," I answered through heavy sobs. Danny nodded. Then the impossibility of the situation came to me.

"But, Danny. You're dead," I said.

"Yeah. I know," he responded sadly, then vanished.

Arriving at the base of Pig Hill, we put on our heaviest down gear. I added a layer of clothing then realized I had put it on over my harness. Removing the layer, I then forgot why I had done so and put the clothing on again over my harness. Realizing my error, I again removed the protective layer, this time taking off the harness. Once again, I put on the heavy down clothing. Turning to walk away, I noticed something strange in the snow. It was my harness. I would need that. I put it on.

Ty also seemed to be struggling as he sorted his gear next to me. He would put on a piece of equipment, then remove it, cursing, and throw it to the ground, put something else on, then likewise throw it to the ground. I finished securing my harness, then looked up to see Harris, Sam, and Mark about ten steps away watching Ty and me. Harris motioned for me to come to them. As I did, Sam said, "Take a knee." Now he, Mark, and I all knelt while Harris stood evaluating Ty's behavior. I was worried about Ty, but, for once, it felt good to be among the watchers.

Ty continued his confused state. His pack was emptied out on the ground all around him. He would stuff everything into it then take everything out again. "Just give him some space," Harris said. It is best to let a climber find his own way back to clarity when he gets loopy. Otherwise, his confusion and frustration might conspire to perceive a tone of confrontation from those who would help. A short fuse to aggression is among the well-documented effects of altitude.

Harris walked over to where Ty knelt, once again removing the contents of his pack. They spoke for a moment, then Ty turned to face us.

"Honest, guys, I'm not crazy," he exclaimed. He looked crazy. Harris spoke to Ty in a tone so soft we could not hear the words. He went on like this for a few minutes, then I saw Ty's shoulders fall limp and his head nod in agreement. It may have been his words or the simple act of getting Ty to stop moving long enough to catch up his oxygen level, but Harris soon had Ty back to normal.

The steep climb up Pig Hill was made more difficult still by deep broken snow. Holding my ice ax by its head, I rammed the length of the handle deep into the hillside. The ground beneath me gave way at random intervals, my legs postholing their entire length down into the snow. Sometimes both legs would sink down until I was hip deep and had to climb up and out. I flailed my way to exhaustion then called for a rest break.

I felt a strange anger well up inside of me as I hunched over gasping for air. I was setting my ax much harder than necessary, clawing at the mountain with the teeth of my crampons. A growl came from me with each exhale, the same sound I had heard come from Axel so many times. I had caught them, the taunting collection of frustrations and hurts that had kept me down for years: my father's abandonment, my childhood in poverty, my brother's death, and the failure of my marriage. They kept coming, one after another, a lifetime of demons intent on keeping me down. But I kept going. I kept stomping and slashing at the mountain, moving higher with each fight. Though I was aware of my own limited resources, I could not summon the prudence to ration them. Where mountains are so often metaphors of life, my life became a metaphor of this mountain.

Then, just as we crested Pig Hill, a sudden peace came

over me. The fight was over. For now. I hadn't vanquished my demons, but I had unmasked them and known each for what it was and the name it could be called by. We would meet again some other day, but they could no longer dance out of reach in the shadows of anonymity.

We rested while Ty set up his tripod and camera at the top of Pig Hill. The summit was clearly visible at the top of a narrow ridge that stood between us. I drug a line in the snow with my ice ax then walked it to see if I could. I felt very lightheaded and feared cerebral edema might be setting in. Failure to walk a straight line is among its early symptoms. But I managed well enough.

Then Harris, roped with Mark, started up the ridge. We watched their careful progress for a few minutes, then Ty, Sam, and I roped together and began our own ascent. The ridge fell off sharply on both sides, dropping three hundred feet down into the Football Field to our left, and six thousand feet to Denali's midflank on our right. Climbers call such a formation a jump ridge, referring to the only means of saving one's team: if a member falls off one side, someone else on the rope team must jump off the opposite side.

The rangers had put a fixed line in place there. We clipped into it, but none of us believed its promise. Under the extreme conditions of Denali's summit, any anchor could easily have worked itself loose. A tiny wisp of wind picked up as we advanced slowly along the apex of the ridge.

We passed anchor after anchor, pausing for each climber

to unclip from the fixed line and then clip back in. I became tangled in my own safety leash at one of these, with the line crossed in front of me as I started to advance. I stopped to examine the situation, but my oxygen-deprived brain could not solve the puzzle. The only solution that came to me was to jump the rope.

Sam watched in horror from his place at the end of our rope as I coiled then sprang into the air. Waiting to see which side of the ridge I would fall off, he prepared to dive off the opposing edge. My left foot made it over the rope, but the long toothy crampons on my right foot grabbed it in midair. I landed squarely on the ridge, balancing on my left leg like a flamingo. Only then did it occur to me what a ridiculously dangerous thing I had done. Slowly, carefully, I reached down to my right foot, still retracted close to my body, and removed the tangled rope.

I knew Sam must have seen the whole thing, what he would later describe as "a pucker moment," and part of me wanted to turn back and apologize right then. But the shame I felt for having endangered the lives of my team-mates was too great, so I scolded myself and pressed on.

I could see Mark and Harris waiting a few steps below the summit, a small snow cone of perhaps ten square feet. They had removed their packs and now stood watching us complete the final ninety feet of the ridge. Sam called out as he arrived at the anchor where I had jumped. As we paused, I looked down the right side of the ridge. Denali fell away sharply, a rasp of jagged stones protruding from its vertical face. Thick clouds had formed a few hundred feet below us. They clung close to Denali, obscuring the mountain but not the territorial beauty that stretched out from it in every direction. Sam shouted, "Clear," and we pressed on.

I set each step slowly, then weighted it as my crampons bit deep into the ice with a reassuring crunch. Advancing cautiously, we allowed time enough for three deep breaths between each step. Ty, Sam, and I were now just sixty feet away. I wanted to burst inside. I wanted to shout and cry and celebrate with my teammates. But it was still too soon. "Focus," I told myself. "Don't blow it."

The rope in front of me went slack. "Anchor," Ty called out. I looked up to see him unclip from the fixed line then turn to face me, smiling proudly. He now stood with Harris and Mark, who shouted encouragement to Sam and me as we resumed our space walk. Ty gathered up the rope between us as I took each step. Plant. Weight. Breathe. Breathe. Breathe. Step. It had been too much to ask for. Any time I had found myself imagining the summit, I pushed the dream away. Now I was twenty steps from it, then just ten. So much adrenaline was coursing through my veins that my hands were shaking. Five steps away. Random thoughts and voices filled my mind, forming a mental collage. Two steps. I was sobbing now. One step. I felt Ty's arms around me.

We stood there for a moment, hugging each other through impossibly thick down layers. Then Ty released me and turned to remove the video camera from his pack. I gathered the rope up as Sam completed the ridge, joining the four of us. Then all five of us stepped up onto the summit together. We were the highest humans in North America. We had done it! In spite of all the team attrition, the cold, the risk, the pain, the work, the sickness, and the ever-diminishing oxygen, we had done it!

There were high fives and bear hugs, shouts and tears.

"We did it, Dave!" Mark exclaimed, throwing open his arms. We hugged, and in that moment, any friction between us was erased. Like the other members of this team, we were now of the same blood, an ozone brotherhood that had risked greatly and together shared one of life's sweetest moments.

DAVE MAURO AND TY HARDT. PHOTO BY JOHN HARRIS.

We took turns posing for photos on the peak. I held up a picture of my sons, my mom, and my best friend Chuck Blair. Then Ty's video camera pointed right at me as he asked, "Okay, Mr. Mauro. Your thoughts?"

"Oh man," I started in a fatigued voice. "I think I probably..." My oxygen-starved brain struggled to construct and deliver a cogent thought. Then I began to laugh, sensing the approach of irony. "I probably look as bad as I've ever looked, and I probably feel as good as I've ever felt. How's that?"

All of my fingertips turned white a few days after returning to Anchorage. They were frost-nipped from taking off my gloves at the summit. It was only a few minutes while I held up photos of family for summit shots, but that was all it took. During my first week back in Bellingham, each fingertip peeled off, revealing the deep pink skin of last resort.

I rode a wave of exuberance those first several days home. I was a man with a secret he wanted to tell. Could anyone walking down the street guess where I had been, what I had suffered, what I had gained? I wanted to share it all, but quickly found it was not sharable outside the small circle of those who had followed my story from the start. If I found myself among people discussing a recent hike and mentioned my summit of Denali, the conversation came to a halt against a barricade built of equal parts disbelief and comparative imbalance. It was like hearing someone comment on the Disneyland ride Space Mountain, then saying I had actually been to outer space. In short, my accomplishment amounted to conversational pepper spray.

I put this disappointment aside, settling for a quiet love affair with my moment on the summit. But soon a familiar nagging started to grow inside me. It was that same feeling that consumed me as I sat on the edge of the futon in my sister's guest room. Somehow, I still did not believe in me.

Maybe that bush pilot had been right after all when he said, "Wounds don't heal up high." Like my pink fingertips, the climb had laid bare the personal demons that dogged me—but had not resolved any of them. The one thing the climb did do, however, was exorcise the debilitating anger that stood between those demons and me. I was now free to address them from a place of peace, having learned that we come to believe in ourselves when we deal with our problems, not by climbing mountains.

I had the profile of Denali tattooed on my right shin, then retired from mountain climbing forever, glad for the experience but gladder still to be done. Like a lucky charm in a pocket, Denali would always be with me moving forward. I sensed great strength emanating from it, strength I would need as I concluded the final two months of my divorce and confronted my personal issues with the help of Doctor Ferguson.

"Hey, look at these," I said, holding my translucent fingertips in Doctor Ferguson's face.

"Oh! Yuck! Put those away," he said. "Shit!"

We talked about what I had learned from the experience of the climb and the work that lay ahead. "This is meaty stuff," he promised. I couldn't decide what order to take them on, but I knew I wasn't ready to discuss the divorce or, more importantly, whether I could ever risk myself in loving again. The wound was just too fresh. But it would soon become apparent the choosing was not up to me or Doctor Ferguson—neither the order of challenges nor my retirement from mountain climbing.

KILIMANJARO

AXEL

HE WAS DYING. I COULD SEE IT RIGHT AWAY. AXEL'S brilliant blue color had faded. Parts of him had gone pale white. Quiet and distracted, he had not been himself since my return from Denali. Somewhere in the last days of June, Axel turned head down, bouncing on his nose against the gravel bottom of his bowl, mumbling quietly.

"New Guinea welcomed us as liberators," I scoffed in my best Dick Cheney voice.

"Heh heh," Axel laughed weakly.

"The French have surrendered, and we haven't even issued terms yet!"

"Good. Yes."

His heart wasn't in it. I added medicinal drops to his water and showered Axel with bloodworms. They drifted slowly down upon him, sliding off his body like curled red streamers. He ate none.

Axel died on July 4, 2007. I buried him next to Cedar Lake Trail in the nearby Chuckanut Mountains. It was a quiet ceremony consisting of Axel, a garden trowel, and me. "You were a good fish," I said, patting the dirt down firmly. I was surprised to find my eyes welling up as I looked down on Axel's muddy little grave.

By the time I returned to my apartment, a constant flow of people were passing by, crowding out onto Taylor Street dock to watch fireworks. The malaise of having come from a funeral left me uninterested in the light show, but being among happy souls seemed like good therapy, so I eased out the door, joining the current of humanity.

Once in place out on the dock, I began eavesdropping on the conversations of those standing shoulder-to-shoulder with me. There was talk of past shows, talk of things to be done in the yard. A child asked where the rockets go after they burst. Then I recognized a familiar voice just behind me. It was Dave Lyon, a casual friend from a few years back. Dave and his wife were nice enough folks but always seemed mismatched to me. It turned out they felt the same way, having ended their marriage shortly after I last saw them. But Dave had fallen in love in the time since. He introduced me to his charming new wife, Shelly. The joy on their faces was infectious.

A sense of hope came over me as I walked back to my apartment that night. It was possible. Dave had done it. A person could bounce back from a failed marriage and even find happiness again. I wanted that. It had been a long time since I had felt happy. Sure, love would be better still, but happy seemed like enough to hope for. In that moment, I decided to try something I thought I would never do, something only desperate people do. I would sign up for online dating.

THE SEARCH

I set the filters to include only nonsmokers, women over thirty-five, and women who described themselves as active or athletic. I also indicated it was fine to have kids, but not to be looking to make more of them. I loved being a father but could see the light at the end of the child-rearing tunnel and did not want to start over again. Preferring a slight height advantage even when my date wears high heels and has her hair up, I chose to include only women who stood five foot five or shorter. Though she existed in the site's database at that very moment, my future soul mate did not survive the screening process because she stood five feet six inches tall.

My divorce had just become final, and I felt alternately excited and unsure about my next steps. "I feel so broken," I commented to my friend, Mark, one day.

"Hey, we're *all* broken," he responded. Mark had divorced a few years earlier and so took it upon himself to act as my mentor.

He asked his girlfriend for a woman's perspective on

what I should do next, dubious about online dating. "We should take him to The Royal," she suggested. "Any guy can get laid there."

Strangely flattered to have qualified as "any guy," I passed on the offer just the same, knowing I had never possessed the skills required for meeting women in bars. To me, it always felt like a job interview where the other applicants were watching. I could usually identify at least four interviewees better qualified than myself and would end up standing before some woman stammering, tattooed with insecurity.

Online dating allowed me to take it slow, messaging back and forth several times before actually meeting a woman. If responses were short and unimaginative, I would close out the dialogue and move on. Sometimes the women would learn something about me they found incompatible and likewise end the process. One woman did so upon learning that I wear a tie to work. To her, this symbolized a sort of servitude to the corporate machine. In all fairness, her objection was no more arbitrary than the height requirement I had placed. I accepted such things at face value, feeling it would be easier to find someone who shared my views than to change the views of another.

A WINK

Lin had already been on the dating website for a few weeks when I enrolled. My profile came up in her searches right away, matching on twenty-one of twenty-three characteristics. The two misses were my height requirement and her own mandate that candidates not still be engaged in raising kids. Lin's own daughter, Rachel, was grown and gone off to college. Her last relationship involved blending families and had been an unmitigated disaster. So, we passed each other by at first.

But Lin found my profile popping up again and again. One day, she clicked the "wink" button, a simple means of saying "Hello there" in the online dating world. I checked her profile and was perplexed she had not come up on my searches. We exchanged messages over the next few weeks and decided to meet for a glass of wine after she finished her shift waiting tables one Friday night. It might have been love at first sight if I hadn't thrown that notion in the Walt Disney trash heap many months prior. But there was no denying that the connection we shared was immediate and powerful. We closed down the restaurant then, not ready for the night to end, sat by a fire in her backyard talking until the sun came up.

Lin and I got together again the following evening at her home. I showed her my photos from the Denali climb, hoping to impress her. We saw one another five of the next seven days, texting constantly on the two we did not. The more I learned about Lin, the more I became convinced of my good fortune. Like me, she had been raised in economically challenged circumstances. Both parents worked to provide for Lin and her seven brothers and sisters. These lessons of work ethic were passed on to Lin as she worked two jobs to raise her own daughter alone. Along the way, she managed to buy a home, saving tips from waitressing and setting aside part of her modest income as a sign language interpreter. I respected this immensely. But I was most struck by Lin's basic attitude toward life. Her natural state was happy. Something could happen in the course of the day to take that away, but she would wake the next morning happy again. Lin wasn't prone to blaming, waiting, or rationalizing. She believed in the basic goodness of people, karma, and the value of silliness.

We didn't see each other during the weeks my boys lived with me. I wanted to focus on being their father and also felt they were not yet ready to see me with another woman. Lin understood this. But this served only to increase the intensity of our relationship during the weeks when we were together, resulting in a vigorous intimacy.

Three months into the relationship, Lin and I stole away to a tiny seaside cottage on Lopez Island. I prepared my signature chicken piccata dish with mashed potatoes and asparagus. Afterward, we lit a dozen or more candles stationed all about the living room and set Norah Jones to play on the sound system. Lin stood when the song "Come Away with Me" played, then signed the lyrics in beautiful, touching form. Her delicate blond hair shifted side to side as the lyrics became a dance. Her blue eyes locked on me, confident and knowing. I was filled with a complete happiness that knew no limits.

When the song was over, Lin sat sideways on the couch, facing me with my hands in hers. "I love you," she said. "But please don't feel like you have to say it back. I just want you to know how I feel."

It was magical and perfect, the one thing I wanted most to hear. It was also the one thing I most feared hearing. The instinct to protect myself emotionally was still too strong. I knew I could not echo her words, even though I felt them crashing around inside of me. I read sincerity in Lin's eyes and felt safe to not return the sentiment.

"Thank you," I said clumsily.

But Lin understood.

THE LION DREAM

That night, I dreamed I was standing in a vast grassland. Wildebeests and zebras grazed casually about me. It was warm, even though the evening light was fading. Suddenly, something large brushed next to me as it passed from behind—a male lion, massive and dangerous. He stopped a few yards away, looked back at me, then walked a broad arch that required me to turn 180 degrees as I watched him. The lion stopped again to look back, then walked off in the direction of Kilimanjaro.

From that day forward, this dream came to me night after night. It was always the same, except that I followed the lion a bit longer each time, drawing nearer to Kilimanjaro. I found myself obsessing about the dream during waking hours, distracted to the point of sitting through green traffic lights. Finally, I told Lin about the lion dream, then added, "I think I am supposed to go to Africa."

"What?"

"Africa. I think I am supposed to go there, and I am supposed to climb Mount Kilimanjaro. I don't know why," I said.

I was prepared for Lin to object. The whole notion was lunacy, especially since I could not say why I was supposed to climb Kilimanjaro or what I expected to come of it. This was to say nothing of the risks. Kilimanjaro (19,410 feet), the most climbed and underestimated mountain on earth, takes fifteen lives a year.

"You should go," she said with a smile.

Lin accompanied me on training hikes and helped me hang posters of Kilimanjaro in my home. For my birthday, she bought me a children's book of African animals. Each morning at breakfast, I would punch out the pieces to assemble a new creature as my tabletop zoo grew crowded. The experience of having a supportive partner fueled my passion for both the climb and our relationship. I felt so fortunate, so loved, so in love. Yet I still could not find the courage to speak the words.

I left for Africa on January 14, 2008, still having never told Lin I loved her.

CASTING THE STONE

The first leg of my flight itinerary left Seattle, crossing up over the Arctic Circle en route to Amsterdam. I had taken a sleep aid with hopes of gathering as much rest as possible in the course of the all-night flight, but something busy inside of my brain woke me at two and would not settle back down.

I looked out the window at the vast frozen landscape thirty thousand feet below and felt a deep sense of peace, the kind of peace that lives next door to loneliness, and the quiet reflective reverence that haunts the basements of both. Moonlight set a soft glow upon the arctic. I tried to imagine some form of life going about its business down there, happily oblivious to the many things the rest of us are told to fear. I had left those things behind. A simpler life awaited me in Africa—a life consisting of the mountain, my hiking boots, and whatever lessons I was meant to learn through this adventure. Like the featureless white world below, I found my thoughts being reset to a blank sheet of paper, a sort of airborne baptism that would deliver me clean with fresh eyes and an open spirit.

ARRIVAL

The presidential election in Kenya had just taken place. Eight hundred Kenyans had died already in the tit-for-tat murderous skirmishes that followed its tainted result. Open battle was being waged with machetes in broad daylight while the military secured key assets—like the airport.

We were led to a room by two armed soldiers and told to wait. I approached one of them after a few hours had passed to ask why we were being held. The soldier told me someone had been shooting at the jets as they took off. Our flight from Nairobi to Arusha was therefore delayed until sundown. Three hours later, a soldier entered the room and announced, "We go now." He led us down a staircase then exited a door out onto the tarmac. "Quickly," the soldier shouted back at us as he broke into a jog. We serpentined between aircraft idling in the darkness, the powerful thrust from props and jet turbines shoving us in random directions. At one point, I became aware that the soldier and I had left everyone else behind. I stopped to go back for the other passengers, but they appeared just then in the night like a flock of confused ostriches. We boarded our jet, which lifted off before some passengers had even managed their seat belts.

I had flown into airports like Atlanta, where a bit of rain creates a scene of such helplessness and confusion that one is reminded of Dorothy and friends being molested by flying monkeys in *The Wizard of Oz*. So, under circumstances bordering on civil war, I had no expectation of ever seeing my bags again. Yet there they were, both of my gear duffels, going around the carousel at the Kilimanjaro International Airport while soft Muzak played over the intercom.

I was greeted by a driver who loaded my things into his

sturdy Land Rover. We rumbled up unmarked dirt roads for the next hour, through armed checkpoints, climbing the jungle-covered lower flanks of Mount Meru. Then a massive set of gates, perhaps twenty feet tall, opened to welcome us into a lodge compound.

THE TEAM RENDEZVOUS

It was almost noon by the time I woke. "Mr. Dorje is waiting for you in the lounge," the front desk attendant said. I had been looking forward to meeting our Nepalese expedition guide, Ang Dorje, ever since seeing his name on the final roster released by climb sponsor Adventure Consultants. Ang was featured prominently in Jon Krakauer's book *Into Thin Air*. He was Rob Hall's lead Sherpa, or sirdar, on that fateful day in 1996 when eight climbers lost their lives on Everest. Ang emerged as one of that day's heroes.

Ang sat alone at a table in the otherwise empty lounge. The open-air room offered breathtaking vistas of the Tanzanian grasslands below. Ang seemed lost in that view as I approached. "You must be Ang Dorje," I said. He stood and offered me his hand, smiling warmly. We were soon joined by teammates Richard Birkill, a South African physician who had immigrated to Canada, and Brian Burkholder, a jack-of-all-trades dreamer from Minnesota.

"Are you the Ang Dorje from *Into Thin Air*?" Brian asked immediately after being introduced. Ang nodded. "Tell us about that day." I felt bad for Ang. It seemed like an abrupt request. But he showed no discomfort, generously taking the time to walk us through his account. Ang's voice broke for a moment when he came to the part where he left Beck Weathers for dead.

"I shake him," Ang said, "but no respond." It seemed clear he was troubled still.

THE FIRST STEPS

Our expedition had chosen the Machame Route, which begins on the lower southwest flank of Kilimanjaro. It traverses the entire south side of the mountain, gaining altitude over the course of five days. We were greeted at the Machame trailhead by our local guide, Zuwadi, and his assistant, Butu. In addition to leading the way, their duties included hiring the porters and managing our camp's food and water. A crowd of men was gathered just outside the trailhead gate, hoping to be hired onto an expedition. The Tanzanian government stipulates a minimum of four porters be hired for every climber, which felt like an embarrassing measure of assistance to me after having none on Denali. Zuwadi selected twenty men then distributed their loads of thirty pounds each.

Team members carried only a daypack with their lunch, water, and a change of clothes. Knowing this would be the case, I had spent months of preparation trying to shed the muscle mass built up for Denali. Such bulk would be added weight on my legs and serve no useful purpose. Worse still, it would compete for scarce oxygen. I had cut out all weight lifting during training and focused on building what I called "badger legs": lean, strong legs that could move for many hours at a time.

We started out through dense jungle, where strange birds called out and colobus monkeys played in the trees high above. A faint herbal scent hung in the air as we passed by exotic flowers.

The route broke out above the jungle just as we arrived at Machame Camp (9,350 feet) that evening. Our tents were already up, including a dining tent with table, chairs, and hot tea waiting. The rain had ceased, so we hung our wet shirts on the bushes and walked about camp, bare-chested in the pleasant warmth of an African evening.

The sound of the jungle's night creatures came to life soon after sundown. Richard and I shared a tent that night, pausing our conversation whenever a particularly strange noise rose out of the darkness.

Richard had grown up in the days of South Africa's apartheid. Though he agreed with the end of that practice, the transition from it had been chaotic in his view. Policies and practices often seemed arbitrary, with greater emphasis on settling old scores than on the creation of racial harmony. Violence against whites increased dramatically. With two young children to think about, Richard and his wife became part of the white flight that followed. Canada welcomed them with open arms, happy to gain highly skilled immigrants. Richard had prospered since then, practicing medicine in the town of Lac la Biche, Alberta.

Richard told me he missed little about Africa. But during the years he lived there, he had dreamed of one day climbing Kilimanjaro. The fact he had not done so felt like unfinished business to him, the one thing that could bring him back.

We continued higher the next day, passing into a strange world of shoulder-high succulents and dry grass. Now well above the trees, we enjoyed broad sweeping vistas of Tanzania and the controlled burns underway as farmlands below prepared for the growing season.

We arrived at Shira Camp (12,500 feet) that evening. Dinner was cut short when a powerful wind swept up the side of Kilimanjaro, forcing us to retreat to our tents. It was my turn to have a tent to myself, so I stretched out with my gear, snacks, journal, and iPod. I tried to film a selfie with my video camera, but it quickly became a shouting match with the wind thrashing my tent, so I put the camera away and turned in for the night.

When I woke a few hours later, the storm had passed. All was cool and still. I stepped outside the tent to stretch my back, already stiff from sleeping on the ground. A gibbous moon watched, yellow and soulful, from what seemed like just a few miles above. I climbed back in my tent and turned on the video camera. "I want to show you something," I said to future viewers. "People ask me what I like about climbing. It's moments like these." I turned the camera away from myself and climbed out the tent door, revealing that haunting moon. Then I stood there, just looking up at that moon while my thoughts drifted to Lin.

I should have told her, I kept thinking. I should have told Lin that I loved her.

THE MENTAL CLIMB

Unlike the low profile I kept with the Denali climb, this time I told a good many people about my Kilimanjaro adventure before leaving. I was excited about it and wanted to share whatever came of the experience. I knew part of Ang's daily duties would be calling in updates via satellite phone to Adventure Consultants headquarters in New Zealand. They, in turn, would post narratives on their website. This made it possible for family and friends to follow along, a notion that pleased me greatly.

I brought my video camera hoping to capture something more from the experience, the way Ty did on our Denali climb. After returning to Anchorage from our Denali climb, we all gathered in his tiny living room to watch the films. Much of the footage was visually stunning. But we learned something unexpected along the way. Ty had interviewed each team member before the climb, asking, "What is it going to take for you to get to the top of North America?" All five of the team members who went on to summit answered this question the same way. In various forms, the successful team members all said they would need to find joy in each day. The unsuccessful team members all stressed maintaining a singular focus, stating, "You gotta keep your eyes on the prize."

Having come of age in the corporate culture of Wall Street, I had heard speakers and coaches preach this gospel of linear thinking for years on end: pick a goal, never take your eyes off of it, and damned whatever gets in the way. Indeed, I myself had embraced this philosophy. But the outcome on Denali strongly challenged this notion. Since that time, I had begun to wonder if this conventional wisdom about achieving goals had been wrong all along.

It's exhilarating to imagine success, to see yourself standing on top. Some climbers will go to that place when they need a lift. You might be struggling one day, so you picture yourself on the summit. But each time you do this, it's like taking an advance on a paycheck you haven't finished earning. Eventually there is not enough pay remaining to warrant the requisite effort to receive it. Then comes the moment when your dream turns on you. You are in pain. You imagine the summit. But instead of being energized by that image, you extrapolate your current condition into an unbearable sum of suffering to come, and that sum easily dwarfs the payoff. You are done.

This would have been me if not for the timing of my divorce and the fact that it had already beaten me down to a point where I just focused on getting through each day. Indeed, going into the Denali climb, I planned to *not* get to the summit. Yet each day I was committed to succeeding. It never occurred to me these notions were mutually exclusive.

POSTSTORM AWAKENING

The next morning, we found our dining tent flattened and its contents scattered by the storm. The porters were busy retrieving the pieces when Zuwadi announced we would be taking breakfast outside. "So, it is a nice morning. There is no reason to put up the tent," he said in a thick Swahili accent. "We will find the table. We will put it here. We will eat. Then we go." Zuwadi smiled warmly as though this had been the plan all along. He then turned to the porters and shouted several sentences in Swahili. The men laughed briefly, then each leapt into action packing up camp. By the time we finished our oatmeal, everything except our packs and the table we sat at was gone. Four porters remained. One cleared the table as we stood, while another put it on his head and left. A third porter stacked the chairs, then left with them atop his head. The fourth handed us our lunches, then left balancing the stove on his head. I looked around. There was no trace we had ever been there.

The sides of Kilimanjaro are raked from top to bottom with deep valleys. Traversing the mountain requires frequent steep descents down into, and ascents back up out of, these valleys. Though most of a Kilimanjaro climb is more accurately described as a trek, it is an extremely strenuous trek owing to this topography. By the time we descended down into the valley where Barranco Camp (13,044 feet) was located, I felt quite spent. A light rain had begun falling a few hours earlier, so we arrived cold and wet. Brian and I climbed into our tent and put on dry clothes.

We rested for a few hours while the porters prepared dinner, then convened to our group tent for curry soup. Each lunch and dinner began with soup, another means of forcing hydration. This was typically followed by an entrée featuring rice or pasta, then decaf tea or coffee.

We lingered at the table, nibbling cookies and talking about climbing as the sun faded. I asked each team member the same question I had been asking myself since leaving home: why do we climb these mountains?

"I think it is a goal," Ang said. "A man has succeeded in life and has a bit of money. He wants a challenge."

"Dopamine deficiency," Richard stated flatly. "We need regular risk-taking thrills to stimulate enough dopamine to compensate for that deficiency."

"I don't know," Brian said. "I guess it's like Ang said. You need a goal. You think it will make you feel good about yourself."

Then Richard turned to me. "Why are *you* climbing this mountain?"

"I honestly do not know," I answered. "I felt compelled

to come here, like I'm supposed to do this for some reason. I'm still trying to figure out what that reason is."

As a man of science, Richard had no use for the vague or transcendent. "Dopamine deficiency," he said.

SLEEP INTERRUPTED

I woke that night with a jolt. My entire intestinal track was on the move, and I had very little time to do anything about it. Grabbing my head lamp, I put on my hiking boots and scrambled through camp toward the outhouse in my underwear. Several expeditions stood in the way, so I dodged and leapt around their tents in a high stakes steeplechase.

I skidded through the outhouse door and crashed against one wall as the wet wooden floor cheated my braking ability. My shoulder dislodged a plank, which then fell noisily among the rocks outside. In a single motion, I lowered my boxer briefs and stepped up onto the blocks on either side of the hole in the floor, surrendering to nature's will.

Back at my tent, I feared the implications of contracting a GI bug at this altitude. The immediate dehydration it brings can turn a sea-level discomfort into a life-threatening condition. My climb was probably over.

I made two more trips to the outhouse that night, waking weak and exhausted in the morning. Ang seemed concerned when I reported my condition to him. Calling

Richard over to our huddle, the two decided I should start a course of Cipro. It was a short three-mile trek that day to Karanga Camp (13,106 feet), so I could continue on while we waited to see what progress the medication made.

Frequent trailside stops made for a longer day than I wanted, but the weather was pleasant and my condition seemed to improve a bit as we arrived at Karanga Camp. Now perched on the southeast shoulder of Kilimanjaro, we gazed out across the Kenyan grasslands. The annual migration of 1.5 million wildebeests was underway, and though we could not see any of these animals from so far away, just knowing they were part of the vast green landscape felt life-affirming.

Ang hung out with me at camp that evening, monitoring my condition and making sure I hydrated thoroughly. In the course of our conversations, I learned how he had started working as a porter at the age of twelve, eventually earning a place guiding climbers. Ang was twenty-two when he first summited Everest and would go on to summit the mountain many more times while working for Rob Hall. In 2001, Ang met American professor Michelle Gregory of Brown University while she was conducting a study from Everest Base Camp. Somehow, in that environment of squeaky air, marginal hygiene, and thick down clothing, they fell in love. Ang immigrated to the United States the following year, and the two were wed. Michelle subsequently took a job with GE in Richland, Washington. They were raising their two children there, just a few hundred miles from my hometown of Bellingham. A devoted family man, Ang called home from the summit of world-class peaks whenever he was able. He had spoken with his young son from the top of Cho Oyu (26,906 feet) recently. When Ang told him it was night where he was, his son asked him to stand on a box and touch the moon.

When not away climbing, Ang worked repairing windmills throughout eastern Washington. He told me he would be returning to Everest soon to fill his role as sirdar for Adventure Consultants in the upcoming season, but he planned to go no higher than camp two. "Too dangerous," he said. Four months later, on May 24, Ang summited Everest for his seventeenth time.

MOVE TO BARAFU CAMP

The two-mile trek to Barafu Camp (15,331 feet) gained 2,225 feet, rising up out of sparse grasslands into a harsh volcanic moonscape. We moved slowly, as if acting the parts of astronauts in a simulated lunar landing. I made a concerted effort to breathe between each step. My strength was returning, but I knew it would be foolish to test its limits just yet.

There was no chatter among us, just a light wind and the sound of loose rock grinding beneath our steps. I thought about Lin and felt grateful for her choice to support me in this adventure, to celebrate it without requiring that it make sense in the context of anything at all. She seemed to understand my need to live this way, listening to life and taking risks.

Zuwadi stopped by our dining tent that evening to brief us on the summit attempt. We would leave camp at midnight after a quick breakfast. Because the final thousand vertical feet of Kilimanjaro is comprised of loose scree, it is important to ascend while it's still firm from freezing in the night. If everything worked out, we would summit at daybreak.

BRIAN

Brian and I lay awake that night in our tent, listening to Zuwadi entertain the porters. He would call out a man's name. That man would call back from his tent. Then Zuwadi would say several sentences, all in Swahili. A roar of laughter would rise up from the tents when he finished. Then Zuwadi would call out another name. It went on like this for some time. Soon we too were laughing, though we had no idea what had been said. A contagion of happiness had spread among us.

Once camp went silent, Brian and I lay awake talking about the very different paths that had led our lives to this place. His included a stint in jail, mistakes with debt, and a process of remaking himself with the help of a wonderful woman who had come into his life. Brian had worked three jobs, including a newspaper route, to get completely debt-free. But the dream of climbing Kilimanjaro had beckoned and, with his wife's blessing, they had spent their entire savings to finance it. "I don't know if that was a mistake," he said.

"There isn't much in this life that can't be lost, taken away, or worn to dust by time," I told Brian. "But the fact you stood on top of *Africa*? That can *never* be taken away."

A shy smile came over his face.

"Yeah, I guess you're right," he said.

SUMMIT LAUNCH

We woke and readied for the climb after only three hours of sleep. Brian and I walked by the light of our head lamps to the team dining tent. Richard and Ang were already seated there, sipping tea. Both inquired about my condition.

"I feel pretty good," I said. "Maybe 85 percent. Good enough to take my shot."

Our cook rushed into the tent with a steaming skillet, then thrust down the morning's offering upon our plates. It was a "spaghetti omelet," a culinary contrivance born of equal parts spaghetti, egg, and convenience. I stared down at my plate, trying to sell the notion to myself: It's egg. You eat egg. It's spaghetti. You eat spaghetti. It's hot. You eat hot food. But I just could not. "It feels like more of a cracker morning to me," I said. I poured some tea and spread several crackers with Nutella, the modestly nourishing chocolate condiment found throughout Africa.

Zuwadi joined us but was not sufficiently awake to engage his talkative tendencies, so we ate in silence.

"I had a strange dream last night," I suddenly piped up. They looked at me. "One of the porters told me he had some bad news and some good news. He said the bad news was that there was a giant yeti eating climbers as they approached the summit."

After a few moments Zuwadi asked, "The good news?"

"He only eats the white ones."

The confused and nervous look that came over Zuwadi's face told me Africa was not ready for race humor. Only Brian chuckled a bit. I turned to him. "Thank you. Tip your waitress. I'm here all week."

THE SUMMIT ATTEMPT

We set out at a slow pace with Zuwadi at the lead, followed by Richard, Brian, myself, Ang, and Butu. High-altitude climbing is all about the distribution of scarce resources, most notably oxygen. Though the brain comprises just 2 percent of a person's body weight, it consumes 25 percent of the oxygen taken in—compared to the 7 percent the heart uses. I was aware of this and knew the importance of keeping simple thoughts. A climber who is fearful or agitated will stimulate reactions in his body that lead it to consume more oxygen. By avoiding such thoughts, the climber leaves more oxygen to go around among the parts of the body actually needed for climbing.

This effect represents the flashpoint where mental and physical strength meet.

I listened to the sound of the night air rushing in and out of my body. Thoughts of loved ones then passed through my mind like photos in a slideshow. We stopped to rest and hydrate at the top of each hour, looking out into the darkness with no visual sense of where we were. My altimeter was the only means by which I could substantiate our progress. In contrast to the high-end battle gear each of us wore, Ang was climbing in tennis shoes and a light coat. Even at high camp, he registered a blood oxygen saturation in the high nineties, while Brian, Richard, and I put up the kind of readings that could start a shoving match between undertakers. Most of the time, Ang climbed with his hands in his pockets. He looked bored.

We came upon the first sick climber around five o'clock. He was sitting on a rock by the side of the trail, slumped forward with his elbows braced against his knees. A local guide was standing beside him, waiting patiently to see if the man's condition improved. There were many more ill climbers, some so sick from the altitude that they lay on the ground vomiting pitifully.

I noticed Brian was starting to waver and pointed this out to Ang. He and Butu came forward to flank Brian on either side. A big man of 245 pounds, I doubted either could do much if Brian fell over, but the modest incline we were on did not pose a risk of serious fall.

We stopped to rest at Stella Point (18,652 feet), the eastern rim of Kilimanjaro's volcanic crater. Huddling from the wind behind a large boulder, the team discussed Brian's condition. His oximeter reading was not particularly low for this altitude, and though certainly wobbly, he did not slur his speech. The remaining 689 feet of elevation to Uhuru Peak, the summit of Kilimanjaro, would cross over the mountain's famous white glacier, but there were no crevasses to contend with or steep trailside drop-offs to worry about. Brian drank twelve ounces of fruit punch Gatorade and reported feeling better, so we set out for the summit.

For the next sixty minutes, we plodded slowly up the southern edge of the crater's rim. I looked down into the dormant volcano, where a broken landscape of pumice and snow retreated to its center in undulating waves. The other side of our trail was anchored by dramatic hanging glaciers now glowing softly in the moonlight. We rounded a massive rock formation and saw the large wooden sign marking Kilimanjaro's summit just fifty feet away. Another expedition was celebrating in front of it, whooping and hugging one another. A sympathetic joy washed over me as though I was watching arrivals at an airport. They were so happy. We were about to be that happy. We were about to stand at the summit. My heart was running wild. I could feel my face shining like a new dime. Then, ten steps from the summit of Kilimanjaro, Brian called out to Ang and collapsed in the snow. He began vomiting as I knelt down to help him. Richard and Ang examined Brian, determining he should descend immediately. But none of us were going to see Brian fall short of the summit when he was this close. We gathered him up to his feet and—half dragging, half supporting—shepherded Brian the final steps to the top of Africa.

A few quick photos were taken, then Butu was dispatched to accompany Brian down to Barafu Camp. The rest of us remained a bit longer. I called my youngest son, Chase, on the satellite phone. "I'm on top of Africa," I shouted into the phone.

DAVE MAURO, DR RICHARD BIRKILL, ANG DORJEE CHHULDIM SHERPA, BRIAN BURKHOLDER. PHOTO BY ZUWADI MARTIN NGUMA.

"Can you see our house from there?" Chase asked. We both laughed.

"I just wanted to call you and let you know I love you," I said just before the connection was lost. I spoke briefly with Lin and my mother then left a voice message for my other son, Trevor.

A bright orange slit appeared on the horizon as January 27, 2008, officially arrived in Tanzania at 6:24 a.m. Standing at the highest point on the continent, we were, for a few brief moments, the only things touched by that light. I would describe the sensation as satisfying, or joyful, or triumphant if any of these words remotely approximated what I felt. But the strange and unexpected emotion that washed through me was much larger than that, and it seemed to come to, instead of from, me. It was warm and peaceful, pure and just. What I felt, standing there in the light of a new day, was love.

Then the sky, the glacier, and the light snow still falling gently upon us all turned brilliant red. Ang slapped me on the back as I stood there weeping. He stuffed a rock into the pocket of my coat and zipped it shut. "We should go down now," he said. I told him I had one quick thing I needed to do first. Pulling a plastic bag from my chest pocket, I opened it and poured out a small amount of my brother's ashes.

DOWN

We descended just twenty minutes before coming upon Brian sitting on a rock. Butu stood next to him, looking unsure. No longer able to stand, it seemed clear Brian's altitude sickness had taken a more serious turn. Richard, again pressed into the role of team physician, diagnosed cerebral edema, fluid building up in Brian's brain. He administered a dose of dexamethasone and said we would need to wait twenty minutes.

Dexamethasone is a potent synthetic steroid. It is often used to counteract the buildup of fluids when treating brain tumors. Altitude climbers carry dex as the heavy hitter in their small pharmacy of weapons. With a potency forty times that of hydrocortisone, it is the go-to choice for a climber afflicted with cerebral edema.

We waited out the medication, making pleasant chit-chat while each of us tried to develop a plan B should the treatment fail. Too heavy for us to carry and too high for a helicopter rescue, Brian would need a litter and a large team to carry it if he could not descend under his own power. This would take time, and the big question in each of our minds was whether Brian would have that much time.

"Let's see you stand," Richard said. Richard and I each grabbed an arm, together hoisting Brian to his feet. He held. "That's a good start," Richard commented. He ran Brian through a series of questions then declared him ready to descend. For almost everything that ails a person at altitude, descent brings immediate improvement. The more Brian could descend, the more he would be able to descend still farther. We got underway with Ang and Butu once again flanking Brian's tall frame.

The combination of dex and descending four thousand feet had restored Brian completely by the time we reached Barafu Camp. But, concerned for the possibility of relapse, we decided to break camp and continue down Kilimanjaro. During this time, Ang and I enjoyed a long discussion on the topic of religion.

I told Ang I had been baptized a Catholic at birth, but not raised as such. Still, the experiences of my life had led me to believe in some higher power. Ang said he, like most Nepalese, was Buddhist. He explained that Buddhists do not believe in God. Such religious ideas, in their opinion, have their origin in fear.

"Buddha said, 'Gripped by fear men go to the sacred mountains, sacred groves, sacred trees and shrines,'" Ang said. "Buda teaches us to understand our fears and accept the things we can't change."

It occurred to me that fear had taken me to this sacred mountain, to Kilimanjaro. My dreams of following the lion had begun right after Lin confessed her love for me. The fear of being hurt had held me back from telling Lin I loved her. That is why my dreamworld spoke to me night after night. I was in Africa to learn something important about that fear, to understand and perhaps even accept it.

DESCENT COMPLETE

We continued descending all the way down to Mweka Camp (9,842 feet), completing our descent the following morning as we arrived at Mweka Gate around noon. Brian, Richard, and I raised a sizable gratuity to be distributed by Zuwadi among the porters then boarded our Land Rover for the return to Mount Meru Hotel. We celebrated our successful climb that evening with a lavish meal in the hotel dining room. I was sad to know this would mean our parting since I was the only one sticking around for safari. The rest of the team all flew home the following morning.

SAFARI

My driver Haffife and I rumbled around in a full-size Toyota Land Cruiser as we set out on safari. It felt strange at first to have a car to myself, but that was just the way things had worked out. Soon I came to enjoy the space, stretching out with my journal, cameras, and various snacks scattered about me.

We visited the Lake Manyara Reserve and the Ngorongoro Crater during our first two days, seeing lions, elephants, warthogs, and monkeys. The third night, we stayed at a lodge on the edge of the Serengeti. A local musician strolled the dining room that evening, playing an endingidi, a gourd with a neck and single string played by pulling a bow across it. He was animated and enthusiastic. The man and his wife joined me at my table when he was done playing.

We spoke of the endingidi and how his uncle had taught him to play it. A year earlier the man had been earning a living making bricks when the impulse to become a full-time endingidi musician came to him.

"Wife," he said, playing back their conversation, "I do not feel joy for making the bricks. But the endingidi makes me happy, and it makes other people happy."

"Then I said," his wife took over, "Husband, you should quit making the bricks and just play the endingidi."

They smiled warmly at one another. Then a curious look came over the man's face.

"Where is *your* wife?" he asked.

"I do not have a wife," I said.

"But you have children?"

"Yes. Two sons."

"Ohhhh. So you are..." He searched for the word. "Devoid?"

"Yes," I said, feeling in some respects his word fit better than the one I was expecting. He seemed deeply troubled by this.

"Hmmm. This is not good," the man said. He went on to speak of how wrong devoid is. Part of me wanted to explain, but it seemed senseless to even try when I was speaking with a man who enjoyed the kind of support where his wife would encourage him to quit their only source of income to instead play a single-string gourd.

AN OASIS IN THE SERENGETI

Two days later, Haffife and I were far out on the Serengeti. I stood atop our vehicle observing hundreds of thousands of wildebeest in every direction. The other grazing species, zebra, impala, and kudu, were mixed in, also numbering in the tens of thousands. Not surprisingly, a host of predators—cheetah, hyena, and leopard—followed the migration.

We made our way to a lush green oasis where a pride of lions was lying about in the grass with full, bulging bellies. Animals that would normally be prey for the lions grazed about them unafraid. They seemed to know the pride had eaten for the day and represented no threat. The animals of the Serengeti lazed about in perfect harmony like the title page in a child's Bible, inviting me to walk among them wearing only a robe and shoulder-length hair. But fed or not, many of these peaceful animals could make quick work of me, even in play, so I remained within the safety of our Land Rover.

Haffife pointed out various plants and flowers surrounding us, noting the cautions that came with each.

"That red flower has a liquid that will blind a man. This bush over here," he said, gesturing to a delicate shrub, "has barbed thorns that dig deeper and deeper into the flesh until infection sets in."

This is the most beautiful and most dangerous place I have ever seen, I thought. Everything about that seemed right to me. By this time, I had come to believe that beauty in the natural world came hand in hand with personal risk, one being fair compensation for the other. And this, it seemed, was part of what drove me to climb high mountains: a hunger to experience nature's beauty, which, in its highest order, came in the form of love. That's the difference between beauty in the man-made world and nature, I thought. The man-made world is designed so we can take without giving, experiencing beauty without risk. We have handrails, sidewalks, fences, and laws. Not so in nature.

I was, of course, experiencing all of this from the safety of our vehicle, the man-made world, and because of that could not know the full rapture of what lay about us. Then it occurred to me that relationships were a lot like the natural world, where beauty in its highest form, love, could only be known when taking great personal risk. The only way to fully experience love is to get out of the car, shed your devices of self-protection, and risk the consequences. Love suddenly made sense to me when I viewed it this way: as part of nature instead of man's invention.

Then it came to me that I had yet to experience the fullness of the love I shared with Lin. All the things I did to protect myself from being hurt emotionally only served to insulate my heart from the purity of love. *That* is why I came here, I thought. *That* is what I needed to learn. I looked at the large male lion lazing in the grass, surrounded by his pride, and said, "Thank you."

HOMECOMING

I passed through international customs and found my way to the escalator that would deliver me to arrivals. At the top I threaded through a small group of people and took two more steps before the image of a woman I had just passed played back in my mind. She was costumed as a cheetah, with fuzzy ears pinned to her braided blond hair. She wore whiskers painted on her face and a long animal print dress. I stopped and turned back to see Lin smiling at me from behind those whiskers. All my fatigue and jet lag vaporized in that instant. I dropped my duffels and gathered Lin up in my arms. We kissed for an embarrassingly long moment, then kissed again. I wanted to tell her right then about the lion and what he had taught me, but I had already chosen a different time and place for that.

I LOVE YOU

Lin and I returned to that same beach cottage on Lopez Island where she first said she loved me. We opened up the door and stepped into the cold stale air within. It was the off-season, and the cottage had sat idle for several months. There was no smell of sunscreen or bug repellant, no incense or campfire smoke, just a whiff of salt and tired dry wood. I flipped the breakers one by one with a satisfying snap, watching the lights and appliances leap to life. Lin began unpacking our cooler while I jogged up the driveway to turn on the cabin's water supply.

I fussed endlessly with the propane heater and the settings on the appliances. I ran the water until it flowed clear then checked to see if the bat that sometimes lived behind one of the flower boxes was there. It was obvious to me that I was stalling, but Lin said nothing. It should have been easier. Lin had already told me she loved me. But I was sweating bullets.

At one point during the first year of my marriage, I had told Jenny I loved her as we took a romantic stroll down a long, empty beach. But she did not respond. When I asked why, she said she came from a family that didn't express such things openly. I was stunned. I could recall her saying it before. Had our love fatigued already? I wanted to press for a better answer, but I was afraid of what I might hear. I knew I loved her and could not bear the thought she might not love me. The empty pause that followed my professions of love came to feel like a game of Russian roulette, invitations to say what she was really feeling, so I stopped telling Jenny I loved her, and she likewise remained silent. Four years passed. By the time we got around to trying the words again, they had come to feel like a phrase learned by rote in some Spanish immersion course.

"Come. Sit with me," Lin beckoned from the couch. We pulled a blanket across our laps and stared into the fire for a long, patient moment. Lin asked me to tell her about the oasis again, so I did, adding color to freshen up a story so recently told. But this time, I told Lin what I had learned. Then I took her hands in mine and looked into her melting blue eyes. "I love you, Lin," I said. "And I knew it the last time we sat on this couch, but I didn't have the courage to say it."

"I knew that," Lin said. "That's why I was fine waiting."

I felt as though I had just set down a sixty-pound pack. Then the tears came, the same tears I had shed on the summit of Kilimanjaro as the light and love of a new day fell upon me there. We held each other, naked to the promise and punishments of love.

ELBRUS

I HAD THE PROFILE OF KILIMANJARO TATTOOED ON MY
right shin, just below the tattoo I acquired after returning from Denali. They looked good together, the third
and fourth tallest of the continental summits. Each held
a special meaning to me, and I wanted to tell their stories.
They were out there, visible any time I wore shorts, and I
welcomed inquires.

"That's pretty subtle," one friend scoffed.

"Yeah, but have you climbed Everest?" another said.

Their reactions, their apparent need to cut down my
accomplishments instead of celebrate them with me, took
me by surprise. I noticed this with a few other people,
mostly guys. "Three months out of the year, you're the
most pretentious man alive," one friend joked, referring
to the seasons I wore shorts.

It was not as though I brought up the topic of my
climbs or forced it into conversations. And these people

certainly never asked about them. Yet they reacted like I had been a terrible braggart. I came to believe that the real problem was a disruption I created in their sense of order. Like myself, these grumblers were in their midforties, comfortable, busy raising kids. It would be easy for anyone to decide that was enough, to live a good and decent life. It is. But for a man to relax and enjoy that life, he must accept that his days of big adventure are behind him—that he is simply too old to do X, Y, and Z. I believe my choices agitated this view, and some people resented me for taking away their comfort.

I began feeling self-conscious about my tattoos and soon chose to wear long pants even on sunny days. As had been the case after Denali, I felt compelled to hide away this part of myself until I better understood why it seemed to bother some people so much.

THAT DAY IN THE CAR

It was the summer of 2008, and both my boys in the year since the divorce had settled into the rhythm of trading weeks between their mother and me. There had been some rough patches, some time in counseling, some acting out. And things were still far from perfect, but we were doing all right. Now fifteen and thirteen, my sons enjoyed robust social lives. They'd reach out to me for rides here and there, but otherwise they were more interested in time with friends than with me. I understood this and was fine with it. Then one day Trevor called and asked that I pick him up at his mother's house. "I need to talk to you about something," he said.

We had driven only two blocks when Trevor said, "I think I'm bisexual."

I eased to the side of the road and turned the car off. We sat in silence for a moment. From the time each of my boys was born, I've told them that I'd always love them, no matter what. I learned this from my own mother, who had gone still further, decreeing, "If you shot someone dead, I would come up with ten reasons why the son of a bitch had it coming." My mom could often be more frank than was necessary.

I turned to face my nervous son. "I love you," I told him. "And I like your chances of finding a mate." His eyes teared as we shared a brief laugh.

Trevor's earliest childhood choices weren't typically masculine. The colors he liked, the games he enjoyed, his mechanisms of social interaction were different from most boys. But, determined to emphasize his given gender, Trevor's mother and I required him to play sports. He hated them. I made him go duck hunting with me. Though he enjoyed putting on the camouflage face makeup, Trevor found little else to like about the experience.

In hindsight, I can see that telling me he was bisexual was Trevor's way of creating a half step. I was supposed to reason that if women were still somewhere in the equation, he might turn out to be straight in the end. That in fact was my thought process as we sat in the car talking. But Trevor never looked back. He came out as openly gay shortly after starting his sophomore year of high school that fall.

FINANCIAL MARKETS

Meanwhile, my work as a financial planner had become particularly challenging.

World financial markets had been in steep decline for several months in 2008. It was not enough that clients were understandably concerned for their declining financial state, but facts had emerged implicating my firm, Merrill Lynch, as being involved in creating the crisis.

I watched helplessly as the Merrill Lynch shares that constituted most of my divorce settlement declined from ninety-five dollars to nine. Completely tapped out of whatever it took to keep forgiving the self-inflicted wounds of the company, I made the decision to move my practice elsewhere, resigning on Halloween, 2008. The next day, my friends and colleagues of twenty-one years raided my client base. One loyalist later told me someone had suggested, "We should tell his clients this is because of his divorce. You know, cast doubt on his mental state." In the final tally, a heartwarming 93 percent of my clients chose to follow me to the new firm.

Still a shareholder of Merrill Lynch stock, I received a copy of their annual report a few months later. It arrived on the same day I received a catalogue from Adventure Consultants, with whom I had climbed Kilimanjaro. I read both documents cover to cover that same day. The Merrill annual report was full of corporate doublespeak and graphs where the x-axis had been stretched out far enough to make a train wreck look like a shopping cart dent. Leadership smiled confidently in photos, framed with quotes harkening back to the proud history of the firm.

The Adventure Consultants catalogue featured pure, white mountains—uncompromising, unchanged, true, real. Climbers smiled brightly, having earned the right to stand at the summit. Exuberant testimonials littered the pages. I hungered for something real, paging through the climbing catalogue like a menu at a steak house. However, the financial markets and my own solvency were still very much up for grabs. I had chosen to keep our family home as part of the divorce settlement and now struggled to meet the bloated mortgage payments. I filed the catalogue away. It just wasn't meant to be.

But one photo from the catalogue kept calling to me: Russia's Mount Elbrus, the high summit for all of Europe at 18,513 feet. There was something about the shape of Elbrus. I found myself going back to the catalogue again and again. The other mountains were likewise remarkable in appearance, but Elbrus rolled over like a giant scoop of ice cream at the top, simple, almost welcoming. Each time I took out the catalogue, I allowed myself to read a bit more about the Elbrus climb. At only twelve days, the time commitment was considerably shorter than that of Denali. Moreover, it would not involve even one night of sleeping in a tent since the expedition was based out of a ski resort with comfortable lodging. Though I would later learn that about ten people die each year on Elbrus, at this point the experience of climbing it sounded more like a summer camp.

The financial markets began recovering in late March 2009. As I found myself drawing those first tentative gasps of relief, the thoughts of Elbrus became more frequent. Lin noticed me spending time with the climbing catalogue and asked if I planned to go on another expedition. I told her I didn't know. Truthfully, part of me did not want to take on another mountain. Climbing a high summit is a lot of work under the best of circumstances, and training for any climb is equally demanding. As well, the Elbrus expedition would cost $5,000 before airfare and travel insurance, and my income had declined to a point where alimony and child support consumed all of it. I was already living off of savings. And then there was the question of why. Why climb Elbrus? What would come of it?

THE CHUCK-IT LIST

A good friend of mine, Jeff DeBruine, died of a sudden heart attack a few weeks before I left for Kilimanjaro. As part of my own grieving process, I carried a photo of him to the summit, thinking often of Jeff along the way. He was only forty-nine. Too young. It got me thinking about my own bucket list. I suppose most people have this experience after losing someone close. But because I believe in the yin and yang of life, at some point the notion came to me that I probably also had a chuck-it list: all the things I would *not* do or become before I kicked the bucket. Some of the items on that list were placed there consciously. For instance, I had decided I would never bungee jump. Nor would I be a physician. I was fine with this. But it seemed to me that other things on the chuck-it list were subconscious additions. I was pretty sure climbing Denali and Kilimanjaro had once been subconscious entries on my chuck-it list.

Independent of these thoughts, I had come to embrace the notion that, in conversations with life, most of us prefer to be the one talking. But we cannot hear life's instructions when we are speaking. My choice to go to Africa had been rewarding on a level I could not have predicted, and that choice came from the decision to listen and trust what life seemed to be saying.

These two ideas then converged as I realized how we turn to our bucket list when choosing where to place our energies. This is us speaking. But every once in a while, something from the chuck-it list *chooses us*. In those instances, it seemed to me that must be life speaking, and, more than any other time, we should listen. It doesn't have to make sense right then. We simply need to trust that it will resonate somewhere down the line. What matters most is listening, trusting, and acting.

In late April 2009, I accepted life's instruction to climb Mount Elbrus. Trusting that some important gift was at stake, I signed up with Adventure Consultants' Mount Elbrus expedition and began training.

I embraced blogging for the first time during my preparations for Elbrus. I was anxious to document and share my experiences. This seemed like an exciting way to do it. Anyone who was interested in my climb could follow along, whether I knew them or not, and those who wanted to ignore the whole thing, like some of my friends, were free to do so. I wanted to post entries with my Blackberry on a daily basis once I was on the climb, like a serial comic strip moving the story forward one day at a time. Like the readers of this blog, I would not know where a given storyline was heading. In this respect, the writing would be much like performing improv, which continued to be an important part of my life back home.

MY INTRODUCTION TO IMPROV

I was coaching elementary school chess when I first met actor and comedian Ryan Stiles (of *Whose Line Is It Anyway?*, *The Drew Carey Show*, and *Two and a Half Men* fame) in the fall of 2004. He and his wife, Pat, had moved to Bellingham to be closer to Ryan's family, living just north of the border in British Columbia. They enrolled their two kids in the same tiny public school my boys were attending. Their son, Sam, joined our chess club.

Ryan and I struck up a friendship, golfing now and then, playing poker with some other guys in Ryan's garage bar. When the PTA decided to tear up most of the playground asphalt and install kid-friendly turf, Ryan volunteered to host a live improv show at the elegant Mount Baker Theatre in Bellingham to raise the funds. They needed $30,000 for the playground renovations and, with Ryan headlining, figured the entire sum could be raised in one show. Ryan called in some favors from his celebrity friends to cast the show, but he wanted a few locals onstage to ground the event to its homegrown origins. My phone rang.

"I'm honored to be asked," I said, "but I don't know the first thing about performing improv. I've seen you do it on *Whose Line*, and I have no idea how you guys think so fast."

"I'll teach you a few things. You'll do fine," Ryan said. He was leaving to film the next season of *The Drew Carey Show* later that day. "You're gonna know most of the audience. It's just a lot of moms and dads from the school," Ryan said. This seemed plausible. Besides, it was kind of like being invited by Michael Jordan to be his teammate in a two-on-two basketball game. How bad could it be?

"Okay," I agreed.

Three months later, I stood behind the curtains, stage left, at the Mount Baker Theatre. A packed house of 1,600 people filled the building with an excited rumble of conversations. Ryan stood next to me as he waited to be introduced. Suddenly I started feeling like I was having an out-of-body experience. What am I doing here? I'm not a performer. I'm a chess coach. I'm a financial planner, I thought. I had taken a beginners' improv class in the time since agreeing to be in the show. But suddenly I could not recall a single lesson from it. My hands were numb.

"My hands are numb," I said to Ryan. He smiled down at me from his six foot six frame. Then I heard his name announced, and Ryan stepped out onto the stage as the entire theater erupted in wild adoration.

In short order, the other cast members and I were introduced and took our places. The next hour and a half passed quickly. I was not good. But whenever my trajectory headed toward awful, Ryan would step in and save the scene. By the time Ryan opened his own improv club, The Upfront Theatre, later that year, I had improved my skills enough to be cast among the original house troupe of six actors, The Upfront Players.

I continued performing improv, sometimes hiding within it during the darker chapters that followed in my life. Improv had taught me the value of listening. In an unscripted story, an improviser must listen carefully to everything that is said so he can add information that fits. This means staying present, not becoming distracted with one's own thoughts, and trusting that the right choice will come when it is time to act. Because I had experienced several years of watching beautiful stories emerge from unscripted performances, and seeing how listening, trusting, and acting onstage as an improv performer seemed to tap into miraculous outcomes, I began to more readily accept the random elements of my offstage life—like mountain climbing.

MOSCOW

I arrived in Moscow late in the evening of July 27, 2010. Richard Birkill, one of my teammates from the Kilimanjaro climb, flew in with me. I had persuaded Richard to join me in climbing Elbrus.

Our preparation for the climb had taken two distinctly different paths. While I had packed water up the steep trail near my home, Richard spent time flying his airplane at altitudes approximating the summit of Elbrus. "You're just going to build muscle mass you don't need and then you will have to oxygenate that mass in an environment where there isn't much oxygen," he argued.

He had a point. As with Kilimanjaro, we would not be packing any real weight during this climb since our camps were fixed at the ski lodge and the upper huts. "But you will have to carry your backup gear, lunch, and water on summit day. That may be only fifteen pounds, but it will feel like fifty at that altitude," I said. We went back and forth on this all during the weeks of training, one never budging the other from his position.

Mike Roberts, our Adventure Consultants guide, introduced himself in his native Kiwi accent as we joined him for breakfast the next morning at our downtown Moscow hotel. I had done a bit of reading on Mike before leaving home and knew he had summited Everest three times and completed the coveted Seven Summits. As high-altitude guides went, Mike was a celebrity. We asked him far too many questions about the climb ahead, yet he was pleasant and affable, confident and patient. Then Richard and I set out to explore Moscow.

Our hotel was located across the street from Sokolniki Park, a sprawling 1,400-acre refuge in the heart of downtown Moscow. Richard and I walked past a long line of chess tables where old men engaged in the nation's official pastime, through a small amusement park, and emerged next to a large tiled promenade full of pensioners who danced to big band tunes crackling from low fidelity speakers. We rode the subway to Red Square, gawking at the Kremlin on one side and the vast array of designer retail shops on the other.

Aside from Moscow's Byzantine churches with their fantastically ornate onion-shaped domes, there was a dearth of color everywhere we went. Sooty high-rise apartments rose up in clusters that traded architectural imagination for brute force function, poured concrete affirmations of a value system said to hold disdain for personal expression.

The other two members of our team arrived that evening: Ankita and Paul, a twenty-something couple from New York City. Ankita was a beautiful and fit woman of Hindu descent. Her parents, who had emigrated from India, were both successful professionals in the United States who still held close to their traditional beliefs about how a proper Hindu woman should live. They had disapproved when Ankita paired up with Paul, the son of Ugandan and American parents. But a lifetime of being raised in the United States had empowered Ankita to follow her own path—dating Paul, climbing Kilimanjaro, and working as a day trader in the financial markets.

ELBRUS: A BIT OF HISTORY

The Greeks knew Elbrus by the name Strobilus and believed Prometheus was chained to a rock at its summit, where an eagle came to feed on his liver day after miserable day, a punishment dealt by Zeus for having stolen fire from the gods and given it to mankind. It is unclear whether Prometheus had a very large liver or this was just an extraordinarily small eagle.

Elbrus was first summited in 1874 by a British expedition led by F. Crauford Grove and occupied for a brief while during World War II by ten thousand German mountaineering soldiers. A few of the barracks these soldiers built at 12,400 feet are used today by teams launching summit bids on Elbrus. Thus climbers, for the two nights not spent at the lower ski lodge, enjoy tentless comfort up high.

We left Moscow the following morning, arriving at the regional airport where we would catch a flight to Mineralnye Vody in the southern part of Russia. Though we weighed our duffels carefully before leaving the hotel, each had mysteriously grown heavier by the time they landed on the scale at our gate.

"Do you see what's happening here?" Mike asked me in a hushed tone.

Our local escort then bribed the airport official with a payment concealed in a stack of documents. Suddenly our bags returned to their original weight, and we were waved through. Though our flights had been booked many months earlier, we were assigned seats in the cramped last rows of the plane. Some sort of ventilation duct consumed the leg space in front of my seat, requiring that I draw my legs in close and pile my carry-ons on top of myself. Mike's tall lanky frame fared no better.

I tried to joke with him about it, but Mike was clearly annoyed. "This is how they treat foreign visitors," he said in a peevish tone. It was true. Still just flirting with the notion of capitalism, most of Russia had yet to recognize the competitive value of service and its promise for bringing more business its way. Where other countries actively courted tourists, Russia seemed at best to tolerate them.

We bounced along through the clouds in our comfortless plane. There was no in-flight service, no movie, no overhead storage, and no safety presentation. Get in. Sit down. Shut up. I snaked a hand into my daypack, retrieving a package of trail mix that I then passed around to my teammates. Happy food.

The occupants were silent, as though we were flying to a funeral. In the brief time I had been in Russia, I noted that the people there were quite stoic. This, I reasoned, was perhaps the consequence of being the children of a generation that had little to smile about. So, it was notable when the passengers of our flight suddenly burst into applause. It startled me. The occasion of their joy? A safe landing.

We gathered our things, piled into our waiting van, and set out on the four-hour drive to the village of Azau. We drove past modest towns, through fields of sunflowers, and down a two-lane road that was often improvised into three. There were lean dogs and motionless burros. Shoeless children played with a kitten near a sad-faced old woman selling watermelons by the side of the road. Incomplete walls protected incomplete homes. There were chickens, hay trucks, cinderblocks, and ruins. These towns all had stories we would never know. We were only passing through, Westerners there for some other purpose. Our van began climbing up a rainy green valley along a river none of us knew the name of. I considered asking our driver its name, but his limited English required supplemental hand gestures. So it seemed, on such a winding narrow road, that it was best to respect the water's anonymity. We slept. We snacked. We arrived.

OZ

Azau was a village being built around a gondola house at the base of Mount Elbrus. If there was a master plan for its development, no one bothered looking at it. Structures had been started and then abandoned, their concrete and dangling rebar telling the sad tale of a dream greater than the fortunes of the dreamer. Other buildings were complete and had rolled out a plywood carpet to beckon customers across the unpaved street over rivulets of muddy runoff. Work continued on one structure as men hoisted buckets of gritty stucco up pulleys then applied the face to an odd, narrow hotel. This might have been a boom if it had not appeared so interrupted, and it might have been a town if there were any order to it. But the placement of these structures suggested a "ready, shoot, aim" process, where men and materials somehow arrived at the worksite before it had been chosen. All of this was intended to become the centerpiece of the 2014 Winter Olympics, which Russia was proud to have been chosen as host. It was a long way from ready and would still not be complete when the games started four years later.

Our hotel sat on a table of land, a short distance below the gondola house. It was a modern-looking structure featuring emerald green glass set into its white three-story facade. Daylight was transformed into an eerie green hue that fell heavy upon the simple furnishings within, a space left otherwise dark due to the proprietor's efforts to conserve electricity. I nicknamed the hotel Oz.

The next day we set out on foot, walking a pleasant trail through groves of birch trees as we made our way down the valley to Terskol. From there, we turned up a side valley and began climbing alongside a glacial stream. The weather was sunny and warm, ideal for trekking. About an hour up the valley, Ankita pulled up lame. An old running injury had resurfaced in the form of progressively worse pain in the arch of one foot. It was decided Mike would escort Ankita back to the hotel while the rest of us pressed on under the leadership of our Russian guide, Alex.

The Russian Government required that all expeditions include a local Russian guide. Though we had every confidence in Mike Roberts alone, compliance with this ordinance was not optional. Thus we hired Alex.

Alex was magnificently gregarious, seeming to embody all the misplaced mirth of Russia. His English was passable, his manner casual, and his facial expressions highly animated. But Alex was also a serious climber, having achieved fame the prior year by solo summiting K2, considered by many to be the world's most difficult mountain climb, in a twenty-seven-hour round trip from base camp.

We fell short of reaching the upper glacier, which had been our objective, but we did make it up to 9,400 feet for some acclimatization and marvelous views. On the way back, we crossed a glacial river, hopping from rock to rock. I slipped as I attempted to hard stick the landing on one stone then fell into the river on the downstream side. The pool I splashed into was deep enough for me to go completely under, pack and all. The glacial water was so cold it gave me an instant headache. I emerged downstream uttering the most primal of words. But aside from introducing an uncertain future for my camera, no real harm had been done. Alex loaned me a spare set of clothes from his pack while my own lay out to dry on the rocks. He then fired up his portable stove and brewed hot tea for all of us. Things could have turned out much worse, but no one wanted to bring that up. It was enough that the sun was shining and tea was sweet.

CLIMB TIME

We gathered our things for the move up to the huts the next morning. An effortless gondola ride would take us there. Though we had legitimately climbed a height equal to that of the huts during our acclimation rotations, I felt sheepish about using the gondolas.

The gondola out of Azau was still under construction, so we drove to the next village over and rode chairlifts up to the gondolas operating there. Every third chair carried a climber from one of the teams ascending that day. The remaining chairs were loaded with propane cylinders, boxes of food, gear duffels, and barrels of fresh water. A team of grizzled Russian men worked frantically to unload the supplies at the top of the chairlift on pace with their arrival. The men passed a flask around as each set down his load and cued up for the next grab. From there, we lined up to board the gondolas.

We had to jog next to the open gondola as it slowly rounded the corner inside the wheelhouse, throwing as much of our things inside before jumping in on top of them. This too was typical of Russia: once inertia's grip was finally broken in a given circumstance, the wheels of progress paused for no one. Paul, Ankita, and I piled into one gondola. Richard and Mike followed in the next.

The gondola carried us to the upper wheelhouse at 11,800 feet. From there, we schlepped our things a short distance to a cube-shaped structure perhaps a hundred square feet in size. Inside, two large wooden bunks hung on either wall, cushioned with horsehair mattresses. A kerosene heater was backed up against one wall. I spread my things out in a lower bunk, and then we all walked to the next cube for lunch.

The dining cube had a picnic table and bench seats inside. Any remaining space was consumed by the tight kitchen operations of a Russian woman who reached over us with steaming ladles of borscht. The table was littered with packets of tea and instant coffee, crackers and various condiments. Anything but glamorous, it was still much better than squatting in a cold tent.

After lunch we climbed up to the Pastukhova Rocks at fifteen thousand feet. We lingered there for about an hour before heading back down to high camp.

REST DAY

After breakfast the following morning, we spent some time working on snowcraft. Mike found a nearby hill with ample incline, then instructed us on traversing techniques, ice ax placement, and self-arrest. I had done all these things on Denali, but did not mind the refresher.

We spent the rest of the morning relaxing. Some of us read. I blogged. It was quiet in our hut. The climb to fifteen thousand feet had taken a pretty good bite out of us, so the downtime was welcome. But the unspoken concern on most of our minds was the fact that our summit attempt the next day would be a much longer climb than the day before, with much thinner air. Mike told the team that climbers pretty typically hit a wall in the saddle, a low depression separating Elbrus's two peaks. "From there, it will be about each individual's determination," he said. Mike then went on to talk about hypothermia and frostbite, making sure we understood the signs to watch for both in ourselves and each other.

After lunch, Richard and I burned nervous energy, examining each piece of gear and packing them for the likely order in which they would be needed. Ankita and Paul giggled in the bunk above me. I posted a photo of the two of them to my blog, not realizing Ankita's father had started following it. I would later learn he had been quite unhappy to see his daughter sharing a bed with Paul.

The six thousand vertical feet that separate high camp from the summit of Elbrus would normally represent an unmanageable stretch for all but the most elite of climbers. But, this being a ski resort, an unconventional, somewhat embarrassing element had come to be regarded as standard practice during the summit push of Elbrus. Diesel snowcats carried climbers from the cubes up to the Pastukhova Rocks. This felt wrong to me any time I thought about it. Try as I might, I could not accept the use of gas-powered machinery as anything other than cheating. But I told myself that we would really just be bookmarking our previous high point from our preparatory climbs. This helped to temporarily salve my climber's conscience.

SUMMIT DAY

There was bad news for the team when we woke at one that morning. Ankita would not be joining us for the summit attempt, though it wasn't her troubled foot that had tethered her to high camp. Instead, she had been up most of the night with some kind of intestinal bug. This left her dehydrated and weak. Ankita had done all the right things: put in the training, bought the expensive gear, hired the best guides, suffered through her foot problem, and endured the chronic discomforts of altitude acclimation.

But in the end, this would not be her day. It's a hard thing to see someone's dream shatter. Paul offered to give up his own summit dream to stay behind and care for her, but Ankita insisted he press on with the climb. Mike and Richard provided her with medications, and arrangements were made to have her taken down to Azau, where the comforts of Oz would provide further relief. I looked back at Ankita as I left our cube that morning. She was sitting in her bunk holding a large ziplock bag over her face as she prepared to vomit again. I offered a sympathetic wave, and Ankita smiled back at me through the bag.

We geared up and boarded the snowcat at two o'clock. Clear skies delivered on the promise of our weather forecast with a brilliant display of stars. By two thirty, we were stepping off the snowcat, crampons on, and starting the first pitch, a grueling incline 1,200 feet up the west flank of Elbrus. We made decent progress for the first hour, but then our pace fell off. I asked Mike if we could move faster. The wind had picked up, and it was difficult to stay warm. He said that our pace was presently being set by Richard. Hearing this, Richard increased his effort and, for ten minutes or so, our progress improved. But I watched Richard from my place at the back of the team and noticed he was working much harder than the rest of us. His efficiency of movement seemed to be slipping away. Something was wrong.

The temperature was down to −5°F, not extraordinarily cold, but with only 50 percent of the oxygen available at sea level, the physiological effect was much colder. Richard would later comment that he felt cold dressed in layers that typically kept him warm plowing snow at forty below back home in Alberta. Then Paul asked if we could move faster. He was losing body heat. Mike called for a break and, explaining that we had to dress for the pace, suggested we put on our heavy summit parkas, overpants, balaclavas, and mittens. I dug each from my pack, put them on, and felt better immediately. Paul put on his parka. Richard added his parka, heavy gloves, and balaclava. Mike and Alex put on their warmest clothing as well. We continued on, our bodies warmer, our pace still slow.

After thirty minutes, I noticed Richard duckfooting his right foot outward and pushing off to step forward and uphill with the left. I called for the team to stop and walked up to Richard. Pointing out what I had noticed, I urged him to not squander his energy with such an inefficient practice. He was breathing hard and complained that his boots were too stiff, making a normal gate impossible.

We finished the first pitch and began the second, a long steep traverse winding northward toward the saddle. Dawn broke, but we were still on the dark side of the mountain. It occurred to me that our problems with the cold would be solved if we could get out of Elbrus's shadow. Then Richard suddenly stopped. A lengthy discussion between Mike, Alex, and him followed. By the time I climbed up to them, it had been decided that Richard would take a dose of Diamox to limit the effects of altitude. He had been talking about turning back.

"We are trying to persuade him to continue on," Mike said, having seen climbers work through such conditions many times and believing Richard could do the same. It would be hard to say how much of Richard's problems were altitude, hypothermia, or general fitness. On some level, each appeared to be contributing. But there was something else.

"I have a bad feeling about this," Richard said. Back in Moscow, he had shared with me a grim premonition that had come to him as he said good-bye to one of his daughters. As she came to him, her angelic blond hair backlit by the sun, Richard had sensed it would be the last time he would see her. This foreboding was now consuming his thoughts—and still more precious energy.

Hearing this, Mike asked if Richard would feel better continuing on if they were roped together, a technique called short roping. Richard said he would, so Mike started rigging the line. Then Mike looked at Paul and didn't like what he saw. "Paul," he said, "you've just been standing there, and you still don't have your overpants on. I'm starting to question your judgment. Don't fade on me, buddy. Put those overpants on now."

Then Mike turned back to Richard, who had a new problem. With all of the standing around, Richard's left foot had gone numb. Mike handled each of these challenges decisively, quite thoroughly validating his reputation as one of the foremost high-altitude guides in the world.

"Right, we will remove the boot and warm the foot," he said, instructing Richard to lay on his back and place the afflicted foot under Mikes upper layers, against the bare flesh of his stomach. I asked what I could do to help and was handed the inner liner of Richard's boot. "Keep this somewhere warm," Mike said. I stuffed it under my parka.

Then I looked at Paul and noticed he was impossibly tangled in the process of putting on his overpants, the crampons of his right foot piercing them in three places. I backed his foot out and opened the leg zippers on his pants. Then I carefully guided each foot through. Mike finished warming Richard's foot and called for the boot liner. As we prepared to get back underway, Richard said he would give it thirty minutes more and turn around if things were not going better. The team plodded on, chasing the edge of Elbrus's shadow and the hope that our climb would emerge stronger in the warm light of day.

We passed into the sun forty minutes later on a section where the traverse flattened out. The combination of warmer conditions and a rest for our legs turned everything around. Richard seemed to find a second wind, and the cold ceased to be an issue. As we paused to hydrate, I turned to Paul. "We will stand on top of this bitch before the day is out!" I said.

"Yeah," he agreed, "I think we will."

The heat of the sun reflecting off the snow can very quickly change the game from hypothermia to heat management and dehydration. By the time we reached the east side of the saddle, we were all removing layers and applying sunscreen. Richard shed his pack at the base of our next pitch, a steep climb rising 1,600 feet from the saddle to the summit plateau. He was still struggling but seemed to have reached down deep and found whatever it is that allows a person to carry on when most of him wants to cash in.

"And now, dear friends," Alex called out, "the final forty meters! Most difficult part of climb." Not only the steepest grade we had seen, this section also menaced us with a sheer two thousand–foot drop off on one side. There could be no mistakes. For the next forty minutes, we methodically scratched our way up the narrow catwalk at the top of the pitch and onto the summit plateau. We rested, hydrated, opened the zipper vents on our clothing, and applied more sunscreen. Exhausted, Richard asked how much farther we had to go.

"You gotta walk the plateau, man," Mike answered playfully.

"I have to have a number," Richard insisted. "How much time?"

"Thirty or forty minutes," Mike answered.

We had been climbing for eight hours and gained almost 3,500 vertical feet from where the snowcat had dropped us off. Now, from where we sat drinking Gatorade, we could see the final rise of fifty feet to the summit on the far side of the plateau. A path to it had been clawed up in the snow by the crampons of earlier teams. It flowed gracefully along the high edge of the top formation with casual wandering curves.

"Are you ready to go to the summit?" Mike asked Richard. Richard looked exhausted and sick.

"Okay, let's get this over with," he answered.

We shouldered our packs and started on the long flattish procession to the summit. A few teams were stretched out single-file ahead of us, a few others behind. I felt as though we were all part of some high-altitude commencement ceremony, more walking than climbing, more reverent than exuberant. I flicked at clumps of snow with my ice ax as we crossed the expanse. Images from the previous twelve months flashed through my mind: Lin crouching down in her flower garden, my son Chase running the mile in middle school track, the trail where I had trained, my mother kissing me good-bye. I thought of the people who had taken an interest and encouraged me in this climb: my assistant Sonia, several clients, the guys at the barbershop, and my new friends Mike and Dick, both dentists from Bellingham who had climbed Elbrus just two weeks prior. I thought of Ty and wished he were taking this walk with me. I remembered him telling me to kick its ass when we spoke on the phone the day before I left for Russia. I thought of my brother Danny and wondered if he might join me for a few steps as he had on Denali.

Each time I looked up from the trail, the tiny riser that formed the summit of Europe had grown larger in the view through my glacier glasses. A wispy breeze raked sideways across the trail, casting a flourish of loose snow into the air, confetti in the school colors of the mountain. Tears pooled up on the inside of my glasses as I looked down to study each foot placement. The salty puddles shifted side to side like mercury from a broken thermometer.

Two teams passed by us as they descended from the summit, carabiners ringing as they swung from their harnesses. Then the trail suddenly steepened as we stepped up onto the stage. Our moment. The moment we had sacrificed so much for. A moment shared. A moment we would always share in the Ozone Brotherhood.

We threw down our packs and came together in a group hug next to the small monument marking the summit of Elbrus, then separated to carry out our own private celebrations. I called Lin and my mother on the satellite phone, then released a bit of my brother's ashes to the wind. We posed for a summit photo and all said how much we wished Ankita were there with us.

Looking out over everything, all of it beneath us for as far as any eye could see, I felt a sense of humility and gratitude. I knew something of value had come into my possession. I could feel it, even if I could not precisely articulate it. It doesn't have to make sense now, I thought. There is time. It will speak the words.

**DAVE MAURO ON THE SUMMIT OF ELBRUS.
PHOTO BY MIKE ROBERTS.**

HOMECOMING

Lin was waiting for me in baggage claim as my flight
set down in Bellingham. We had emailed back and forth
frequently during my absence, but other than our short
conversation on the satellite phone at Elbrus's summit, we
had not spoken for two weeks.

I had guarded my mental focus throughout the climb, storing away the many moments when I missed Lin. But now, with the climb completed, they all came tumbling down upon me like the contents of an overpacked closet: the time I woke from a bad dream and reached out a hand to find her, the moment I was underwater after falling into the river, the certainty I felt that Lin would hate borscht. I had stared into each sunrise wishing Lin could see it with me and felt her spirit when I stood on the summit. Lin had fully supported my going on the climb. She made no demand for quid pro quo, nor did she ask me to promise this would be the last time I left her behind to worry. I had felt free to explore the strange path my life was following, and something about that freedom only made me love her more.

Lin once again wore a costume to the airport. This time, she dressed as a Russian babushka, swaddled in rags with a headscarf tied beneath her chin. For grandmotherly effect, she slumped forward, supporting her weight on a cane. It wasn't sexy, but it was funny. We stood there for a moment just laughing at her costume. I noticed other travelers glancing sideways at us, knowing something was going on, but not sure what. Then I gathered Lin up in my arms and hugged her. Then I kissed her in ways one does not kiss a grandmother, probably making observers more uncomfortable still.

I slept most of that first day home then woke in time

to do two shows at The Upfront Theatre. Ryan was in the cast that evening. He and the other actors asked me about the climb while we waited in the greenroom before the first show. They were happy for me. In contrast to the vocal minority of doubters in my life, none of these people seemed threatened by what I had done. Scaling continental summits did not fit the profile of an improv performer, but that did not matter to them. Improv by its very nature involves making sense of a nonsensical world. The more disconnected two facts appear to be, the happier improvisers are with them. But this had not occurred to me before that evening, so I had kept a low profile when it came to my mountain climbing, especially after experiencing pushback from other people in my life. It just seemed simpler if improv people only knew me as an actor, just as clients only knew me as a financial planner and blog readers only knew me as a climber.

We walked out onstage, and the audience erupted—as they always did when Ryan Stiles was part of a show. "Hey, everybody," Ryan said once the applause quieted down, "Dave here just climbed the highest mountain in Europe." Again the audience clapped enthusiastically, but this time the applause was for me, the mountain climber.

I had also enjoyed applause in the form of positive comments from readers of my Elbrus blog. By the time I returned from Russia, I had published twenty-eight articles, and the blog had received over two thousand page views.

Not bad for a first stab at blogging. People from Germany, France, Ireland, and Israel had all followed along. It was everything I had hoped for, a chance for others to experience an adventure through my words.

My sessions with Doctor Ferguson came to a close, with us exploring my general sense that something had changed in my life since leaving for Russia, though it was not yet clear exactly what that was. I knew I preferred the supportive response I was getting over the critical comments that had driven me into hiding. But it was more than that. Every part of me felt braver. And it wasn't because I had made it to the top of Elbrus. Something else along the way had made that happen, but I could not yet say what.

STAND IN YOUR TRUTH

The Upfront Theatre often held workshops for cast members. These were typically taught by highly accomplished talent from Second City or some other well-known theater. I took part in one such session about a week after returning from Elbrus.

The instructor was talking to us about character development in improv, how important it is to vest fully in the part you play. "If your character is a bigot, then be the world's biggest bigot," he said. "If your character is happy, then let that pour out of you." He looked at us and paused for a moment, then said, "Stand in your truth."

I heard nothing the instructor said for the next ten minutes as my thoughts triangulated between Trevor, Ankita, and my tattoos. They were all telling me the same thing. My son had shown amazing courage by coming out as gay in high school. Ankita had stood in her own truth, defying the cultural restrictions of who she should be—and triumphantly summiting Elbrus the day after us, laughing in the face of both sickness and injury. And the ink on my leg put a part of me out in plain site to be judged. The judging had sometimes been unkind, other times enthusiastic. But neither could matter any longer. This was what the Elbrus experience had taught me: to not just sing my song, but to sing it out loud, to stand in my truth and live all the incongruent aspects of who I was—financial planner, actor, mountain climber—freely and unapologetically.

I had the profile of Elbrus tattooed just below that of Kilimanjaro a week later. Lin held my hand whenever the vibrating instrument crossed over my shin. It felt like the needle was bouncing off the bone.

"Maybe you just like getting tattoos," she quipped, suggesting the mountain climbs were mere window dressing.

"Or maybe I just like shaving my leg," I added, a necessary precursor to getting a tattoo there.

People started asking me if I was going to climb all of the Seven Summits. I was tempted to answer yes. A bit of small-town celebrity had come to me through the first three climbs, and I did not mind the attention. But I always responded that I didn't know. It was an anticlimactic response to offer someone who only wanted to be excited for me. I felt bad about that. But it was the truth. I had not risen from the couch one day and declared my intent to conquer every continent. Rather, each of the mountains I had climbed called *me*. I wanted to keep things that way: listening, trusting, acting. If no further calls came, I was prepared to be done with climbing.

ACONCAGUA

DON

EARLIER IN 2009, BEFORE DECIDING TO CLIMB ELBRUS, I had floated the idea of an Aconcagua climb to my brother-in-law, Ty. It was a rainy winter evening, and I sat nursing a Manhattan in the lounge of the restaurant where Lin waited tables. I could see her darting about the dining room like a hummingbird that paused to hover before patrons. She did this week after week, putting in forty hours Monday through Friday as a sign language interpreter for the school district, then waiting tables on Friday and Saturday nights. This had been her life as a single mom for twenty years. Still, Lin found the energy to smile brightly as she tended to her customers.

I, however, was sulking. I felt pissed off and once again ready to quit my father—stop caring, stop calling, stop taking on responsibilities for a man who no longer seemed to understand them or fully appreciate what it took for me to fill this role on his behalf. Don and I had argued earlier that day. He was still angry that I had sold his truck a few months back while he was laid up in the hospital being treated for a heart attack. I knew he would be unhappy when I did it, but in the interest of public safety, I could no longer allow my father to get behind the wheel. In separate instances over the prior two years, he had driven through a fence, through his garage door, over a fire hydrant, and into opposing traffic. As well, Don was suffering from periodic seizures, which made driving particularly dangerous, and though his driver's license was suspended for six months each time he had a seizure, Don drove anyway. Menaced by the fear my father might harm someone, I invoked power of attorney and sold his battered GMC while he was recovering from surgery.

I tried to be as sensitive as possible to Don's dignity, telling him this was an economic issue, that his finances could no longer support the costs associated with his truck. There was truth in this, as his insurance rates had gone sky-high. I arranged for a ride service and enlisted the help of a kind neighbor to whom I sent gas cards each month. But nothing could replace the easy independence Don had enjoyed with his own automobile. Every time we spoke, he complained bitterly about what I had done, sometimes behaving aggressively with his words and actions. Like so many times before, I weighed the negatives of having

Don in my life against an empty ledger of positives and the resentments I carried for all he had never been. There must be some kind of safety net out there, I thought, social services or some other agency that can step in and take over for me.

I stared out into the darkness, through windows streaked with wind-driven rain. I'm sick of this weather, I thought. I'm sick of dealing with my father. I need a break. I finished my drink and ordered another, already resigned to the notion that Lin would drive me home after her shift. That drink was followed by another, and one more after that. I don't recall much about the thought process that followed except that I wanted to run away to a warm place and knew it was summertime in South America. Somewhere along the way, I sent a text to Ty: "Are you down for Aconcagua in January 2010?"

"Absolutely," he shot back.

Done. We did not speak about it again until nine months later. In the meantime, I had forgotten about my drunken invitation and gone off to climb Elbrus. Then, in October 2009, Ty sent me an email with information he had gathered about how we could hire a mule team to pack our provisions into Aconcagua Base Camp. At first I was confused. Then I found my text.

By this time, my father's mental condition had deteriorated still further. Where he had behaved like a rebellious teenager a year earlier, Don was now childlike and simple.

Everything I read about dementia (now Don's formal diagnosis) suggested it was best to leave him in his home as long as possible. So, my sister and I cobbled together the many cogs of a complex gearbox designed to meet our father's varied needs in methodic synchrony.

The Elbrus climb had provided me with a much-needed respite from these responsibilities. But after returning, the demands of taking care of my father quickly taxed my strength to the point of frustration. Ty's email about Aconcagua began occupying my mind during idle moments, and the forces of rationalization took hold. It wouldn't have to be as costly a climb as Elbrus and Kilimanjaro had been. For one thing, we wouldn't have to hire a guide. Google satellite images showed a well-worn route. That combined with handling all our own logistics would cut thousands off the cost. All in all, I estimated we could attempt Aconcagua for about $3,000 each. That was still a goodly sum, but I could swing it somehow. And having Aconcagua in my future would help me through the challenges of dealing with my father. I ran the idea past Lin. She supported it, saying, "I think you need something like this right now."

MY MOM

"Are you going climbing this January?" my mother asked when I saw her at Thanksgiving. I told her I was. "Where to?" she inquired, sounding annoyed.

"Aconcagua," I said.

"Where's that?! Is it in Indonesia? Because our neighbor, Steve, has a friend who was trying to climb the Seven Summits and gave it up. He tried to climb some mountain in Indonesia, it scared the hell out of him, and he said, 'That's it!' A man after my own heart."

I told her Aconcagua is in Argentina. "It's the high summit for South America."

"Well that's not where this mountain is. What is the name of that mountain? I have it written down somewhere. Oh damn it! Where is that piece of paper?!"

I reassured my mom that this was not the same mountain that had so sadly ended the dream of her neighbor's friend.

"Well, promise me this, at least. Promise you will never climb Everest," she said.

"I cannot make that promise," I answered. "I have no plans to climb Everest. But I also had no plans to climb Kilimanjaro. I'm just kinda taking this as it comes."

"Oh. Shit," she said.

TRAINING

We would be carrying our provisions above base camp, so I needed to return to the bulked-up physique of Denali. I dug out my notes from the workout sessions when I was preparing for that climb and began sorting through them. I lashed together a series of exercises specifically designed for leg, upper body, and core strength. My legwork included one-legged squats while hugging a twenty-pound medicine ball, platform leaps, and stair climbing while wearing a lead-weighted vest. I used kettle bells and rope climbing, in addition to weight lifting, to bring my chest and shoulders up to scale. Various sit-ups, curls, crunches, and planking exercises toned my core. These sessions lasted two hours each Monday, Wednesday, and Friday. On Tuesdays and Saturdays, I would carry my pack, with eight gallons of water in it, up a steep trail. It was back to the weight-forward Neanderthal body type for me, a complete transformation from what I had known the prior two years. By the time my final week of training drew to a close in early January 2010, I was a lean 191 pounds, trail-ready, and eager for the hill.

FOOD PROVISIONS

Ty and I made arrangements for Grajales Expeditions to pack our provisions into base camp by mule and provide all meals while we were there. We would be responsible for any meals above base camp. Our strategy for those meals closely mirrored that of Denali.

For each day of climbing, Ty and I each had a two-gallon ziplock bag containing a breakfast, lunch, and dinner. For breakfast, we each packed two packets of instant oatmeal, cocoa, Starbucks instant coffee, freeze-dried banana chips, and trail mix. Lunch consisted of beef jerky, a Cliff Bar, freeze-dried pineapple slices, a candy bar, Gatorade, potato chips (ultimately crushed to potato powder), fruit leather, and more trail mix, all within a separate ziplock bag placed inside the two-gallon bag. Dinner was typically comprised of one freeze-dried Mountain House meal for two (though we each ate a complete packet). These are lightweight but offer a solid five hundred calories. I ate a different meal each night, ranging from freeze-dried lasagna to freeze-dried chicken and mashed potatoes. Ty packed the same meal for every night, the freeze-dried Teriyaki chicken. I had seen him eat this night after night on Denali, each time proclaiming it to have been the best meal he had ever eaten. A packet of instant soup (chicken or onion), candy bar, cocoa, and a peanut bar rounded out each dinner.

Each morning, we would take out a fresh set of meals, remove the lunch bag to somewhere accessible on our packs, eat the breakfast items, then stow the remaining dinner items for later that day. As bags were emptied, they could be compressed tightly within each other to conserve space. Any leftover food items from each day would be consolidated into a two-gallon bag. This would provide important backup in the event we were forced to dig in and supplies ran low.

All told, a day's rations weighed about two pounds and totaled approximately five thousand calories. Even so, we knew we would probably burn more calories than that. On similar rations I lost seventeen pounds climbing Denali, and I had been fairly lean going into it. But the converging factors of load weights and an inability to ingest more calories argue against a person adding still more to his rations since most climbers suffer a loss of appetite as they reach into higher altitudes. For me, it had always amounted to force-feeding any time I was above sixteen thousand feet. This stands in direct opposition to the body's needs. Aside from the obvious and ferocious caloric burn rate that accompanies such strenuous endeavors, the altitude also brings a steep increase in a climber's metabolism. For instance, a climber at Denali's high camp (17,500 feet) burns an estimated six thousand calories a day lying in his sleeping bag. This same person would burn just two thousand calories in the course of a normal working day at sea level.

MENDOZA

One of the pure pleasures associated with traveling to the southern hemisphere is trading a January winter for a January summer. I knew we weren't in Argentina to stroll about its fabulous vineyards, but I still felt Ty and I were getting away with something as we stepped off the plane into a warm sunny day in Mendoza. The scent of barbecue danced in the air while a congress of automobiles chatted among themselves with short, polite beeps. A beautiful Argentine woman in abbreviated apparel shuffled past us as we made our way through the terminal. "I guess we're not in Kansas anymore," Ty commented. Our airport transfer dropped us at the Hyatt Hotel, a grand marble structure in the old-world fashion of the official residence of some high-ranking regional politico. Independencia Park sat just across the tree-lined street. We checked in, then immediately changed into cooler clothes, heading out on foot to explore the neighborhood.

Pulling a few exploratory loops out and away from the hotel, we noted most businesses were closed for siesta. The 98°F heat eventually chased Ty and me into the shade of the park, where a few locals napped on the grass and teenage boys tried to impress teenage girls with their bicycle acrobatics. Many empty vendor stands were assembled along the large circular promenade running the perimeter of the park.

Later that night, around 11:30 p.m., I stepped outside our hotel to gather a last breath of warm summer air before calling it a night. I was stunned to find the park before me was a busy nocturnal playground. The sounds of an amplified voice drew me into the park toward an outdoor stage where street performers were just finishing a magic act. I watched for a few moments then raced back to the hotel to get Ty. Together we wandered the park, marveling at the sizable crowd everywhere we went. There were children clamoring on lit playground equipment, lovers picnicking on the grass, great crowds of shoppers grazing the diverse offerings of vendors along the promenade. We watched actors, acrobats, musicians, and painters. There was no festival or important holiday responsible for all of this.

The occasion was nothing more than a Sunday summer evening for a people who live broken days, with siestas setting a Latin rhythm to their lives of patient comfort.

Two days later, after obtaining our climbing permits, we traveled by van to Los Penitentes, a winter ski resort about three hours from Mendoza. We were greeted there by climbing legend Fernando Grajales. Many years earlier, Fernando had made the first ascent of a very difficult route up Aconcagua. He was subsequently honored with that route being named after him, The Grajales Colouir Route. Fernando was now a man of advanced years, relying on many lieutenants to run Grajales Expeditions, but he still took the time to shake hands with each climber supported by his organization.

We sorted our gear the next morning, cramming most of it into four heavy-duty duffels to be packed in by mule. Then Ty and I were dropped off at the trailhead for the Vacas Valley, our approach route to Aconcagua. We checked in with the ranger there and set out up the valley. Everything about the picture we walked into was large and interesting. Steep rock walls rose up from the Rio Vacas, tumbling by, noisy and cocoa-colored. A Panavision sky provided dramatic backdrop to the rugged stone gates, which opened one nudge at a time as we pressed farther into the canyon.

My mind drifted to Trevor and Chase as the miles passed. At some point I started noticing that whenever I thought about my sons, my father also came into the picture. Weird.

Ty and I arrived at the outpost of Pampa de Lenas and set about choosing a campsite. A team from the American Alpine Institute was already setting up there. I recognized someone I knew in that group and called out to him.

Brian had been on my Kilimanjaro team a few years prior. That was a first foray into high altitude for him, and it had not gone well. I was surprised to see Brian attempting Aconcagua, given that its summit is a full three thousand feet higher than Kilimanjaro's. Yet I did not feel it was my place to say anything. Climbers can have different reactions each time they go into thin air. Brian was an adult, and it seemed important to respect his personal choice. We chatted about our prior climb and caught up on what the other members of our Kilimanjaro team had been up to since then. Brian looked thirty pounds lighter than he had been on our last climb. His features were lean and trail-hardened, his movements efficient and smooth.

"I've been climbing some of the volcanoes in Mexico," Brian said.

Though none of these had been as high as Kilimanjaro, I hoped the lessons and conditioning he gained might compensate for Brian's difficulties with acclimation.

Soon the air grew dusty as the mule trains pulled into Pampa de Lenas. Ty and I built our camp, ate a modestly tasty freeze-dried meal, and settled in for the night. As we lay there too excited to sleep, coyotes called to one another from across the canyon. I thought about Don. I had told him I would be away for several weeks and had outlined the climb. But time had become an elusive concept for my father. I wondered if he understood my absence. Don's half sisters would be checking on him, as would my sister, Michelle. He would be looked after by his neighbor Laurie, his physical therapist, and various other parties who were paid for their efforts. Don would be fine. I had no concerns about that. But more than anything, I wondered if he missed me.

We set out the next morning farther up the Rio Vacas with much of the trail on broken rock that left our feet feeling beaten up. The heat came on, hitting 102°F as we neared Casa de Piedra, an apologetic ranger station built out of a small cave in the side of a massive boulder. Rich black smoke stains tarnished the area above the cave opening, evidence of the rangers' cooking fire. Ty and I checked in then threw down our packs on a suitable campsite. We were well ahead of the mule trains, and thus without our gear, so we killed time soaking our feet in a nearby spring creek.

ARRIVAL AT PLAZA DE ARGENTINA: BASE CAMP

The first part of the next day's trek involved crossing a (mostly) dry river valley about a mile and a half wide. A knee-deep river of glacial runoff twenty feet wide tumbled down the center of the valley. Typically climbers made this crossing while holding onto the downstream side of a mule, but at this late part of the Argentine summer, the knee-deep ford could be made unassisted.

We arrived at Plaza de Argentina (13,800 feet) late that afternoon, hydrated, and built our camp behind a stacked stone wall constructed by teams that had come before us. Comparing notes, as we did after each move, Ty and I both reported feeling good, better than we felt pulling into a similar altitude on Denali.

A charming young lady who worked for Grajales Expeditions showed us to the dining tent where we would take our meals while at Plaza de Argentina. She brought us a plate with a variety of meats and cheeses, and a large pitcher of orange drink. Having already accepted the inevitable death of comfort that comes with a mountain climb, Ty and I were giddy with the prospect of knowing some further civilized satisfactions. Our dining tent provided a place tall enough to stand in and yet be sheltered from the wind. Though we still needed to set up our sleep tent, we would at least have a place to go for the days at base camp, a place to read and socialize with Brian's team, who had been assigned to that same tent.

CARRY TO CAMP ONE

One helicopter had taken a sick climber out of Plaza de Argentina on our rest day. Two more choppers lifted sick climbers out of base camp the next morning as Ty and I prepared to make our carry to camp one. I suspected some helicopter lifts were economic choices as opposed to medical necessities. Climbers made the long trek into base camp and started suffering from altitude sickness. Realizing they would not be going up, and not feeling good enough to trek out, these climbers opened their wallets and called for a bird. But still, each helicopter that came and went symbolized a noisy broken dream for someone, and that sadness hung in the air.

Ty and I started up toward camp one, navigating through a large field of penitentes, snow-ice formations that reach upward in a spire formed by the unique sun and wind combination of this climate. Our progress was steady for the first 1,400 feet, but then I started feeling the thin air and found myself stopping to breathe quite often. Though I had come of age as a climber since Denali, Ty was still much stronger than me. He never seemed to tire. I envied this about Ty and briefly considered the notion of smothering him in his sleep with a filthy sweatshirt.

We finished the carry and cached our gear at camp one in a nice spot looking out over the Vacas Valley. Ty and I retreated to our dining tent after descending to Plaza de Argentina, quickly drank two quarts of juice, and discussed the work ahead while elevating our tired feet. Our first day of climbing had been successful, but it took a lot out of us. We decided to rest the following day then, dependent upon weather, pack the remainder of our base camp up to camp one, establishing ourselves at that new higher elevation.

MOVE TO CAMP ONE

There was much talk of strategy during our rest day, most of which was being done by the members of Brian's team. Having gotten a good look at the steep ascent during their carry from base to camp one, a keen interest in hiring porters had emerged among them. In the end, they decided to share the cost of three porters, allowing each of the five climbers to lighten his load accordingly.

At this point in time, Aconcagua was still considered a nonportered climb. In the eyes of the mountaineering community, a kosher summiting included each climber carrying their own gear. But porters had become available on Aconcagua in recent years, and we could see them being used by other teams as the steepness of the mountain challenged their confidence. I suspect, in time, Acon will become like Kili—which will be too bad. Something in the personal test, the demands, and the rewards will be lost. But still, it takes a monumental effort to get to the top of Aconcagua at 22,700 feet, and respect is owed those who achieve it—whether they carry or not. For our part, Ty and I never raised the possibility of hiring porters. We wanted Aconcagua on our terms, two men giving it all they had to see if that was enough.

As Ty and I pulled into camp one, the wind picked up, and the temperature dropped sharply. Having noted a weather pattern of heat in the afternoon and snow in the evening, we wasted no time building our tent and gathering water. By the time the storm hit, we were well-sheltered. Ty and I took turns bracing the ceiling with our hands through the worst of the gusts then retreated to the comfort of our sleeping bags as the wind died down.

"You did good today," Ty commented. "I'm proud of you."

Like many Alaskans, Ty tended to speak when spoken to, but otherwise did not typically have much to say. But now and then he piped up with something so devoid of pretense and bullshit that it hung with me for days. I thought about Ty's comment as I waited for sleep to come. It struck me as fatherly, an odd notion coming from someone four years my junior. My own father had said the same words to me, but the bad baggage that was also part of Don seemed to zero out the sentiment. This felt different. Ty had nothing to prove, no mistakes to make up for.

In the course of our days together on the trail, Ty shared how he too grew up with an absent father. His parents divorced when Ty was six. Like me, he had moved in with his father later in life, but he was pushed out by wife number four.

"I'm not one to look backward," Ty said during a lunch stop one day, "but I do pray my kids have better memories than I did and also know I have their back no matter what." I was struck by the absence of lingering resentment as Ty talked about his father. At another point, he commented, "I don't have any bad feelings for my dad. He drew a bad hand with myotonic dystrophy, and I'm sure that played a role."

I wished I could know the peace Ty had somehow found with regard to his father. Nothing about that failed relationship seemed to dog Ty, and he had gone on to be a model husband to my sister, Noelle, and father to their two children. I wondered if part of his healing involved being a father to everyone, offering comments like the one he had just made to me, backfilling paternal ditches wherever he found them.

CARRY TO CAMP TWO

I suffered broken sleep that night, with constant bouts of Cheyne-Stokes breathing. We considered canceling our planned carry to camp two, but tired as I was, I had already grown sick of camp one and needed to feel we were laying the groundwork for a better place, a place that would hopefully offer some kind of drop toilet in lieu of the "go where you like and put a rock on it" strategy that had turned camp one into the kind of place where each loose stone was viewed with suspicion. The park service did offer one official alternative: a large, thin-gauge plastic bag issued to each climber at base camp. We were advised to accumulate our waste in this bag and pack it along with us over the mountain. Climbers had voted their disapproval for this plan by the clearest means imaginable.

Camp two would be less crowded, as the splintering of routes dispersed the crowd of dung landscapers far and wide. It would also offer a higher vista and a sense we were making progress. I began to feel better as we got underway. The rugged surface of the moonscape we climbed through was interesting and provided dramatic contrast to the snow-capped peaks around us. We made excellent time and pulled into camp two that afternoon, still feeling strong.

On our maps, camp two was labeled Guanacos Camp, so named for the alpaca-like creature that lives in these mountains. However, most climbers called it Helicopter Camp for the scattered pieces of metal that cautioned against the notion of trying to land a chopper at eighteen thousand feet. Though camp two also had no drop toilet, the smaller number of climbers alone made it cleaner. Additionally, climbers had conscientiously isolated their leavings in an area on the downhill side of the glacial moraine so as not to contaminate the runoff used for drinking and cooking. In the course of climbing to Guanacos Camp, we had traversed around to the sunny side of Aconcagua. The afternoon heat there melted the icy tail of the glacier we camped next to, providing a plentiful supply of clean water. It was a climber's paradise.

We cached our loads in two canvas duffels, locked them to keep the ravens out, and headed back down to camp one. A helicopter dashed in just over our heads en route to a late afternoon extraction from Plaza de Argentina just as the first flakes of evening snow began to fall.

I felt good as we boiled water for our freeze-dried dinner entrees. We had taken a load to camp two. It was possible to summit from camp two. We had no intention of doing so, but it was possible—and that made this thing real. I kept thinking, "Now we are dangerous. Now we are definitely in the hunt."

MOVE TO CAMP TWO

There is a game I play with myself whenever I move camp. It starts with a conviction that the preceding carry was more than half the total weight of our camp, and thus the move will be easier. This inevitably proves incorrect. As I stand swaying beneath a load that would humble the Grinch, I point out to myself that this will be a one-way trip, as opposed to the carry, which requires a return to the lower camp. That should make it easier than the carry, I think, and the overnight acclimation will make climbing into thin air easier than it was during the carry. This all makes perfect sense, of course. It just never turns out to be the case. A heavy burden is a heavy burden is a heavy burden, and all you can do is gut it out step by step.

We started out slow up a modest incline that ran out of camp one and through the penitentes. The trail through them was so narrow in places that our massive packs had trouble passing. Then the route turned up a steep ascent, rising 1,500 feet along the side of a rocky bowl formation. We stripped our upper layers down to just T-shirts as the combination of work and warm sun quickly shifted the balance of concern from cold to heat management.

It was late afternoon as we closed in on camp two. I was stopping to breathe hard every five minutes or so. My water was gone. The once magical vistas around me had become visual white noise. I was a drooling, lumbering beast, an ogre in North Face clothing. Ty waited patiently for me each time I stopped. Strong as ever, he did not appear even to be winded. Adding our packs to the previous day's cache, Ty and I then stretched out for a nap like reptiles on a hot rock.

We woke an hour later. Ty boiled up a pot of water for our dinner entrees while I pump-filtered four liters of drinking water from a hole in the glacier. We enjoyed hot mugs of Lipton Chicken Noodle Soup, followed by freeze-dried entrees. I forgot to bring a bowl along for the climb, so I was forced to use my thermal mug for everything: oatmeal and cocoa in the mornings, soup in the evening, whatever else in between. It bothered me at first, but by this time I had learned to block out the ancillary tastes and just focus on "the big flavor" before me.

HIGH CAMP

Ty and I woke at camp two to another day of ideal weather. As I ate my oatmeal/chicken soup/cocoa, Ty said, "We've already skipped two rest days, but the weather says go. How do you feel?" he asked.

"I feel good. Ten hours of sleep. I'm rested. I'd rather carry a load than hang around camp all day. You?"

"Same," Ty said. We both knew there might be a price to pay for skipping rest days, but high camp was only four hours above us, and we were anxious to check it out. If we got tired, we could cache our loads next to the trail wherever we were and head back to camp two. If the carry wore us out and we woke the next day beat, we could take a rest day then. It made sense. Enough sense, anyway.

We loaded a carry into our packs and climbed up to high camp, caching our supplies in a good, level campsite. The plateau that forms high camp is large enough for perhaps twenty campsites, falling off sharply on three sides with halting views across all of the Andes. In an area noted for electrical storms, this anvil formation was an easy target for lightning strikes. Our strategy would be to get in, summit, and get out.

Ty and I returned to camp two for the night then broke camp the next morning, packing all our remaining provisions and gear into massive loads that towered high above our shoulders. Clear, windless skies made for perfect conditions, and we both felt recovered from our previous day's carry. But the eighty-plus pounds each of us schlepped took a toll as we clawed higher up the mountain. We stopped to rest at least once an hour, hydrating and gobbling down fast energy GU packets. I encouraged myself with the promise this would be the last day we packed provisions uphill since our summit attempt would be a fast and light affair. We arrived at high camp, elevation 19,620 feet, and set up our tent.

NOT OUR DAY

We had planned to make a summit attempt the next day. We woke to a brilliant sunrise. The wind was light. We both felt strong. All of the work leading up to this moment had been like the coiling of a snake. Coiling, coiling, coiling. Now all that pent-up energy would be released in one exacting strike at the summit of Aconcagua.

Aside from attaining the summit, I had another powerful reason to welcome the successful execution of our goal: we could go home. We had given much to the climb, and I felt depleted. A loose accumulation of minor injuries spoke to me constantly, and I had grown sick of every form of foodstuff among my remaining provisions. I could not even enjoy the comfort of music since my useless iPod headphones had soaked in the sweat pools in my ears and frozen.

I fired up our white gas stove, put the pot on, and filled it with snow Ty had gathered the night before. But something was wrong. The stove was putting forth a lame effort, burning a quiet blue flame instead of its typical roaring jet. At this rate it would take hours to generate the water we needed to leave high camp. Ty diagnosed the problem, then disassembled the pump system and lubricated the compression cup. He reassembled the stove, and it worked perfectly. But this took time, and now it was too late to leave for the summit. We would end up too high on the mountain too late in the day. "Besides," Ty reasoned, "we don't have enough snow gathered at this point to melt that much water."

He was right, but I was unwilling to let the day go, such was my desire to be headed home. "I think we can still do this thing," I said, then grabbed the snow bag and my ice ax. "I'm gonna go get some more snow."

The nearest snowbank was two hundred feet up the mountain, which was enough exertion to take the edge off my mood—an angry, pouting, mumbling-to-myself grumbler. It was 5°F, but with the altitude, it felt like −30°F in the thin air. What had seemed like adequate layers as I left the tent soon were not. Before I had even started raking at the snowbank with my ice ax, all the fingers inside my heavy summit gloves had gone completely numb. I worked harder at the snow, believing the effort would warm them. It did not. I turned back toward camp with only half a bag of snow, cradling its contents in my arms because my fingers would not bend to grasp it properly.

I cast off my gloves as I climbed back into the tent and jammed my hands into my armpits. At first they did not respond. I examined my fingers for the powder-white color that marks the first sign of frostbite. Ty just looked at me, uncertain of my mood and where it was going next. "We're not going anywhere today," I conceded peevishly.

Slowly, my fingers started coming back to life, and the pain left me swearing through gritted teeth. A deep groaning sensation began in the bones, emanating outward through knotted tendons and burning flesh. If there had been anything I could have done to buy even a moment of relief from the agony within my flash-frozen hands, I would have done it. I asked Ty if any hot water was left over from the last melt so I could thaw my fingers. He said there wasn't, that he had put it into the water bottles, where it had quickly cooled. I felt the pain and frustration inside me crash into each other like the twin tails of a boat's wake. "I just want to get off this fucking rock!" I yelled.

I knew that thinking about the summit was the classic climber mistake. At some point, they always realize the suffering to get there will outweigh any satisfaction realized. That's when they quit. But worse still, I had shifted my focus past the summit, past the comforts awaiting us in Mendoza all the way home—to Lin, to my boys, and, strangely, to my father.

Feeling and function gradually returned to my hands. I had been lucky. No lasting damage had occurred. It seemed incredible to me that I had made such poor choices in the course of my emotional meltdown. I knew better. I needed to reset my thinking, not just for the sake of reaching the summit, but also in the interest of safety. Ty and I ate our oatmeal in silence as I cleared my head item by item. If something wasn't important to what would happen that day, I placed it in a mental box and stored it away.

BRIAN UP HIGH

Brian's team moved into high camp that afternoon. Ty and I chatted with them as they set up next to our tent. I watched Brian carefully, evaluating his stability, efficiency, and energy. In a candid moment, several days prior, Brian admitted to me his concerns over how he would do up high. "I just want to make it to high camp," he said. "That's my goal."

"That seems like a reasonable goal," I said. "You can always see how you feel from there." I had a pretty good idea how Brian would be feeling and privately expected that if he made it to high camp, he would not remain there long. I was wrong.

Brian looked solid. His footing seemed confident, his strength intact, and contrary to the quiet inward persona of a sick climber, Brian joked among his teammates, commenting, as was his habit, with too much information on his private bodily functions.

Brian's team planned to rest the next day while Ty and I took our shot at the summit. They were excited for us. We were vested in one another's story lines and wanted nothing more than happy endings. It showed in their eyes, the looks that said, "Show us it can be done." Yet something stood in the way of actual words and outright expressions of encouragement. That something was honesty.

By the time a climber arrives at high camp, he *has* whatever he is going to have. The state of his physical and mental strength is the best he is able to manage. And if circumstances should require something much more, it will have to come from the person that climber is deep down inside. Inspirational words had nothing to do with it. At this stage of an altitude climb, encouragement was bullshit. And we all knew it.

THAT EVENING

Five inches of fresh snow fell that night. Ty and I celebrated the convenience of scooping pure fallen snow right outside the tent door, not even having to leave the comfort of our shelter to harvest the raw material for that day's water. We had decided to leave at seven. Since the first several hours took us up the south side of the mountain, we would be in the frigid shadow of Aconcagua. But, in spite of our best efforts, it took longer to get ready than we had expected. The thin air slowed everything down. Bending over and tying a bootlace required a dizzying pant-fest to recover.

Only one other team appeared to be attempting the summit that day, the International Mountain Guides (IMG) team we had been traveling with in tandem from the start. They had already started up the route by seven fifteen, moving single file at a slow, deliberate pace.

It was eight by the time Ty and I left high camp under windless clear blue skies. Ty led for the first stage, 1,150 vertical feet up out of high camp. His pace was typically swift. I didn't mind the work at first since it encouraged the generation of body heat, but eventually I found myself wishing for the more moderate pace of the IMG group. Not only was their pace more agreeable, but they had also opted to break left of the main ascent halfway up, carving a lateral traverse with a kinder grade. As we approached this fork, I hoped Ty would likewise go left but, as is his custom when faced with two trails headed to the same place, Ty chose the steeper option. I felt frustrated by this, aching to ask Ty if it would be at all possible to pick a more difficult route up the damn hill. Later that day, however, the clarity of that moment and the layout of the scene would come in handy.

We arrived at Independencia Hut as the IMG group was finishing its break. We hydrated and ate a snack while Ty removed his left boot to thaw his big toe against the warm sunlit boards of the small abandoned structure. The sun rapidly became more intense as we sat there, so Ty and I each shed a layer. But as we stood to continue toward the long traverse, Ty noticed something below us. "Uh oh," he commented. "Take a look at those." The entire hemline of Aconcagua was crowded with clouds that would almost certainly envelope the mountain as the day progressed.

If we continued up, we could expect a rough time getting back down. But we had the heavy clothing to gear up if needed during the descent—and we had certainly traveled in bad weather before. Ty and I determined we could manage the downhill fight if the weather brought one. It was one of those decisions a climber makes with the best information he has at the time.

01/23/2010

TY HARDT. PHOTO BY DAVE MAURO.

I led the next stage, which took us in short order to a balcony preceding the traverse. Deceptively steep and interminably long, the traverse cut a long grade up a quarter-bowl formation that normally would have been bare rock. But the snows of the night before had fallen and frozen, raising the ante by creating a toboggan hill that a climber would rocket down some two thousand feet if he fell.

"I wasn't expecting this," Ty commented with dread.

"Me either," I said. "I don't suppose there are any fixed lines since this is normally all rocks and dirt."

"No, I doubt there are," Ty said. We cached our trekking poles and put our crampons on. Then, ice axes in hand, we set out on the traverse, careful and measured.

We caught up with the IMG group again at the base of the Caneleta, a steep eight hundred–foot ascent weaving around and over boulders the size of cars. I had saved something extra in my energy reserves for this, having read many accounts of climbers whose will was broken by this pitch, the final challenge to the summit. A month earlier, a man attempting to be the first person from Thailand to summit Aconcagua so completely expended himself on the Caneleta that he died upon reaching the summit. There his body laid for several weeks while authorities tried to figure out what to do about it.

As Ty and I hydrated and made minor gear adjustments, the IMG group started for the summit. Knowing we would catch up with them, we took some extra time to rest in the safety of a small cave-like hollow at the base of the wall. Snow was falling lightly, and the dense fog that had followed close behind us during the ascent now began consuming our surroundings.

The first four hundred feet of trail dodged in and out from beneath a low overhang at the base of a rock wall. The route threaded scant passages up ambitious inclines like a Gregorian staircase. We stopped often to breathe, sometimes taking only a few steps before having to stop again. I scrutinized my efficiency of movement and repeated the mantra: "Simple thoughts, simple thoughts." My body was on automatic pilot, a function drummed into its reptilian brain through the many hours I had spent training.

As we made painfully slow progress up the final four hundred feet, I stopped bothering to check my altimeter. I knew we were going to the summit. Normally this realization brings me a burst of energy, but on this occasion, I felt nothing beyond a primal need for oxygen. I would plant a foot uphill, transfer my weight to it, and take five deep breaths. Each time I did so, I closed my eyes to focus only on breathing. The image of Trevor and Chase appeared in my mind during one such rest. They were standing together, arms hanging loosely at their sides. Their faces were expressionless, as though watching butter being spread on toast. I opened my eyes, placed the next step, transferred my weight, and then closed them again to breathe. Again I saw my sons, but this time my father was standing with them. I placed the next step and again closed my eyes. I saw Trevor and Chase standing next to Don, but this time he was their age. He looked nervous, shuffling his feet as he stood there. Each time I closed my eyes, Don grew younger. He was twelve, then eight, then six years old. I found this so unsettling that I tried to push him away in my thoughts, just focusing on my sons. But the next time I closed my eyes, Trevor and Chase had vanished, leaving only my six-year-old father. He was crying and frightened. I wanted to gather him up in my arms. I took another step and closed my eyes. I saw my hand resting on Don's shoulder and heard myself say, "It's all right, son."

Then I heard Ty shout, "C'mon, Mauro, lets finish this together!" He was standing thirty feet above me, a few steps from the summit. I watched Ty throw down his pack and motion for me to continue toward him. Step after painful step, I paused to breathe. I saw no images now when I closed my eyes, just a soft light. I looked up at Ty ten feet above me then placed my next step. Bracing one arm against my uphill knee, I took eight deep breaths. I threw my weight forward and added a second step before stopping to rest again. My heart was racing. No matter how many breaths I took, my body did not seem to find any oxygen. I looked at Ty again, now an arm's length away. I knew he would not reach out for me, and I did not want him to. This last step was the one all climbers think most about. It is the culmination of many months' training and all of the other steps it took to get here. It is the place where will is tested and honor granted. Ty said nothing. He just smiled down at me and waited. Then I heaved myself forward wretchedly and might have stumbled past Ty had he not caught me up in his arms. We hugged for a moment, then turned and walked the last steps across a mild incline to the small monument that marked the summit of Aconcagua, 22,841 feet above sea level, the highest point in the Americas.

I handed Ty my camera and pulled out the laminated pictures of my boys, my mom, and Lin. After posing for a summit photo with each, I traded places with Ty to record the moments he would share with family on the summit. Then IMG guide Ben Marshall said, "Team photo! Here, let me get a picture of you two together!" I handed him my camera, then offered to do the same for his team, having reached the summit a short while before us.

Then I dug the satellite phone from my pack and called my mother back in Monroe, Washington. I told her I was on the summit and couldn't talk since the weather was going bad and we needed to start down. She congratulated me and offered cautions for a safe descent. Then I called Lin. When I heard her voice, the numbness that had been my existence for hours broke open, and a flood of emotion came gushing out. Tears were already running down my face as she answered. "Hey there, you sexy stack of pancakes," I said, offering what had long ago become a standard greeting of ours. I felt myself cascading into an emotional purge and fought back against the impulse, knowing I would still need everything I had left to get down to high camp.

I was kneeling on the ground as I shouted into the satellite phone, my face down to avoid the snow and growing wind. When I looked up, the entire IMG group was gone. "Hey, you wanna call your fam?" I asked, extending the phone toward Ty.

He looked very nervous and unsettled. Ty's eyes grew large and he shouted, "Whoa!" He started backing around in circles, shouting, "Whoa, whoa, whoa!" Then he threw down his hat and rubbed his head frantically. "My hair is crackling," he exclaimed.

I stood to approach him, and as the steel points of my crampons contacted the ground, an electrical current passed through my legs. It was then I realized we were in the middle of an electrical storm. Being the highest points on the continent, I knew Ty and I were perfect lightning rods. "We gotta get the fuck off this mountain," I screamed through the wind and thunder as I threw my pack off the summit in the direction of the trail. Ty, having already put his pack back on, dashed down the trail with me close behind. We came upon my pack thirty feet below the summit.

"Do you think we should get rid of our axes?" I asked him, considering their conductive properties.

"No way," he argued. "We're gonna need 'em to get down, dude."

We descended at what seemed like a frenetic pace. We were charged with adrenaline and squandering precious oxygen with the useless racing of our hearts. "Focus, Dave," I said to myself, aware of the consequences of one ill-chosen step on the steep pitch. The lower we descended, the thicker the fog became. Visibility soon closed down to a few feet, but the trail winding down among the boulders was clear and well-beaten. Suddenly, an IMG guide appeared in front of me. It was so sudden that I almost ran into him from behind. He had one of their climbers short-roped already.

"Do you need any help here?" I asked him.

"No," he replied. We passed them and two other climbers before coming to the next IMG guide, who also had a climber short-roped. A few moments later, we all arrived at the base of the Caneleta. Ducking into the cave, we started gearing up for what already looked like a helluva fight to come. I put on my down summit coat, heavy mittens, balaclava, and goggles, then zipped all clothing vents shut.

Ben, the friendlier of the IMG guides, approached Ty and me. "Hey, if you guys wanna tailgate along with us, that's cool." We accepted, believing greater safety lay in numbers and glad for their Argentine guide—who could probably find the way down blindfolded.

We followed along just behind one guide, still short-roping a climber who complained that he could not see. The wind and snow were obscuring the tracks in the trail, making it very difficult for the short-roped climber to judge depth. As a consequence, we were falling behind the rest of the group. I climbed up and around them, dropping down in front to break trail in fresh snow that was now almost knee-deep. We caught up with the rest of the IMG team at the balcony, where ice axes were traded for the trekking poles we had all cached there during the ascent.

A sense of relief showed in the faces of the climbers. We had made it down the Caneleta, crossed the traverse, and now had only 1,400 feet of relatively easy descent down to high camp. There was no exposure to falling. This was a wide-open ski slope-like hill we had all been able to study at length from high camp. We were practically home.

Ty decided to add some heavier clothing, so we remained at the balcony as the IMG team resumed its descent. Just before leaving with them, the Argentine guide put a hand on my shoulder and smiled. "Good luck," he said. He apparently thought we had decided to separate from the group. He meant it kindly and sincerely, but it wasn't the kind of "good luck" a person gets very often. It wasn't like the "good luck" you get when you are trying to pick up a spare at the bowling alley. It wasn't like the "good luck" someone offers as you leave for a job interview. This was the kind of "good luck" that says, "I hope you make it down alive." The year before, a guide and climber had not. They became lost below this point and froze to death.

"Go ahead," Ty urged me, concerned about holding us up.

"No," I said. "I am *not* leaving you!" I peered over the edge of the balcony. The IMG team had all disappeared into the fog below.

Ty finished with his gear, and we started down the hill. Again we caught up with the group at the next ledge. Then, in one long single-file line, we all resumed our descent toward high camp. By this time, it had been ten hours since we left for the summit. Many of us were out of water. Most of us were out of energy. The adrenaline had worn off. I assumed we were close, an uneventful slog down to the tents. Had I looked at my altimeter, I would have realized we were still two hours away. I had been running on empty for at least two hours and wasn't even sure what was keeping me going. My feet were chunking down hard, the skeletal structure of my legs forced to go it alone in spite of muscles no longer able to set me down easy. My vision blurred slightly with each jarring step, steps I was no longer consciously taking. It was like sitting in a chair while someone whacked it with a cricket bat.

Ty and I were in the middle of the IMG group at first, separated by one of their climbers, but the order kept changing as some climbers descended faster than others. Ty, a fast descender, passed two more IMG climbers, assuming I was passing them with him. I, however, am a slow descender under the best of circumstances. Even the short-roped climber at the very end of the line passed me. Soon after that, I realized I was alone, watching unfamiliar landscape go by and not much caring. The twelve climbers in front of me left a clear trampled trail into the fog. I would just follow it. Though I was now far enough back that I could no longer hear them, I continued on without worry. After all, I reasoned, we had to be very near camp.

A few minutes later, Ty realized I was not right behind him. He stepped out of the line, expecting to see me mixed in with the IMG group, but I was not there. Ty stood looking up the trail as the IMG group passed, then disappeared into increasingly heavy snowfall. Then I appeared from the fog uphill. "Hey there, Super Climber," Ty said as I came upon him still waiting on the trail.

"I'm gassed," I said. As we stood there talking, the fog cleared for a moment, and I thought I saw a group of four climbers packing a carry past from right to left through the clearing below us.

The dense fog quickly consumed this window as Ty and I descended down into it. There, the trail we were following became interspersed with several other sets of tracks, some of which were traversing, others descending, and still others now impossible to interpret owing to the snow that had already filled them in. Nothing about the large boulders around us looked familiar. We realized the IMG group was now gone and we would have to find our own way down.

"I just need to sit down for a minute," I told Ty, plopping down right where I stood.

He studied me for a moment then said, "I sure would hate to get lost right about now." Then it hit me. This was exactly how it happens. An exhausted climber sits down to rest and never gets up. They say death by exhaustion, like by freezing, is a relatively comfortable death. At that moment, I was very comfortable. I could have sat there for hours, sat there while the last of the light faded, sat there while the snow hid any remaining tracks. I stood back up.

Ty and I resumed debating the various trails before us. Why didn't this scene look familiar? Then I recalled how the IMG group had veered left that morning at the fork where Ty chose the more aggressive line of ascent. "They took a different route up the hill," I said. "That's why nothing looks familiar. They must be descending by the same route they took up!" I told Ty how he, head down and grinding uphill, had taken the steep ascent to the right that morning while the IMG group traversed to the left around some boulder outcrops.

"Are you sure?" he asked.

"Absolutely. I was mad as hell at you for taking the most aggressive line of ascent."

"You were?" he said with surprise.

"Yeah! I thought you were being a real shithead," I said gleefully. I started down the trail, but Ty did not move.

Still seeking some form of concrete proof, he posited, "So *a* decision is better than *no* decision?"

"Yes," I responded. Ty started down toward me, still unconvinced but willing to go along. Then an idea came to him.

"Crampons," he said. "The IMG group was still wearing crampons. The group traversing would not have needed crampons!" We studied the tracks in the trail below carefully. Crampon marks scarred them thoroughly. That was good enough.

A few hundred feet lower, we came to the fork in the trail where our two paths had separated that morning. "This is it," I said. We continued down the trail until a modest cluster of tents appeared below and to our left. It was the IMG group. We knew our tent lay less than a hundred feet below this. We were home.

It was eight when we stumbled into camp. Brian's group had become worried and already made up hot bottles of an orange energy drink for us. They had even begun discussing the notion of launching a rescue attempt. I called Lin on the sat phone to report that we had made it safely back to camp. I was spent. Removing my boots and crampons seemed like a monumental task. I crawled into my sleeping bag, still wearing full summit clothing, and passed quickly into a deep, deep slumber.

THE DAY AFTER

By the time Ty and I woke the next day, Brian's team had left for the summit. We had slept almost thirteen hours. I crawled from our tent squinting like a nocturnal animal drug out into the light of day. Though our plan was to descend all the way to base camp on the opposite side, Plaza de Mulas, Ty and I moved casually about, aimless and slow-witted. I considered the notion of just resting for a day. But there would be no point in staying another night at high camp. To do so would most likely result in still further deterioration of our condition.

Ty and I packed up our tent. Unwilling to carry a load down then climb back up for the remaining provisions, we had become resolute with the scheme of taking everything,

120 pounds each, down at once. Each of us would shoulder the burden of a double load—the heaviest carry yet in what was our weakest condition of the trip. This was a choice born not of ambition or machismo, but of the complete lack of other acceptable options.

We started down the steep trail toward Plaza de Mulas beneath monstrous loads. The risk of falling forward on such a treacherous pitch led both of us to err on the side of balancing our packs toward the mountain. As a result, our loads hauled us backward against the hillside many times, only to skid in graceless humiliation on our rumps. Each time I fell, I lay on the ground for a moment assessing the pounding my elbows and ass had suffered, then positioned my feet downhill and carefully shifted the weight of myself and pack over them to stand. Individual ligaments ached in isolation at various points up the length of my legs. My knees felt as though they had been beaten with a nightstick, and something was wrenched out of place in my left shoulder. But we pressed on. I felt blisters forming then the dampness of blood filling one boot as my toenails were jammed loose. Deep sinewy muscles within my gluteus tightened in spasms as we stopped for our first break.

We made deals with ourselves to descend at least eight hundred vertical feet before resting again, but I never lasted that long. As our first glimpse of Plaza de Mulas came into view, minuscule and taunting, the weather rolled over into a cold, wind-driven pellet snow. We stumbled on, finally arriving eleven hours and five thousand feet below high camp at the tent city of Plaza de Mulas.

I threw down my pack outside the Grajales cook tent. Snow-caked and spent, I tromped inside and sat on a plastic milk crate while the camp boss dealt with a British climber who needed a helicopter out for one of his team members. It was warm inside, and the tent smelled of chicken, onions, and peppers frying in pans. I felt a large clump of snow slide off one shoulder and fall to the floor beside me. The cooks and camp boss looked me over critically. In this tiny space, their tiny space, I was breaking the rules. Camp etiquette called for not entering the tent until it was my turn, then leaving immediately thereafter. They may have liked to chase me out, but the kitchen crew had seen my kind before. They knew it would be a mistake to have anything to do with me since an exhausted climber is capable of only two reactions: quiet compliance or explosive aggression. Guessing which one they would get probably seemed like a poor wager. Somewhere inside me, the survival instinct that had been active for the better part of two weeks relaxed as I sat on that plastic crate. I felt my head bob as slumber wrapped around me, kind, soft, complete.

The camp boss woke me and in short order confirmed the services Ty and I would need.

"And do you need beds?" he asked.

"Beds?" I questioned, certain he could not mean what he said.

"Yes, beds."

He led me to a large Quonset hut tent with several bunks lining each side. A bare plastic mattress on each bed offered forgotten comforts. I immediately agreed to rent two bunks for twenty bucks each... even though snow blowing in from the tent corners was covering them. We would not have to sleep on the ground or set up our tent in the blowing snow. We might even make some new friends among the ethnically diverse bunkmates who peered at me from the breathing holes in their mummy sacks.

"Dude, you look like hell," another climber said to me from across the table that night at dinner. There was no cause to doubt him. My forehead had burned and blistered in the intense sun of the last few mornings. My lips were so swollen and cracked they felt like flaps of leather that met without joining. The area around my nostrils was peeling away. I laid a hand to my face, and everywhere it touched, ragged bits of flesh turned up like autumn leaves on a lawn. My eyes were bloodshot from the ceaseless wind.

Though we were still at 14,500 feet, an altitude equivalent to the summit of Mount Rainier, this was low enough to feel the thicker air, low enough to trigger physiological changes. At this altitude, injuries could begin healing, but first they would make themselves known, springing forth from hypoxic dormancy. "You remember that rock you fell back against three days ago?" my body would ask. "Well, here's the bruise I promised you!"

I thought about my sons as we settled into our bunks that night. I imagined them warm and comfortable in our home on Lake Samish and wondered what had been going on in their lives the last several weeks. The experiences of the climb had awakened a vast appreciation for how much I had to lose, and I missed my boys like never before. I thought about Don and hoped he still understood my absence.

THE TREK OUT

We woke the next morning and set about sorting our gear in one of the empty Plaza de Mulas dining tents. Light daypacks were readied with our lunches and a layer of waterproof clothing. The remainder of our things was bundled and tagged for the muleteers to pack out.

Ty and I set out down the Horcones Valley on foot. We listened to our iPods and stopped to snack. Occasionally we were overrun from behind by trotting mules, their dust consuming us as they dodged by wide-eyed and skittish like chickens being chased.

As we trekked away the hours, I thought back on the strange imagery that had appeared in my mind while climbing the Caneleta. It meant something, a message from the mountain, and though it wasn't clear exactly what that message was, I sensed some path had been laid before me, a path toward healing and forgiveness with my father.

Ty and I hung out for three days in Mendoza, touring

wineries and eating fine Argentine beef, drinking watermelon juice and laying by the pool. Word came on the third day that Brian and his team had summited Aconcagua.

COMING HOME

I stepped out onto the tarmac in Bellingham after twenty-nine hours of travel. The timeless catatonia of international flight cleared from my head as cool Pacific Northwest air settled upon me. I knew Lin would be waiting in baggage claim and felt the anticipation that had been building slowly over several days suddenly spill over. I walked faster toward the terminal, limping on my declawed right foot then broke into a jog, weaving around passengers who trailed small children and roller bags. Ongoing airport renovations funneled me into a plywood cattle shoot that dodged left and right at random angles. Still, I kept jogging.

I always feel I am bringing something home with me when I return from a climb, something I do not exclusively own. Most of the time, I don't fully understand what has come to pass beyond the simple fact I stood on top of a continent. But the people who stood with me in spirit each paint upon a canvas with their own color, adding texture and nuance in the shape of their fears, their hopes, and the audacious possibility that had, for a short while, become a part of their daily lives. It is a painting to which I add my signature, having never held the brush.

Lin always places the first mark, representing all the

times she feared I might not return to resume the life and love we share. My climbing is, to her, at once a punishment and affirmation of love. Her courage is tested, her patience fatigued. But something in the process touches a place so pure that her trust in the forces at work only strengthens.

As I emerged into baggage claim, I saw Lin standing in a clear area back from the crowd. I paused to look at her. She smiled back at me and placed a rose between her teeth, striking a dramatic Argentine tango pose. The voluptuous black and red dress she wore had been concealed until the appointed moment by a trench coat thusly cast down at her feet. I felt my smile crumbling to a whimper as I walked toward her. I wanted to apologize. I wanted to thank her. Still smiling, tears ran freely down Lin's cheeks. As I reached for her, she threw both arms around my neck and leaned her weight against me. We kissed. A peck, really, a sort of test kiss that asks the question, "Do you remember me?" Then we embraced in the kiss that answers that question.

I spent most of the next day sleeping. It was good to be in my own bed and move about in my home, personal space so stark in comparison to the last month that it was at once comfortable and disquieting. I milled about aimlessly for an afternoon before deciding to check in with my father in Anacortes, Washington.

"When are you leaving on that mountain climb?" he asked.

"I just got back," I told him. There was an awkward pause.

"Hey, that's a pretty good deal," I added in an attempt to spin positive. "It all worked out, and you didn't have to go through the worry."

"Yeah," he agreed tentatively. We talked a bit about the climb, a bit about the dogs he was taking care of for various neighbors. I invited him for Sunday supper.

It would be a full week before I felt my rhythm return, a month before I went back to the gym. Several times I met up with someone who had read my blog and seemed interested in talking about the climb. But most of the time I just found myself parroting journal entries, feeling it had all been said. But it hadn't.

I had not written about my father in any of the blog entries and told no one about the sequence featuring him that had appeared in my mind as I approached the summit of Aconcagua. The imagery of Don's regression to a frightened six-year-old boy haunted me as I struggled to understand it.

I decided to take Don along with me on a short trip to Phoenix so I could observe him more closely and see how he did outside the familiar surroundings of his home.

Don required detailed instructions with each step of the airport security process.

"Okay, Dad. Now step through the metal detector. Good. Now walk over to the belt and find your things. That's it. Put your shoes on. Now we are walking to our gate. This way."

He smiled kindly each time then paused for further instruction. My father seemed to respond as much to the tone of my voice as to what I said, so I made a point of being pleasant, positive… fatherly. Our flight had just lifted off when it came to me, and I understood the visions from Aconcagua. It was not enough to be the father to my sons that I never had. If I was truly going to break the chain of failed fatherhood, I would also have to be the father that Don never had. In this context, my father's sickness was in fact an amazing healing opportunity. For me.

VINSON MASSIF

THE DECISION

MY EARLIEST MEMORY OF ANTARCTICA COMES FROM A Godzilla movie I saw as a child. In this feature the Japanese find the Lizard King frozen in the Antarctic ice. They carve away the area where Godzilla is entombed and tow the massive ice chunk back to Japan for reasons that are never explained but must have been hotly debated later by Tokyo city council members.

I was twelve years old the next time Antarctica came to my attention. Conspiracy theorists claimed the United States' moon landings were faked, having been filmed in Antarctica. NASA did base some of its astronaut training there, but of course maintained that the moonwalk film was authentic. Then the sudden emergence of bigfoot sightings stole attention away from the conspiracy theorists' claims, only to reemerge a few years later, during which time they theorized that the US Government had faked the bigfoot sightings to avert the discovery of their faked moon landings. Thirty-nine years passed before Antarctica again entered my sphere of awareness when a friend mentioned it as we sat having lunch at a burger joint in Bellingham.

"I got a call from Phil Erschler," Dick said. "He wants me to join his Antarctica expedition this December."

I did not yet know who Phil Erschler was or his remarkable resume of climbing accomplishments (first American to summit Everest via the North Wall), so I focused instead on what I did know. "Aren't you concerned about Godzilla?" I asked, certain the Japanese had returned him there.

Mike, our other lunch companion, and Dick had been climbing partners for several years. Together they had summited Elbrus, Kilimanjaro, Aconcagua, and several lesser mountains. A few of these climbs had been led by Phil Erschler's International Mountain Guides.

"Really? Are you gonna go?" Mike asked.

"I don't know," Dick said, tapping his fork against his plate. "That's just four months from now." Like Mike, Dick was a successful area dentist. Blocking out the three weeks needed for such an expedition would require a fair bit of scheduling coordination with his practice.

"And the price tag is kinda high," Dick continued, "about $35,000." Mike and I were astonished, but Dick's smile suggested he had already made his decision.

"What would you climb there?" I asked.

"Vinson Massif. High summit for the continent. Sixteen thousand and forty-eight feet," Dick said.

By the time the three of us met for lunch again a week later, Mike and Dick had both decided to join the expedition. They invited me to come too, but I was already committed to the Aconcagua attempt Ty and I planned to make at about that same time. Their attempt was successful, and on January 6, 2010, Mike and Dick stood with their team on the summit of Vinson Massif, the top of the bottom, as climbers call it.

In turn, Ty and I went on to summit Aconcagua, an experience that yielded rich personal dividends to me. One of those was the love I found for writing about climbing, both in blog and journal form. I came to miss this writing greatly in the quiet months that followed our Argentine expedition. During that time I continued to meet with Dick and Mike for lunch and found myself captivated by their stories and photos of Antarctica. Eager to learn more, I scoured the internet for firsthand accounts from others who had climbed there, but very little had been written. Since first being spotted by a US Navy plane in 1957, Vinson Massif had been climbed by fewer than a thousand people. This made for soil too fertile for my writer's compulsion to turn away from, so I began seriously considering Vinson Massif for the December 2010 expedition season.

My eldest son, Trevor, had graduated from high school the prior year and moved to Chicago to start college. His younger brother, Chase, was entering his junior year of high school. Having already climbed Aconcagua in January, I wanted to make sure that Chase would be okay with my leaving again in December of the same year. We agreed that it would be, but my climbing would be put on hold after that through Chase's senior year. Between sports and special functions, there would be a lot going on that year, things we wanted to experience together.

Lin also supported my going to Antarctica. At this point, we both held the view that Vinson Massif was nowhere near as dangerous or difficult as Aconcagua had been. A full vertical mile shorter, Vin Mass sounded more like an exotic climber's holiday. I signed on with Adventure Consultants, with whom I had climbed Kilimanjaro, for their December 2010 Vinson Massif expedition.

I began blogging the Antarctica expedition four months before leaving. Readers of my prior two blogs quickly picked it up and began commenting, mostly voicing concern.

"Dave, I read your blog last night and we wish you lots of luck and happy climbing, but I have to tell you I think you're a little crazy," one reader wrote.

Another wrote, "My uncle spent like ten years climbing all over the Antarctic as a meteorologist for the USN. He's a totally hard-core, decorated, retired, been there done that type. I asked him what he thought about climbing Vinson Massif for sport. He laughed and said, 'Your buddy's nuts.'"

I decided they might have a point. The expedition catalogues put out by climbing companies rarely speak of risk in the thin verbiage that dances around the impressive photographs adorning their pages. I decided to look into it.

Matador Trips had just published an article titled, "11 Most Dangerous Mountains in the World for Climbers." I was shocked to find Vinson Massif ranked seventh, ahead of Denali (tenth) and Everest (ninth). The rationale behind this was the extraordinary remoteness of Vin Mass, making anything outside of self-rescue a nonoption. But my continued research turned up numerous other reasons to rethink the risks of this climb.

Antarctica is the coldest place on earth. During the Antarctic summer, December, the average inland temperature is still −20°F. During winter, it is much, much colder, having once reached −135.8°F, the coldest naturally occurring temperature ever recorded on earth.

Antarctica is the windiest place on earth. In places like the East Antarctic Ice Sheet, a mean annual wind speed of fifty miles per hour howls day and night, 365 days a year. Wind is the chief foe of mountain climbers. It strips away body heat, challenges efficient movement, and complicates the most mundane aspects of existing on a high reach.

Antarctica is the driest place on earth. Classified as a desert, the continent sees less than two inches of annual precipitation (in the form of snow) inland. There would be no rainwater gathered off the roof of our tent, no glacier meltwater to harvest at leisure. All liquid would have to come from melting hard-packed ice that was decades old, and we would need much more of it as the dry air increased the demands of hydration.

Antarctica is the tallest continent on earth. Ninety-eight percent covered in ice averaging one mile thick, the landscape gives climbers a five thousand–foot head start on their Vin Mass journey as soon as they land. But living on that ice, combined with the low angle of sunlight, means the only warmth climbers know is whatever their own bodies can generate.

It seemed Antarctica was a land of superlatives—all of them worthy of being taken seriously. Yet for all of this, I could not find a single reference to a climber fatality on Vinson Massif. Like Shackleton's infamous Imperial Trans-Antarctic Expedition, which famously survived a shipwrecked winter in Antarctica without losing a single man, Vinson Massif climbers had likewise enjoyed the fruits of thorough preparation, expert technique, and damn good luck. Yet one could not help but wonder at the motives of these climbers.

Vinson Massif (*massif* being French for mountain) is named after Carl G. Vinson, the US congressman from Georgia who first persuaded the US Government to pledge support for the exploration of Antarctica. Explore it they did, though curiously the United States never laid claim to any part of the continent. Those who are quick to charge the United States with imperialism should note that they were beaten out by the countries of Russia, Chile, New Zealand, Britain, and France. Some parts of Antarctica are claimed presently by as many as three different countries. While there is evidence to suggest this causes some tension among them, the continent's Monopoly-equivalent value of Baltic Avenue prevents the kind of escalation that might prompt them to take up arms since they'd only freeze to death holding them.

Vinson Massif is not a prominent summit. Many taller mountains exist in places much more accessible. It is not a trophy name. Few outside the climbing community have ever heard of Vinson Massif. Surely the Matterhorn would be a better choice if you wanted to raise an eyebrow at some social gathering, even though, at 9,500 feet, it is easily dwarfed by Vin Mass (16,048 feet). Further, one could not label a Vinson Massif expedition easy, safe, or cheap. Given all of this, the question remained: why do climbers take on Vinson Massif?

Being nothing short of a compulsory for anyone wishing to complete the Seven Summits, the vast majority of climbers who join Vinson Massif expeditions are seeking to add their names to the very short list (perhaps 350 people) of those who have managed to "touch 'em all," standing atop each of the Seven Summits. But this was not my own motivation.

I still did not consider myself a Seven Summiter, even

as I prepared to take on the fifth of the Seven Summits. Indeed, I had become a mountain climber over the course of my prior adventures, but I did not love the mountains, not like most of the climbers I met. Life was hard in the mountains—and dangerous. Still, the calling I felt from each mountain seemed clear, and the rewards that followed were rich. Over the course of my life, I had given myself over to listening, just as I did each time I performed improv. And when the calling said, "Climb," I climbed—though I hoped it would say, "Beach." But this time, the calling said, "Write," so that is what I set out to do. Antarctica was simply the topic of that writing, chosen largely because of my discussions with Dick and Mike. That is why I decided to go to Antarctica: to both write and have something worthy of writing about.

TRAINING

I researched the physical requirements of climbing Vinson Massif: heavy pack loads, pulling a sled full of gear across the ice, severe cold, and stingy air. I already possessed the body type needed for this, having so recently climbed Aconcagua. The only thing left to do was condition the muscle groups used in pulling sleds. I fashioned a plywood sheet with an old tire, in the middle of which I could add jugs of water for weight, and began dragging it around on the streets of my neighborhood. "Hey Dave, what are you gonna climb now?" people would ask as they drove by slowly. I had become "that climber guy," "that crazy fucker who's going all over the world climbing big-ass mountains," "Denali Dave." It felt good. Any time I was in the barber chair, my barber would bring up the topic of my climbing for the entertainment of other patrons. I was somebody.

Day-to-day life rolled on during the months I trained for my trip to Antarctica. My son, Chase, turned seventeen. I hosted Thanksgiving and took my father to various doctors' appointments. My workdays grew longer as more and more was forced into the shrinking time that remained. I took walks with Lin and spent time trying to allay my mother's fears. There were holiday candles, leaves to be cleared, and the wearing of my favorite red flannel shirt. I scrutinized the details of the climb, inventoried my equipment, and Skyped with Trevor.

By the time I entered the final week before my departure, I had already started to miss my loved ones, even as they sat across from me at the dinner table. Part of me had already left. Obsessing over the vast minutia of what would come, I mumbled to myself like that crazy guy you pass on the street, jabbing a finger in the air as issues of note scrolled by on an invisible crawler.

I loaded Christmas music onto my iPod, theme songs for Antarctica, and purchased an audiobook about the Shackleton expedition. I scrambled frantically as the last few days passed. Then, as I said good-bye to Lin on November 29, it all fell away. Life was simple again, portioned into single days with well-defined objectives. The first two of those days would be spent aboard airplanes as I made my way to the southern tip of South America, the rendezvous point for my team in Punta Arenas, Chile.

THE END OF THE WORLD

I landed in Punta Arenas—"the city at the end of the world"—on December 2, 2010. Established in 1584 by the Spanish as an outpost to prevent high seas crimes by English pirates, Punta Arenas was originally named Puerto del Hambre (Port Starvation). Indeed, all but one inhabitant perished (largely from starvation) during the first three years of the settlement. Ironically, that lone survivor was rescued by the notorious English pirate Thomas Cavendish. Later renamed Punta Arenas (Sandy Point), the city's location at latitude 53° south makes it the world's southernmost city and therefore the ideal launching point for an Antarctic expedition.

THE TEAM

I had already spoken with one of the teammates I would soon be meeting, Guy Manning (thirty-six), an attorney from the Cayman Islands. We chatted on the phone a few weeks before departure. During that call, I asked Guy why he was doing this climb, and though he had been considering the question since I emailed it to him a few days prior, the answer still eluded him. "You think the answer is obvious," he began in his native British accent, "but then you don't know." This difficulty articulating motivations was typical of other altitude climbers I had met. While most people would require a clear rationale for undertaking a difficult and often dangerous task, altitude climbers do not. If anything, they get by that much the better for the lack of such encumbrances. "I love to travel," Guy added in the tone of a man headed out on a fall foliage tour.

"If you are successful summiting Vinson Massif, what will this experience mean to you three years from now?" I asked during our telephone conversation.

"A sense of achievement," Guy said. "Something only a small number of people have done. An experience that will not fade."

Phil Drowley (forty) had summited Mount Everest two years earlier. Along the way, he used public awareness of his attempt to raise funds for Ronald McDonald House. The first person from the Isle of Man to ever stand atop Everest, Phil was welcomed home to great celebrity. The Manx flag he held in his summit photo was placed on public display, and Phil was called upon to speak at schools and civic organizations.

Steve Novick (forty), a US expatriate living in London, had found himself battling cancer at thirty-six. The difficult treatments he endured taught Steve how much suffering he could take, a valuable lesson later referenced during hard moments climbing. At thirty-eight, two years after beating cancer, Steve stood on the planet's highest summit. He and Phil met as members of that same team, forming a close bond that carried into the Vinson Massif expedition.

Mitchell Halsey (sixty-two) was a New Zealand native who had relocated to Johannesburg, South Africa. "I would like to encourage people to look at their lives," he commented during an interview after returning from his Everest summit in May 2010. "There are so many fantastically exciting things to do." It seemed he had done many of them, having already stood atop six of the seven continental summits. The Vinson Massif climb would serve as an exclamation point to Mitchell's philosophy of living, his seventh summit, and a place in history among the very few humans to have touched every continental peak.

Our guide, Doug Bates (thirty-eight), had already led successful climbs on each of the Seven Summits, as well as Cho Oyu and Ama Dablam, in his role as senior guide for Adventure Consultants.

RUBBING THE TOE

Introductions were made the morning of our second day, and soon our team settled into the friendly cadence of six crows perched on a wire. We reported to the headquarters of Antarctic Logistics Expeditions (ALE) shortly after breakfast to attend a required preflight orientation. Sitting among the forty other passengers with cause to be in Antarctica (climbers, trekkers, scientists, and penguin watchers), we listened as the speaker told us what to expect during our time aboard the Ilyushin IL-76, the Russian-made jet contracted for our flight.

The presentation then shifted to a discussion of frostbite. Several graphic photos drove the point home. "If you freeze part of your body," we were told, "don't thaw it unless you are sure you can keep it thawed." The speaker said that a medical tent was available at the Union Glacier Base Camp for treatment and stabilization of injuries until the afflicted person could be flown out. However, no special flight would be ordered outside the normal weekly IL-76 visit unless the condition was life-threatening. To frame this last point, she stated that frostbite and broken appendages were not considered life-threatening.

I lunched with Guy and Doug after the meeting then set out to explore Punta Arenas, finding my way to a stately park where vendors of inexpensive handcrafts manned booths around its perimeter. In the middle stood a massive bronze statue commemorating Hernando De Magallanes—commonly known as Ferdinand Magellan in English—who in 1520 was the first European to arrive on this shore. Years of harsh weather had fatigued the statue's finish to a mackerel gray, save one big toe, rubbed to a shiny brass luster by the many fishermen and southbound adventurers who believe that doing so will assure their safe return to Punta Arenas. A few grizzled men passed between the statue and me as I stood back admiring it, each dragging a weathered club-like hand across the toe. Though I am not a superstitious person, I did feel the stakes had been raised for whatever would follow, so I stepped forward and touched the shiny bronze digit too.

GEAR NOT

Though all of my gear arrived in Punta Arenas, my backpack was soaked clean through. It seemed clear the baggage handlers in Atlanta had left it out in the rain the entire night I spent there. I unpacked the contents and hung them like prayer flags from a complex web of lines I rigged, crisscrossing my hotel room. It could have been worse.

None of Phil or Steve's gear arrived. Iberia Airlines then held a séance wherein the ghost of Amelia Earhart revealed the location of the missing gear. "Your luggage is in Madrid," they were told. Though no one with the airline could offer eyes-on confirmation, Steve and Phil were reassured their wayward gear would arrive in Punta Arenas later that day. It did not.

Since our flight to Antarctica was scheduled to leave sometime that night, Phil and Steve had no choice but to set out on a retail feeding frenzy, each spending over $4,000 to completely reoutfit themselves with gear sufficient for a high-altitude arctic expedition. The proprietors of several equipment shops gladly extended their hours of operation to accommodate the pair. Back at their hotel room, Steve and Phil had just finished removing the price tags from their new possessions when our scramble call came at 2:40 a.m. Sleepless, they left for the most extreme environment on earth relying on untested kits.

HALF THE FUN

Our bus rumbled through the quiet dark streets of Punta Arenas then out onto a southbound highway toward the airport. An airport official led us out onto the tarmac, where we were instructed to wait before a massive cargo jet, the IL-76.

The most logistically challenging aspect of the Vinson Massif expedition was the transportation of our team and considerable provisions 2,174 miles from Punta Arenas to the interior of Antarctica. The distance is too great, the cargo too heavy, and the conditions too severe for most conventional aircraft. Fortunately, the Soviet Union had the same problem many years earlier as it struggled to move military equipment in and out of remote locations where it officially had no military presence. They needed a medium-range, heavy-load cargo jet that could handle harsh conditions and rough landings. To this end, Soviet engineers created the Ilyushin IL-76. At 152 feet long and with a 165-foot wingspan, the IL-76 is capable of carrying up to 144,000 pounds up to 2,700 miles. As the round trip to Antarctica and back totals 4,348 miles, a good bit of cargo space would need to be dedicated to the barrels of jet fuel used to bring the aircraft home. Ours would be a nonsmoking flight.

This Russian jet and crew, contracted out by ALE, was the only lifeline to Antarctica. That being the case, the $16,000 per-person round trip fare they demanded made sense. There simply were no other operators willing to make these flights. Indeed, it was rumored that this crew, no strangers to missions of opportunity, financed their ongoing operations by running guns in Afghanistan in the same aircraft during the off-season.

Each of us walked through a tray of disinfectant as we boarded the jet and found our seats within the dark belly of the beast. Red velvet upholstered theater chairs had been bolted to pallets, which themselves had been bolted to the cargo runners in the floor of the forward bay. They were torn, stained, and rickety seats that in some cases would not sit up straight. We were given no preflight safety discussion, no demonstration of how to buckle our seat belts. It seemed clear no oxygen masks would drop from the ceiling in the event of sudden loss of cabin pressure. We were cargo on a cargo jet. The humorless navigator glared at us, bleary-eyed, from his chart table. Shortly before liftoff, he slumped forward and fell asleep.

I was expecting the IL-76 to ride like a garbage truck with wings, but the monstrous hulk sped down the runway with smooth efficiency, its four jet turbines howling fiercely. Loaded with forty-five passengers, their gear, provisions for Union Glacier Base Camp, barrels of fuel, and a passenger van on snow tracks, the IL-76 lifted off, slicing through high winds with impressive stability.

It had started. Our journey suddenly felt very real and a little bit scary. Unlike my other climbs, this one involved going somewhere I could not easily escape. Though each of us had been required to show proof of evacuation insurance, with a minimum $200,000 coverage, before boarding the plane, we had also been told in the clearest terms that there would be no evacuations.

The even whine of our jet engines retreated to a reassuring hum once we reached cruising altitude, allowing most passengers to reclaim lost sleep during the first half of our flight. I awoke after two hours to find people moving about the cargo bay, ghostlike as they appeared and vanished in the thin gray hue of a single overhead light. A German climbing team was passing around a plate of open-faced sandwiches and cups of Sprite. I partook of each as I joined them, socializing near our still-dozing navigator. What I had assumed to be charts in front of him turned out to be a Russian crossword puzzle. It seemed clear his skills were a backup in the event cockpit GPS should fail. I hoped dearly that it wouldn't, as the smell of alcohol radiated from the navigator like a green cloud. I used the restroom, crawling through a tiny Alice in Wonderland door, then returned to my seat for the remainder of the flight.

The flight crew tinkered endlessly with engine speed and pitch as they brought the big jet down, ever closer to the ice. These adjustments were done so precisely that the first touch of wheels to glacier was barely perceptible.

Then the jets roared as their thrust was reversed. We had arrived in Antarctica.

UNION GLACIER BASE CAMP: AN ISLAND UNTO US

A powerful wind grabbed me as I stepped off the gangway onto the ice. It spun me around as I skated sideways and backward until I hung up on a patch of snow. I made my way, hopping from patch to patch as though crossing a river on the backs of turtles, to a small portable structure where hot tea and a kerosene heater provided welcome comfort. The room packed tightly with other passengers then thinned out as groups of eight boarded the passenger van just driven out the tail of the jet. With the benefit of snow tracks instead of wheels, it easily crossed the eight-kilometer snowy expanse to Union Glacier Base Camp.

Three large Quonset huts had been arranged to form the core of camp. Two were laid out inside with rows of tables for dining at the front and kitchen facilities at the rear. We would eat all our meals there while at Union Glacier. The third hut was designated as a common place for quiet activities like reading, journaling, or board games. A set of four plastic porta-potties were arranged opposite the dining tents, each decorated with multilingual instructions detailing how visitors were expected to keep solid and liquid waste separate for later transport back to Chile. Climbing teams pitched their tents around the perimeter of camp, past which a string of flags delineated the safe zone. We were living on a glacier: a moving, cracking, expanding, contracting piece of frozen water. Crevasse falls were a very real risk outside the safe zone. Leaving it was a strict no-no.

Our team lingered at Union Glacier Camp for two days before the weather cleared enough to set out for Vinson Massif Base Camp. We loaded ourselves and gear into a DC-3 fitted with skis. A company that contracted out to fly mail into Canada's remote provinces during the summer months had been retained by ALE to fill this role for us. However, this aircraft could not land on the short landing area at the base of Vinn Mass, so we were dropped in the middle of a nearby glacial valley with our mountain of provisions.

I watched the DC-3 lift off and then grow small. It banked to the right around the Ellsworth Mountain Range and was gone. In that moment, it was easy to imagine we were standing on a spot where no man had ever been. Most probably we were. I felt tiny and vulnerable. Prominent foothills flanked our valley on either side, powder-white with speckles of black stone showing through where the fall line was steepest. The glacier we stood on disappeared into yesterday in one direction and tomorrow in the other, while a vast silence stood next to us, the kind that fills the space between echoes, an auditory wedge separating statement from affirmation.

We held our position, waiting for another aircraft, a

Twin Otter, to come ferry small loads into Vinson Massif Base Camp. This, like everything else in Antarctica, would be weather-dependent. The plane might arrive later that day or several days hence. There was no way of knowing. But if need be, we could build a camp right where we were and survive comfortably on our provisions.

A few hours passed as we took photos and milled about the perimeter of our gear pile, then the distant hum of engines eased into our silent world. Phil spotted the red dot of our Twin Otter descending into the valley several miles away. "There she is, mates," he announced, jabbing a finger toward the only clear patch of sky.

Once in place at Vinson Base Camp, the team began shoveling out level platforms for tents. Thick clouds had moved in, cheating us of the sun's warmth, and it looked like a storm was coming. We hastily set up three two-man tents and a group dining tent that covered the four-foot deep rectangle we dug down into the snow.

I felt chilled the moment I stopped working. The temperature had dropped to –35°F. Doug called for us to join him in the group tent for hot tea and biscuits, but even that did not seem to warm me.

"I'm cold," Phil declared. "Me toes are numb."

"Mine too," I agreed.

The cold crept into all of us as we sat on our ice bench seats watching Doug work on two camp stoves and assemble our dinner of chicken chunks in pasta.

"It could be thirty degrees colder at the summit," he said. By the time we retired to our tents at eleven, I was chilled through. I climbed into my -40°F down sleeping bag and closed the top behind me. I lay there, curled in a fetal position, for almost thirty minutes before feeling returned to my feet. I tried to listen to my audiobook about the Shackleton expedition, but it only made me feel colder. So, I turned on my head lamp and journaled with pencil and paper in the comfort of my cocoon, as far from home as was geographically possible.

EXERCISING A VIRTUE

We were aware of at least three other teams attempting Vin Mass at the same time as us, and radio chatter the next morning confirmed that they too had been brought to a frozen halt. One team was dug in at high camp, unable to summit or descend due to powerful winds. Theirs was a dangerous circumstance. Not wishing to further complicate our own challenges, we chose to remain another day at Vinson Base, rigging our provision sleds, practicing our rescue techniques, and walking the broad perimeter of our safe zone in an effort to generate body heat.

We passed the time drinking hot tea in our group tent, the colorful collage of our varied dialects braiding itself like a rope. Occasionally, we would ask one another to explain an unfamiliar term, but there were other times when I understood almost nothing being said by my teammates.

"Are we talking about cricket?" I would ask. Invariably, the answer was yes.

The storm surged the following day, delivering thirty-five-knot winds and still colder temperatures. The team stranded at high camp reported being down to twenty-four hours of food and a few members suffering frostbite. Doug commented that such conditions start to enter the realm of life-threatening. Still, there was nothing anyone could do for them.

The upside of living in a frozen world is that nothing spoils. A climber can bring food provisions to such an expedition he would otherwise never consider. To this end, Doug had stocked fresh vegetables that we cut up and thawed in our entrees. Asparagus, peppers, mushrooms, onions, and carrots thus found their way into several meals. Meat was also on the menu. We feasted on chicken, beef, and lamb. Doug had even brought along a pint of Glenlivet we used to fortify our postsupper cocoa. These luxuries went a long way in pushing back against the low-grade suffering that typified our waking hours. We welcomed that. But we also knew the weight of such comforts would require us to leave them behind as the going got steeper.

MOVE TO LOW CAMP

The team woke to broken clouds and a kinder −10°F temperature. I crawled out of the tent I shared with Doug, shielding my eyes from the intense reflective glare as I stumbled to our dining tent in loose-fitting camp booties.

After a leisurely breakfast of oatmeal with freeze-dried milk, we packed our sleds and broke camp. Unlike Denali, where moves were typically preceded by a carry, our strategy for Vinson called for fewer days and provisions, allowing us to move directly to low camp without a carry. Our initial load would be quite heavy, but that would abate as we cached provisions at low camp. This approach had worked well for Doug and the teams he had previously taken to the top of Antarctica.

Another important aspect to our strategy involved light management. The temperature lift that comes from direct sunlight in Antarctica can mean as much as a twenty-degree difference between standing in sunlight or two feet to the side in the shadow of a cloud. Our first move would involve pulling our sleds up a glacial valley that was shaded until the midmorning sun shone down into it. As the angle of light then passed, the valley would go dark again. We planned our departure from base camp to enter the valley just as light settled into it and then push hard to get out the other side before the sun was once again eclipsed by the Ellsworth Mountain Range.

After the tents were struck and everything packed, we used our dinner plates to scrape the ice surface where our group tent had been. This removed even the smallest of crumbs that had fallen to the ground, in compliance with the strict "leave no trace" ordinances authored by the consortium of nations laying claim to Antarctica. The scrapings were bagged and cached at base camp for later removal upon departure. These same ordinances also required us to remove all garbage and solid human waste, to stay within established routes and camps, and dispose of urine only at a designated hole at each camp. This meant pee bottles had to be used even when on the move.

A stationary cloud dogged us from above as we got underway, roped together in two teams of three. Every time we seemed close to exiting its shadow, the cloud advanced, keeping us in a deep freeze. I braced myself for a trying day, but the cloud melted away after an hour, leaving us with the happy problem of heat management as both the sunlight and its reflection off the ice quickly pushed the thermometer to 28°F. At this temperature we were all overdressed, so the team paused to shed layers and apply sunscreen. We snacked on energy bars and sipped our water. It was the first time I had felt comfortable outdoors since arriving on the continent, and I realized how my mental focus had been consumed with just coping. I knew this was bad form. A person can cope for only so long. I made a note to myself to work on this, to find some piece of joy in each day.

There was tired celebration with halfhearted high fives as our team pulled into low camp. We dropped our packs and immediately set about constructing an outpost, cutting blocks of ice with a saw, and stacking them to form a protective wall for our tents. There is little to oppose the wind as it sweeps across the ice of Antarctica. Even in the mountains, the wind seemed to barrel by with impunity, with a moderate gust carrying enough force to peel up an unprotected tent and roll it, with occupants, across the ice like a tumbleweed.

It was eleven by the time we ate dinner, a fabulous meal of vegetables, instant potatoes, and lamb shank with gravy. Gravy, my spirit animal. Outfitters will quickly concede that the only thing they can absolutely control is the menu. Smart outfitters, like Adventure Consultants, make certain that box is checked with a flourish.

The team bedded down at twelve thirty. Absent the clouds, there was plentiful daylight even at that hour, so I walked to the edge of camp and called Lin on the satellite phone. As always, we did not speak of any hardships thus far. Instead we talked about our upcoming Christmas plans, a rendezvous with my two sisters and their families in Arizona. I asked Lin if she had gotten the flowers I arranged for in advance. She had. They were beautiful. We talked about how much we missed each other, then I lost contact with the satellite. The air had grown fifteen degrees colder in the course of our conversation as the sun eased lower, skating atop the icy horizon. I climbed into my sleeping bag and journaled the day's happenings, planning to call them in later to my work assistant, Sonia. I had been doing this every few days, reading my journal installments over the satellite phone, thusly recorded on the other end then transposed by Sonia to my blog. I wanted readers to experience the climb with me as close to real-time as possible.

A CARRY UP THE HEADWALL

We slept late the following day, resting up from our move to low camp. The air was still, and the sky was clear as we emerged from our tents, comfortable in our light coats. There had been another team at low camp when we arrived the night before, waiting out the same storm that kept us at base. They were gone now, having left for high camp in the early morning hours.

We ate breakfast then loaded our packs for a carry up the headwall. Far too steep for sleds, the climbing that remained between us and the summit required us to carry everything. To that end, each of us shouldered fifty pounds of gear and provisions as we set out in roped teams, arriving at the headwall an hour later.

The headwall of Vinson Massif rises two thousand feet up from the lower glacier. It is steep enough that a climber can stand plumb while touching the hill with their hand. Any fall would be a long one, so prior teams had set fixed lines for protection, which they left behind as a courtesy to those who followed. Each subsequent team was expected to maintain these lines, and the last expedition of the season would remove them. Doug clipped into the line with his ascender and safety leash then started up the pitch.

The team that left low camp that morning was completing the face, now tiny black dots far above us. Comprised of US Air Force personnel, they were climbing the Seven Summits to honor US servicepeople who had fallen since September 11, 2001. I enjoyed meeting them the night before as we built our camp next to theirs. They were led by Phil Erschler.

Phil had been gregarious and outgoing, welcoming each of us to low camp the night before with a handshake made of stone. It might as well have been his continent for all the climbing Phil had done there, but he didn't act that way. And if anyone was not aware of his historic place in American climbing, Phil made no attempt to fill them in. We were all just a bunch of guys a long way from home. Phil and I talked about the team that had been stranded at high camp. Their battered members had descended that day and passed by each of us as they limped down to Vinson Base.

"I think I saw frostbite on all of 'em," Phil had commented with the hard gravelly voice of a fishing boat captain. "But they should get a ride back to Union Glacier tomorrow. They'll be all right."

I clipped into the fixed line then started up the headwall. My body responded, with lungs and legs settling into a cooperative rhythm. I passed Mitchell after ten minutes, then team members Steve and Phil, who were squabbling over which side of the rope they should be climbing on. Pausing at each anchor point, I took a moment to look out across the vast icy landscape below. As far as I could see, the flat glistening ice reached outward and away in a featureless sheen that fell off the edge of the horizon. I was awestruck by its beauty. But the visual magnificence of what I saw seemed to tug at something inside of me, like an emotional vacuum on the other side of the horizon. It pulled me in the direction of anywhere else. It may have been the difficult days we had already endured, or perhaps something else, but I could not deny the strange feeling that Antarctica wanted me to leave.

I am not supposed to be here, I thought. I am an uninvited guest.

It was the complete opposite of how I had felt on every other climb. Even during some of my greatest moments of suffering, I had always felt I belonged right where I was, on my path, following the instruction of a greater voice. Not this time.

We rested at the top of the fixed lines, three-quarters of the way to high camp, and cached our provisions, planning to gather these items up as we moved to high camp the following day.

Back at low camp, we enjoyed another sumptuous dinner prepared by Doug: chicken curry over noodles. This was followed by our customary cocoa with Glenlivet and updates on the Ashes, a cricket tournament between Britain and Australia held every two years. The British team seemed to have a firm grip on victory. This led to a discussion of nationalism and the changes underway within each of our home countries. Mitchell said gay rights were the issue of the day back in South Africa: "Just because someone wants to stick his business up another man's bum doesn't mean he should get special rights," he complained.

None of my team members knew I had a gay son. The topic had not come up, which is what made Mitchell's comment particularly surprising. He must have assumed we would all be of the same opinion, that gays are nothing more than whiny sexual deviants. But the pensive glances exchanged among team members suggested Mitchell did not have a quorum.

I felt deeply offended by Mitchell's comment and wanted to challenge him on it. I wanted to point out that there is nothing "special" about equal rights. This is a topic I gladly weigh in on whenever I am confronted with ignorance and narrow-mindedness. The anger welled up inside of me, and I wanted to let it out, but I knew I could not. Team cohesion is a fragile and essential element in mountain climbing. If I mixed it up with Mitchell, there would be a rift running down the middle of our group, and even if I were willing to sacrifice my own expedition in the name of a core value, it would be unfair for me to also sacrifice everyone else's. For all I knew, there might be other team members who felt the way Mitchell did. We could end up in a full-out shout-fest. Then, when those moments came where each of us placed his life in the hands of the other, where would we be?

I wandered over to the edge of camp after breakfast the next morning and called in several blog entries on the satellite phone. Aware of how quickly the information loop can be completed, even in Antarctica, I was careful, as always, to only speak of teammates in positive tones. The incident with Mitchell was not mentioned. I put the phone away and returned to camp, passing Doug along the way.

"That sounded fairly dramatic," he commented in an annoyed tone then stalked off. I was surprised by his reaction, replaying the entries in my head to guess at what part he objected to. I could think of nothing. I knew the staff at Adventure Consultants headquarters was following my blog and also spoke to Doug as he called in updates each evening. They could reassure him there was nothing to object to, I thought. Nothing more was said.

We packed up the remainder of low camp, caching a modest quantity of provisions. Conditions were ideal. I could feel the enthusiasm among team members. If the weather forecast proved correct, we might leave high camp for the summit the following day. Again organized in two rope teams—with Steve, Phil, and Doug on one and Mitchell, Guy, and me on the other—we set out for the headwall.

We had been underway only thirty minutes when Doug called for a break. Walking back to where I stood, he leaned in, speaking in a low voice, and said, "I know when someone is mocking me! I'll leave you behind in that crevasse, mate!"

I was stunned to silence. Before I could assemble the words to ask Doug what the hell he was talking about, he had turned around and started the rope teams underway again.

My mind was scrambling to make some sense of what had just happened. Was it the part where I quoted him, saying, "Those are conditions that start to border on the realm of life-threatening," as we discussed the team stuck at high camp? That was the only part where he was mentioned. Why would that bother him so much? Did he hear something different? Even still, what kind of a guide threatens a client? I was relying on this guy to keep me alive in one of the most dangerous places I have ever been, and he just snapped.

I decided to take Doug aside for a talk the next time we stopped for a break, certain that a simple misunderstanding of some sort had set him off. But when that break came at the foot of the headwall, Doug acted cheery and upbeat. Maybe he just had to let off some steam, I thought. Maybe we could just move on now that he said his piece. I probably should have talked with Doug anyway, but doing so felt risky given his sudden mood shifts. He was happy now. Happy was good. I decided to just leave it be.

We stowed the team ropes in our packs, then Doug clipped into the fixed line and started up the headwall. I hung back, creating some separation between us as Guy, Phil, and Steve clipped in one by one.

My legs felt strong, assisted by an ice ax in one hand

and my ascender in the other. I was breathing hard as I climbed into thinner air, resting occasionally to take in the remarkable scenery beneath me. But as I took it all in, I was again consumed with a sense that I was not supposed to be in Antarctica. I didn't understand this feeling. It frustrated me. I had sacrificed mightily for this adventure and only wanted to share it with others through my writing. Where had all the magic gone? Then I began to brood over Doug's threat to me, unable to set it aside. I climbed faster in an attempt to blunt my anger, but it did not help. As I threw down my pack at the top of the fixed lines, I told Doug, "When I write about the headwall in my blog, it is going to be *quite dramatic!*" He said nothing. But I wished he had. By that time, I was aching for a fight.

MITCHELL HALSEY, GUY MANNING, DAVE MAURO.

We added the items to our packs that had been cached the day before. Doug also asked Guy and me to take on a few items to lighten Mitchell's load, as he seemed to be struggling. At this point, my pack felt truly substantial, perhaps a hundred pounds. The team then trudged the remaining hour and a half to high camp (12,450 feet).

After putting up tents and eating a freeze-dried meal, we quickly turned in for the night. The six of us crammed into two two-man tents, having left one tent behind to reduce the weight we packed up the headwall. I thought about the comment I had made to Doug at the top of the headwall and regretted it. It showed poor emotional discipline on my part and could not be expected to yield any positive results. True, Doug had stepped way out of line, but aside from that instance, he had also been an excellent guide—cooking, organizing, and watching us to the point of caring harassment. Maybe there is something going on in his life outside of climbing, I thought. That must be it. The whole exchange had been weird, troubling, and out of place, but I again resolved to let it go.

THE TOP OF THE BOTTOM

I struggled inserting my plastic climbing boots into their neoprene outer layers as the team prepared to leave high camp the next morning. Then my crampons refused to attach properly over them. Doug helped me sort them out and, for a moment, it seemed things were okay between us. But then he commented, "That's okay. You've probably never put those on before," suggesting that I was a complete rookie. So we're still doing this, I thought. But I said nothing.

As we got underway, I set about coaching myself for the seven-hour climb ahead. "Simple thoughts," I repeated. I evaluated the efficiency of my stride as we started the modest incline out of camp. My crampons bit into the hard snow with reassuring purchase. Probably a symptom of lingering frustration, I was setting my climbing poles much harder than necessary, so I eased back. My legs felt good, my toes uncharacteristically warm. As the rising sun would be shining on my left side for most of the ascent, I had worn a much heavier glove on my right hand than that on my left. As well, I had activated a chemical hand warmer inside my right glove. In Antarctica, whatever the sun does not touch is either frozen or will be in very short order. A woman on Adventure Consultants' earlier Vin Mass expedition that season had frostbitten one hand by not taking such considerations into account.

I set the soundtrack in my head to "Linus and Lucy" from the *Charlie Brown Christmas* album. There is a ridiculous dance the characters do with this song in the cartoon. Lin and I can't help doing that dance whenever the song comes on. I pictured us bouncing around our kitchen back home and caught myself smiling.

We cruised up a meandering route of moderate incline

for the first hour out of high camp. Cresting a ridge, the landscape opened up to a glacial field two miles wide. The tracks of earlier teams navigated its various crevasses in broad, lazy arches. The day's real climbing awaited us on the other side of this expanse. There, a more inclined pitch up to a saddle was followed by a very steep icy slope, gaining a thousand feet of elevation to a small exposed balcony.

We had enjoyed perfect weather up to this point, with clear sunny skies and very little wind. But the forecast from the day before warned that these conditions would deteriorate quickly by midday. They did, with fierce winds shredding the high flank of Vinson Massif and temperatures plummeting to −40°F as we reached the balcony. We had to shout at close range to hear one another as we added balaclavas, heavy mittens, and massive down parkas. The final pitch looked down upon us, a steep and narrow reach of ice-covered rock one hundred feet tall. I felt my gut tighten with apprehension as I imagined how easily a gust of wind could pull a climber free from that face.

Doug led Mitchell and me on the first rope team. We clawed with ice axes and crampons that too often bounced off hard stone. There was too much slack in the rope as I closed in on Mitchell, who was delayed for some reason just past a shelf above me. I shouted for him to belay me up, but the wind easily consumed my squawking. I looked down at Phil waiting to advance his rope team. We just shook our heads at each other. I tried to hold my position on the rock face, but a growing sense of vulnerability got the best of me. Pushing the rope aside, I swung my ice ax above me several times until it found a solid hold. Trusting all my weight onto it, I pulled myself up, mounting the ledge.

Mitchell had been delayed as he tried to understand Doug's instructions for using the boulders as running protection. Though the wind let up momentarily, it was still impossible to comprehend one another through our thick balaclavas. Doug finally gave up the effort and continued the climb.

Just fifty yards separated us from Vinson's summit, but the route there was a narrow, almost flat catwalk of icy rocks that fell off to oblivion on one side. We advanced, careful and methodic, using what anchored protection we could find. A thin veneer of ice broke loose from a rock as I weighted my foot placement. I could feel the harsh rasp of my crampon teeth as my foot skidded against stone. Catching myself with a handhold on the rocks, I paused to breathe. I looked toward the summit, now just twenty yards away. Doug was standing a few feet below it, belaying in the rope as Mitchell and I advanced. A moment later, the rope went slack again. Mitchell had arrived and now stood next to Doug. All that remained above them was a snowy pinnacle of ice that cantilevered out and over all of Planet Earth, from the bottom up. Mitchell backed up and onto the pinnacle just as I arrived. Doug took a summit photo of him, icicles hanging from his bushy white mustache, a look of childlike joy painted across his face. I extended a hand to Mitchell as he stepped down. "I'd like to be the first to congratulate you on conquering the Seven Summits," I said. He smiled broadly and in that moment seemed to touch something he had chased his entire life. Though we clearly had our differences, I felt a simpatico with Mitchell and a gratitude for having witnessed his triumph.

I pulled my camera from the pocket of my parka and switched it on. Nothing happened. I examined it closely, turning the function from on to off and on again. It still did not respond. It had frozen. Seeing this, Doug said, "No worries, mate. I'll get your photo on my camera." I backed up onto the summit and, at a count of three, pulled my goggles up and my balaclava down for a hero shot against skies so blue they didn't look real.

As each team member completed his summit photo, we gathered at a wide area below and off to one side. There I uncapped a tiny metal cylinder, and in an instant my brother's ashes were swept away like the pilot canopy of a parachute, my parachute, the one that would float me back to the earth I knew and the places I belonged. Danny and I had enjoyed one hell of a ride with our mountain climbs, but in that moment, my heart said the ride was over. I turned back toward the team, only to be gathered up in a congratulatory hug from Phil. Overwhelmed with emotion, I began sobbing. "I know," Phil said. "I know."

We had descended to low camp two days later, a victory in our pockets and all major risks behind us. It was midnight, and though the long daylight hours of that strange season still fully illuminated our white world, the low angle of the sun cast definition to the wind-scalloped snow before Phil and me as we stood looking out across the glacier. A lone figure was approaching as we spoke about the motivations of climbers. It was a patient and introspective discussion, handed back and forth like a Rubik's Cube. Then Phil said something that spoke to the core of my own experience as a mountain climber.

"Look at this bloke comin' down the mountain. There's no celebration, no people cheerin', and that's not what he wants either. This man has been at war... really, with himself."

I felt that had been me all along, a man at war with himself. It never was about the mountains. They were just the battlefields where I fought the demons that had haunted me: my failed marriage, my fear of intimacy, my brother's death, my relationship with my father. I felt I had won each of those battles—yet somehow I had not won the war.

By the time a climber takes on Vinson Massif, they have already served numerous tours of duty on high-altitude battlefields. Some of us are missing fingers. Others bare the tattoos of frostbite. Many have no visible scars, choosing to speak of days spent surviving at thirty below as though it were an afternoon at the zoo, stoicism and denial being their standard-issue carbine. But the people at my table, that first morning back at Union Glacier, were the walking wounded. Comprised of the team that had been stormed in at high camp for six days under truly horrific conditions, each bore the black flesh of frostbite. One would probably lose the tip of his nose, another his left ear. I tried to engage them, asking, "What, ten years from now, do you think you will most remember about this trip?"

All were silent for a long moment. Then the woman seated next to me said, "I just want to get out of here."

I got up from our table to fetch a cup of coffee and found myself staring into a mirror hanging near the dispenser. Examining my reflection for the first time in two weeks, I was surprised by how little I resembled myself. My lips were swollen, cracked, and bleeding from the effects of sun and cold. My facial hair had grown out in a two-toned agreement, dark at the cheeks with a gray stripe running down the middle from my mouth as though I had choked while consuming a bowl of indifference. The end of my nose was chafed and red, my hair matted and greasy. Suddenly I felt aware of my many minor hurts: the blisters on my feet, the numbness of my fingertips, the tingling in my toes, and a deep ache in my shoulders. By comparison with those seated at my breakfast table, Vinson had treated me fairly kindly. But there was no denying it had also kicked my ass. I could not imagine climbing again. Something had changed. That thing that had driven me through the first four of the Seven Summits seemed to be quieting. Vinson had not beaten me. I stood on its summit. Yet, more than ever, I felt ready to declare peace.

My teenage son, Chase, often spent time teaching me the expressions used by rappers. These came in handy whenever I found myself improvising the part of one onstage. Being as middle-aged and white as a person can get, such words struck comedic contrast when they came out of my mouth. A real crowd-pleaser. It was Chase's voice that came to me as the IL-76 lifted off for our departure from Antarctica. Dressed in heavy down and packed together like chicks in a nest, we rumbled across the ice gathering speed. The jet and everything in it shook violently, but a soothing darkness enveloped us, warm and homeward bound. I could feel myself drifting off to sleep, that early dream state when voices come to you. The nose of our aircraft lifted, and the landing gear went silent. In that moment, I heard Chase declare, "We out dis bitch."

A PENGUIN IN THE DESERT

I arrived in Phoenix a few days ahead of Lin for our planned family Christmas. With past climbs it had always been Lin picking me up at the airport, dressed in a manner that spoke thematically to whatever far-flung place I had been. But this time we would be reunited with me picking her up at the airport in Mesa, Arizona. So I decided I should be the one to dress up, keeping our quirky tradition alive.

Nothing symbolizes Antarctica better than a penguin, so this seemed like the clear choice for my costume. After many phone calls, I found what had to be the only penguin costume in the desert. The downside was that it had been made of a rug-thick material guaranteed to cook the occupant when worn anywhere warmer than Antarctica. I took it.

I pulled up to the Mesa airport ten minutes late and in a panic. The whole effect would be lost if Lin walked off the plane and I was not there to greet her as she had me so many times. Hurriedly, I climbed into the costume and headed for the terminal. The realistic design of the garment pinched my legs close together at the ankles, making anything better than a fast waddle impossible. I was breathing hard inside the headpiece. Sweat ran freely down my face. My penguin feet were slapping hard on the pavement. I could see passengers pouring into the baggage claim area. With both flippers waving madly, I bum-rushed the lot of them.

Unfortunately these people were exiting the flight from Great Falls, and I only succeeded in fostering a festive sort of confusion. Lin's flight from Bellingham was running one hour late. Families with young children assumed I had been hired by the airport to bring a little holiday cheer to the otherwise mundane experience of waiting for relatives to arrive. I found myself posing for photos and allowing kids to touch my beak. But a few people asked why I was dressed as a penguin and, having time on my hands, I shared the story of my trip to Antarctica and the many themed reunions Lin and I had enjoyed. The story spread throughout baggage claim.

I noticed something strange going on as passengers filed into the room. The party meeting them would linger instead of proceeding to the baggage carousel, waiting to witness the penguin's reunion. Most of the passengers had deplaned and become part of the large crowd around me by the time Lin walked in. She was dressed as a snowflake. There was glitter on her face, and she wore a homemade headdress of cutout paper snowflakes. Her blouse and pants were a flawless white, and her fingernails and toenails were painted red with tiny white snowflakes attached. Lin's blond hair was braided back with all the delicate intricacy of ice crystals.

LIN LEHN, DAVE MAURO.

It is perhaps a testament to how specifically her eyes searched for me that Lin did not notice the six-foot penguin standing among the crowd now watching in silence. She passed me by. But as she did, I honked at her. She stopped and looked back at me. I honked again. A brilliant smile came to Lin's face as she rushed into my open flippers, cheers and applause erupting around us.

CLIMB NO MORE

I spent a lot time thinking about the expedition in the weeks after my return to Bellingham. Though the scenery was spectacular, the climb successful, and the pleasure of meeting Steve, Phil, and Guy rewarding, I could not shake the feeling that my decision to go had been a mistake.

Doug and I never did reconcile our differences. Possessing the only photographic evidence of my moment on the summit, he continued to own the advantage in our rift. When the postclimb evaluation survey arrived by email, I returned it with only positive feedback, certain my picture would be accidentally deleted if I caused any trouble for Doug. He sent me the image shortly after that. But when I examined this aspect of the experience closely, I did not feel it was the cause of my misgivings for having gone on the expedition. I can work well with people I do not like. Sometimes it is part of a larger learning experience.

There had been a physical price to pay. My frost-nipped fingertips all turned white and peeled off within a week of leaving Antarctica. As well, random episodes of intense hot and cold sensations in my toes suggested I had suffered some measure of nerve damage as a result of the prolonged exposure to severe cold. But I had accepted the possibility of such injuries before ever signing on. This too was not the source of my regret.

The more I reflected on the Vinson Massif expedition, the clearer it seemed that the real problem had been the absence of a calling, the sense that some greater purpose was being served. This had driven all my prior climbs, filling me up with life and learning, awakening my sense of wonder even in the midst of horrific moments. Standing on a continental summit would be plenty of reward for any mountain climber, yet this time it had not been enough for me. This led me to conclude that I was not, and never had been, a mountain climber. I was a seeker: someone who follows a calling, regardless of where it may lead him, to find the gift at the end of its trail. The calling is everything to a seeker. It is the scent he tracks and the music that plays in his head. Without it, the seeker is simply wandering. I had decided to go to Antarctica so I would have something worthy of writing about. I wanted to keep blogging. It was a conscious choice. I decided. But, as such, I had stopped listening and probably missed whatever true calling might have come.

I was glad for having promised Chase I would take the next year off from climbing. Suddenly the whole notion of mountain climbing felt ridiculous and wasteful to me. In the idle months ahead, I could find my way back to listening, back to my own personal path. Who could say where it might take me next? It might be a calling that was close to home, cost little money, and did not involve risking my life. I liked this notion. Mountain climbing had been very good to me, and I was grateful for the emotional healing it had sponsored. But quietly, in the back of my mind, I doubted I would ever climb again.

CARSTENSZ PYRAMID

MY CLIMBING RETIREMENT

THE FIRST THING I DID AFTER RETURNING FROM VINSON Massif was reread *Into Thin Air*. I think I was trying to add a note of finality to my retirement from climbing. This book did the trick. The death, suffering, and sacrifice featured in the author's account of his own Everest attempt exceeded anything I could remotely imagine myself taking on. I had never said no to a mountain, but I decided this time I would. What's more, I would do it preemptively. Right then. If someone called with an invitation or if I found myself dreaming about Everest, my answer would be a swift and clear no.

This ruled out the Seven Summits. No Everest, no seven. As such, there would likewise be no point in climbing the only other mountain on that list that I had not yet summited, Carstensz Pyramid in Papua New Guinea. All I knew about that mountain was getting to it involved trekking through jungles inhabited by former (and rumored to be still) cannibal tribes. It's hard to put a positive spin on cannibalism, I thought. Better I should skip that one too.

So that was it. I was done, and it felt great. As my uncle Claus put it, "Five out of seven is not bad." I had learned a lot, grown a lot, healed a lot. The whole epic adventure had swept me up and changed my life over the course of five years. For this I felt profound gratitude. But I would not miss the months of hard training, the punishing financial toll, the time away from loved ones, the nights of sleeping on ice, and the general suffering that was part of each climb. At forty-eight, I was already crowding the demographic for what is widely considered a young man's sport. The time had come to take my bows and enjoy life's comforts.

Life had indeed become more comfortable over the course of my climbing years. The financial markets had recovered, and with them my career as a financial planner. Where there were days in 2008 when I thought I might lose my home, I was now back on firm financial footing. My relationship with Lin had strengthened and deepened, and I came to know a love I never thought possible, a Walt Disney kind of love, a love that crushed the cynicism that had been my shield all through the divorce period in my life. My sons were doing well. Trevor was away studying architecture at Illinois Institute of Technology in Chicago. Chase had been voted student body president of his high school.

Though my father refused to even discuss the notion of leaving his home, an equilibrium had been reached between his diminished state and the many varied services I integrated into his life. He was still angry with me over selling his car, but sometimes he forgot about it and we were able to have nice visits. By this time it was apparent that something about Don's advancing dementia affected his ability to differentiate at times between memories of his own life and movies or news features he had recently seen. At Thanksgiving, the prior year, he told my sons about his high-stakes adventures as a civilian coordinating the pursuit of a rogue Soviet submarine. They were astonished that I had never shared this with them then disappointed when I pointed out that their grandfather had recently watched *The Hunt for Red October*. This sort of thing disturbed me at first, but eventually I came to embrace it. In his own mind, my father lived a wildly exciting life while incurring no personal risk in reality. His brain had found a way around nature's rule that risk and reward are equal.

My mother and stepdad, Jack, living an hour away in Monroe, were doing well at this point. Though my mother had suffered a heart attack the year before, her recovery had been complete. At about that same point, Jack lost several toes to a circulatory disorder. Absent his big toes, he gave me back the pair of flip-flops I had gifted him for his birthday. In a dark way, it was kind of funny. We both laughed about it. In the time since, Jack had learned to walk a little different, but walk just the same, his signature upbeat attitude unharmed by the setback.

Michelle, the sister I had moved in with when Jenny and I separated, had fallen in love and married. For as long as I could remember, my sister had chosen men who treated her poorly. But she had figured a lot of things out about herself and relationships during the ten years since her own divorce. Colin was the first man I had seen my sister with who seemed to care more about their shared happiness than his own.

In Anchorage, my other sister, Noelle, had steadily moved up the ranks in various capacities working for the Boys & Girls Club. By this time, she was one of two lobbyists representing the organization's interests nationwide. Her husband, my climbing partner Ty, had left network news broadcasting to take a prestigious position handling public relations for the Arctic Slope Regional Corporation, a multibillion-dollar consortium of native peoples, funded through the vast profit sharing coming from the oil companies extracting crude on tribal lands.

It was a good time in my life and the lives of those I loved, one of those rare periods when a person tries to bank some happiness for the inevitable trials ahead. It was the perfect place to end a story, my story of mountain climbing. I had the profile of Vinson Massif tattooed on my right shin, the fifth in a series of tiger stripes clustered neatly together, then called The Upfront Theatre and had my name reactivated for casting.

LEARN AGAIN

The first show I did after returning from Vinson Massif was a one-hour improvised performance in the film noir genre. I held back in the wings as the other improvisers slowly built a scene with various characters all gathered outside a speakeasy. There was a private detective, flappers, a few bootleggers, and a man buying prohibition moonshine. It was a rich scene with all kinds of potential. I could see it going great places, but it was going there without me as I stood frozen stage right. I began to panic as I schemed how I might force my way into the story. A hit man, I thought. These films always had some guy with a tommy gun. I entered the scene miming a machine gun in my arms and, without speaking a single line of dialogue, crossed the width of the stage laying down a furious hell storm of hot whistling lead. Bodies crumpled to the floor as the audience gasped in disbelief. Ten minutes into a sixty-minute show, I had gunned down the entire cast.

It was the kind of thing that happens when an improviser is caught up in his own thoughts, not listening. In the context of improv, listening refers to two distinct functions. The first is the literal act of listening: hearing what is said so you understand the who, what, where, and when of the scene. But the second and more difficult form involves listening to the creative voice that speaks to you. This voice will not compete for your attention. Any distractions, any thoughts you are shuffling around in your head will quickly chase it away. Much of the training improvisers go through is designed to teach them how to clear their minds, how to trust their creative voice, and how to commit to wherever that voice may lead them. Listen, trust, act.

I stood alone at the edge of the stage, suddenly horrified by what I had done. The audience looked at me. I looked back at them. Then the tech booth dimmed the lights to black. Show over.

I continued to struggle onstage. After my third frustrating month, I told Lin I was going to quit improv. It made sense. Every other part of my life was so nice. Improv was like a rock in my shoe. Maybe I had outgrown it, or maybe it had just run its course. Besides, since Lin had finally quit her job waitressing, we now had weekend nights open for going out together. I wanted that. I met with the creative director for The Upfront Theatre, Billy Tierney, planning to tell him I was done. But I never got around to that. Instead, we talked about improv and the things that make it magical. As I listened to Billy share his philosophy of the craft, I found myself remembering how it had once been for me, recalling how improv had, during my darkest times, been the *only* place I felt good. I had been glad to clear my mind during those periods, to be someone else for eighty minutes. But now I liked who I was. I liked the life I was living, and I didn't want to separate from it.

THE PROBLEM WITH COMFORT

I kept mulling over my meeting with Billy, trying to reconstruct the departure of my improv skills. In an honest moment, I had to admit they had been declining for the last few years as my personal life improved. Slowly the notion came to me that comfort was essentially the problem. There seemed to be a clear inverse correlation between how unpleasant my day-to-day life was and the quality of my performance improv.

Yet I also knew excellent improvisers who seemed to enjoy pretty good lives offstage. Ryan Stiles was one of them. He was already enjoying vast success, appearing on three different television programs and various national commercials. As well, he was admired and respected for his generosity to the local community, including charity work for the public school system and a summer camp for burn victims. But Ryan's improv skills were among the best anywhere. I could see them turn on like a green light as soon as he walked onstage. Ryan's connection with his creative voice was so strong and so direct that it was often like watching a man grab a high-voltage power line. I would get so caught up in watching Ryan perform that I sometimes forgot I was in the scene.

It seemed better skills could be the answer to my improv malaise. So instead of quitting improv, I recommitted to the craft and began rebuilding my skills from the ground up. It all came together one night in December 2011. From the moment I stepped out onstage, I was the man gripping the high-voltage power line. Everything I did worked fabulously. It was magic, intoxicating. I could hear audience members commenting, "Oh, here he comes again!" as I entered scenes. Characters I had never known came out of me with casual ease. Dialogue passed through me as though spoken by someone who knew the script. Laughter hit the stage in great rolling waves, interrupting scenes for long obtuse pauses. And it wasn't just me. The whole cast was perfectly in sync, supporting each other, giving space, and finding satisfying closure to scenes. Nights like this would remain the exception for me, but I knew I had found my way back. My creative voice was still in me, and I could clear the way for it to speak again.

THE CALL

The only times mountain climbing entered my mind during the fourteen months following Vinson Massif was when someone asked what I would be climbing next. I always said that I didn't know, finding this easier than telling people I had quit. After a while they stopped asking. I was glad for that. I just wanted to move on.

Then a freak snowstorm hit in February 2012, blanketing Bellingham as the cast for that evening's show chatted in the greenroom.

"Maybe we will all get snowed in and have to stay here," one cast member speculated.

"We could last a few days on ice cream bars and Ryan's liquor stash," another said, referring to the only items in our greenroom refrigerator.

"Then we would have to eat each other," someone said in a Vincent Price voice. We all looked around as though sizing up who we would eat first.

"I had an idea for a sketch about stranded climbers who are forced to eat each other," Ryan commented in my direction. "They would be real casual about it. 'More Phil?' 'No. I'm full.'"

RYAN STILES AND DAVE MAURO. PHOTO BY KRAIG PENCIL.

It's hard to explain, but as the laughter faded, I felt as though a great bird had gripped me in its talons. I knew this bird. It had gathered me up before and taken me places far, far away. Oh no, I thought. Please no. I struggled for a few moments, but knew it was futile. It was as if Ryan's comment had opened some door. Cannibals plus climbers equaled Carstensz Pyramid. The voice I had worked so many months to reconnect with through improv was now telling me something I did not want to hear: I was not done climbing. I was supposed to go to Papua New Guinea. By this time, I had come to trust that voice, believe in that voice, and confidently hurl myself into whatever circumstances it asked. I accepted the reality laid out before me, listening for what would come next, then walked out onstage, knowing I was headed to Carstensz Pyramid.

Lin and I spoke of the matter a few days later. I didn't tell her how the notion had come to me, but simply that it had, that I sensed I was supposed to attempt Carstensz Pyramid. Her gentle smile told me she both supported the idea and had never really believed I was done with climbing in the first place.

I had told Lin, when I retired from climbing, that I wanted any future adventures in my life to be the kinds of things we could do together, shared experiences we could relive in our later years. However, though quite physically fit for a woman of fifty, Lin simply had no interest in climbing mountains. So, we devised a different means to incorporate her into the Carstensz experience. We would both leave on June 30, 2012, I bound for Papua New Guinea and Lin headed to Munich, Germany, where her daughter, Rachel, worked as a preschool teacher. Lin would enjoy time with Rachel while I climbed, then she and I would rendezvous in nearby Bali when I came back out of the jungle. It wasn't going to be cheap, but through a combination of savings, credit card points, and accumulated airline mileage, we could manage. It was perfect. I would be following a calling, Lin would enjoy rare time with her daughter, and then we would experience an exotic place we had both dreamed of seeing.

RESEARCH

It's probably not a good idea to base your research of an actual place on a fictional romance novel that happens to be located there. But I had mentioned my upcoming adventure to good friends Jeff and Leslie, and shortly thereafter they mailed me a copy of *The Seeds of Singing* by Kay McGrath. Set in Dutch-occupied New Guinea in the 1940s, this novel offered the promise of a World War II historical context, interactions with indigenous peoples, the observations of anthropologists, and a worthy mingling of flora and fauna, so I decided to start my reconnaissance by reading it. *The Seeds of Singing* delivered all of this, often at the same time, as forbidden desires were indulged by the side of jungle pools. Though my prudish sensibilities were, at times, alerted, my academic needs were given just enough to keep them going. So, in the interest of research, I pressed on, finishing the five hundred–page volume in a matter of days. Here is what I learned:

1. It was almost impossible to get a good mint julep in 1940s New Guinea.
2. My money is always on the guy with the poisonous blow-darts.
3. A leech can fit through the lace grommet of a boot.
4. Headhunters are not so much bad humans as misinformed collectors. Let's not judge.
5. The heat of the jungle can act as a sort of moral kryptonite.
6. Malaria is so prevalent in New Guinea that, prior to pharmacological preventatives, you might as well have just laid out naked in the evening air and gotten it over with.
7. The tribes of New Guinea really really really dislike one another.
8. It is advisable to yield on price when bartering at the point of a bayonet.
9. There used to be a really good living in growing rubber.
10. The natives upriver like white men—lightly braised with a plantain gravy.

WHY NOT AUSTRALIA?

Unlike the other six continental summits, Carstensz Pyramid is not located on an actual continent. New Guinea is in fact an island, the second largest island in the world, and part of a region known as Oceania, which includes several Pacific islands and the continent of Australia. The high point for Australia is Mount Kosciuszko, or "Koz" as climbers call it. Until Rawson Pass was closed in 1977, it was possible to drive to the summit of Koz. At just 7,310 feet tall, it is little wonder the climbing community went looking for something more substantial to define the high summit for this region. So, the search was expanded to include Oceania—and thus Carstensz Pyramid, which stands at a more respectable 16,023 feet.

Carstensz Pyramid is considered the most technical climb of the Seven Summits. In contrast to the drawn-out grind up a snow-covered slope as characterized by the other mountains, Carstensz involves a bold frontal assault of the mountain's three thousand–foot rock face. Added to this is the remoteness of Carstensz itself, the nearest village airstrip being a five-day jungle trek from the mountain. That trek passes through the tribal lands of various indigenous peoples, most notably the Dani. These tribes have a long and storied history of cannibalism exacted upon one another. Frequent flare-ups of intertribal hostility, combined with broader geopolitical dysfunction, resulted in access to Carstensz being closed completely in

1995 and more recently in 2005. Fewer than fifty climbers attempt this peak each year, and fewer than six hundred have summited.

My first inclination was to sign up with Adventure Consultants for their planned Carstensz expedition in mid-July. I had climbed with them on three of my expeditions and found the organization to be exceptional. But Doug, the guide I had clashed with in Antarctica, was leading that climb for Adventure Consultants, so instead I chose to go with IMG on their early July attempt of Carstensz. This shift in providers would later prove fortuitous when the Adventure Consultants expedition was taken hostage by a group of armed rebels in the jungles of New Guinea.

HUMANS: OUR BIGGEST RISK

In addition to the risks typically associated with any climb, I added humans to the list for Carstensz. Western New Guinea is a very poor and desperate place. This unfortunately plays out in several forms relevant to any expedition passing through it. The first of those is the practice of kidnapping for ransom.

The largest employer in Western New Guinea, and therefore the largest taxpayer to the Indonesian Government, is the Freeport Mine, an open-pit excavation so massive it can be seen from outer space. Locals allege that the Freeport Gold and Copper Mine takes much and gives little to the people of Papua. Despite this, the Indonesian

Government appears to turn a deaf ear to the plight of Western New Guinea's people in return for the estimated $1 billion per year the Freeport Mine pours into the national tax coffers. Frustration over this has, in the opinions of some, given rise to a robust kidnapping-for-ransom trade throughout the region. As very nearly all Caucasian residents are employed by the mine, the two have become synonymous, thus making anyone of European decent a viable target for the collection of ransom from the wealthy Freeport Company. This would be a concern for our largely Caucasian climbing team during the time we spent in Timika, Western New Guinea's largest city.

Farther away from Timika, in our launch village of Ilaga, the human risk would shift to that of roaming paramilitary bands still trying to further the interests of Papuan independence from Indonesia. Small bands of indigenous freedom fighters roam Western Papua staging acts of sabotage and engaging the Indonesian military in brief skirmishes. They fund this ongoing campaign through crimes of opportunity against non-Papuans. On several occasions, this has included robbing climbing teams at gunpoint.

Lastly, there was the issue of cannibals. The Korowai reportedly still practiced ritual cannibalism. A 60 *Minutes* episode filmed in 2006 documented this. I should note, in the interest of political correctness, that when I say "cannibal," I mean it in the kindest way possible. While these people do indeed consume human flesh, it is not as though they will eat just anybody. The cannibals in New Guinea will only consume another person when he is believed to possess valuable shamanistic powers, the likes of which they themselves hope to embody... literally. So, unless you are David Copperfield, or make the mistake of performing card tricks, you're probably not in any danger. Probably.

The bulk of our journey would travel through the tribal lands of the Dani, a native people who were believed to have abandoned the abhorrence of cannibalism for the sweet, sweet taste of cash. With a vested interest in seeing our safe return, the Dani natives we would hire as porters could be relied upon to serve as both passport and protector.[1]

LEECHES

The other form of risk unique to this climb was leeches. Most leeches live in still or slow-moving water. It is a quiet life with few demands to fill their days. One might expect these creatures to have developed some higher order of intellect with so much leisure time, but for all appearances, there is one thought that plays over and over in the leech's

---

1 It has long been the policy of the Indonesian Government to officially deny that cannibalism still occurs within its domain. Few things are worse for tourism. But the government came clean shortly after I left Western Papua, announcing the arrest of twenty-nine indigenous persons on grounds of cannibalism. The suspects did not deny these charges. Indeed, they readily admitted to their actions, failing to see what was wrong with them. All resided in the territories my climbing team had twice passed through.

thirty-two brains: "I could *really* go for some blood right now."

The jungle trek to Carstensz Pyramid would involve wading through many streams where leeches almost certainly lived in abundance. But New Guinea is one of the few places that are also home to terrestrial leeches—leeches that live on land, under leaves, and in the trees. They rain down if you stand in one place for too long. They scrape off onto your pants as you pass through the brush. Once it's on you, the leech will seek out warm areas beneath your clothing, typically the ankles and armpits.

I know that sounds pretty awful, and it would be easy to disparage the lowly leech, but they are as our creator made them, and closer examination reveals the leech to not be the villains we think of them. Here it is, play-by-play, what happens when a leech bites a person:

1. The leech attaches to the skin by way of suckers located at the mouth and tail. This creates a sound, stable adhesion. The engineers among us can certainly appreciate such solid structural site preparation. Absent the second sucker on the tail, a leech would flail about causing more damage, like a vicious dog escaped from your neighbor's yard. Indeed, compared to such dogs, leeches are kindly and gentle.

2. The leech injects a local anesthetic before biting. Who else does this? I've been bitten by hamsters, ponies, and

a first-grade classmate. None of them cared the least for my pain. Leeches are caring.

3. The leech then bites you and injects an anticoagulant called hirudin. This thins the blood and speeds up the draw process. Vampires skip this step. That is why Hollywood must use time-lapse photography when filming a vampire sucking the blood of his victim. It takes a really long time if the blood is still thick. Many vampires become exhausted and have to nap. This is to say nothing of the victim, who is probably already late for the opera. By thinning the blood, leeches are in fact doing you a favor. You are welcome. They are saying, "Let's make this quick and painless and get you on your way." Leeches are sensitive to your needs.

4. The leech fills its body with blood. Your blood. Enough to triple its size. I want to point out that its takes the bad with the good. There may be elements of your blood that include residuals of a misspent youth. They are now the leech's problem. Leeches carry the burden of your poor choices.

EQUIPMENT

I had used all equipment necessary for a Carstensz expedition before. The climbing poles, ropes, ascender, and harness were all old friends by now. Tent construction gave me no trouble. I could purify water by several means.

But the one unique item for this trip would be the rubber boots, which would be worn for the entire seventy-mile trek in and out.

It rains almost every afternoon in Western New Guinea, even during the drier months of July and August. This means mud. Lots of mud—slippery, wet, and hip-deep in some places. The boots would fail to keep a person's feet dry under such conditions of course, but that wasn't the point. They served as protection against unseen roots and rocks beneath the mud.

TRAINING: YOGA

I had a friend named Larry Teeters when I was six. I still remember him and his younger brother Roland. If there was trouble to be had, they had it first and best. They were fast and tough in ways the neighborhood kids came to assume was typical of Swedes, as they and their immigrant parents were the only we had known. So, it was hard to believe when his father enrolled Larry in ballet classes. "He thinks it will make me a better boxer," Larry explained. None of us understood this or why, for that matter, he would go public with such information. But we liked Larry, so we just let it go. I never saw him box, but I did see Larry perform ballet. There he was in tights, bouncing around onstage with a bunch of girls. I felt bad for Larry, who looked as though he was fully engaged in feeling bad for himself.

Then Roland saved the day! He somehow slipped away from his parents and entered stage right. With arms stretched out wide in a mock ballet pose, Roland crossed to center stage, leaping and kicking at the air until he fell on his can. All the while, his face displayed the elation of a human acting out the single best idea he has ever had.

I thought a lot about Larry Teeters most Wednesday evenings while training for Carstensz. That is when I went to yoga class. I was learning yoga because I believed it would make me a better mountain climber. This was highly recommended in the training guide for the Carstensz climb.

TRAINING: ROCK WALL

Carstensz is not so much a mountain climb as it is a long trek with a three thousand–foot rock climb in the middle. When I say "rock climb," I mean near-vertical inclines, ropes, harnesses, and anchored protection. Recognizing my complete lack of skills in rock climbing, I enlisted the help of my good friend David Hutchinson, who had been a climber for over forty years. Each Tuesday night, we met at the YMCA climbing wall for two hours of one-on-one instruction. When we first started working on my climbing technique, I was all will and no skill. But David taught me how to read a route, when to rest, and how to hang from my skeletal structure instead of by my muscles. He taught me to use parts of the rock and parts of my body that I would not have thought of. By the time I left for Carstensz, I was still not good, but I was good enough.

LAST DAYS

I began blogging about the Carstensz climb shortly after deciding to go, though I consciously chose not to post any updates during the actual climb. Though readers of my Vinson Massif blog seemed to enjoy the real-time aspect, I felt in retrospect it had proven too much of a distraction. Instead of experiencing everything fully, I had experienced some things, then rushed off to write about them. It seemed possible this may have contributed to the general disconnectedness I experienced during that climb. Instead, I planned to keep a written journal while on the Carstensz expedition, scratching brief notes about the day's events each evening before bed then building them out as blog entries once I was back.

June 30 arrived and I saw Lin off on her flight eastward to Munich, by way of Iceland, then boarded my own plane headed west to New Guinea by way of Taipei. In a matter of hours, we were as far from one another as is earthly possible.

I thought a lot about my calling during that flight. As I looked back on prior climbs, it seemed clear I had benefited from the help of others along the way, especially on Denali. Though I had served my role as a team member in each instance, I could not recall a time I had gone out of my way to lend special help to another, to vest so completely in that person's goal that I was willing to sacrifice my own. Is that why I had been called to this adventure? That would make sense. I owed a debt, and the repayment of it would be a suitable act of gratitude for the people and forces that had taken me so far.

TEAM MEMBERS

I met Lead Guide Jason Edwards and Assistant Guide Dan Zokaites while checking in for my flight out of Seattle. As IMG is based in Ashford, Washington, just a few hours south of Seattle, I was not surprised to find we were on the same flight. The two men were quite different, yet complimentary, with Dan's mellow, ponytail-sporting demeanor balancing well against Jason's energetic talkativeness. We chatted a bit during the flight to Taipei then some more as we continued on to Denpasar, Bali. There we met up with some of the other team members: Carol, a sixty-five-year-old PhD from Salt Lake City; Roger, a patent attorney from Dallas; and Deni, an urban planner from Alma, Canada.

The six of us found rooms at a small hotel located off a back alley in Denpasar. We ate, slept, and returned to the airport that night for our two-in-the-morning flight to Timika. Once there, we boarded two vans with dark-tinted windows and headed for The Grand Tembaga Hotel, a four-story oasis in a landscape of disturbing poverty. Garbage filled a concrete river channel running past tin-roof shanties and purveyors of suspect foods. Shoeless children played in dirt alleyways, dodging in and out of the colored blankets that served as the front door to their homes. Our vans bullied their way through a river of sputtering scooters then paused briefly while a security gate opened, granting us access to the inner sanctum of our hotel compound. There I met the seventh member of our team, Dr. Pal Tande, who worked as head of cardiology for a hospital in Tromsø, Norway. All team members had experience on continental summits, including Carol, who at age sixty-one had summited Mount Everest.

LIFE IN TIMIKA

We spent our second day in Timika sorting through equipment, wandering about our walled compound, and otherwise killing time as we prepared to fly to our remote launch village, Ilaga, the following morning.

I started the day drinking instant coffee and watching television in the hotel restaurant. A news program featured footage of a water buffalo running amok in one of Indonesia's small cities. The rogue animal trotted through an open market and into traffic, goring the occasional car as he loped along. Eventually he was diverted into a neighborhood, which proved less hectic for the people, but much more dangerous for the water buffalo. A slight, shirtless, barefoot man emerged from his cinderblock home with a pistol as the cameras rolled, then he shot the massive animal in the head at a range implying low confidence in his marksmanship. End of story.

I climbed the stairs to the hotel's rooftop pool and sat scratching notes in my journal. Kenny G's Christmas album, *Miracles*, was playing on the sound system. His rendition of "The First Noel," enjoyable even in July, was drowned out by the call to prayer from a mosque several blocks away. It was a strange moment in a strange place.

We were introduced to several more members of our expedition that evening. Fully half our team consisted of the Smick family. Don, forty-seven, and Julie, forty-six, owned a company that prepared medical school aspirants to take the MCAT entrance exam. They brought their four teenage boys—Bob, Jered, Jakob, and Nate ("Nano")—each standing somewhere between six foot one and six foot four.

Jason and Dan addressed the group after dinner in what would become a regular update at the conclusion of each day. A conflict among neighboring tribes had erupted in Ilaga, so the decision had been made to switch our launch site to the village of Sugapa. As well, the plane we intended to use had crashed the day before. So there was that. Our backup plane was also unavailable, as it was undergoing repairs after being shot at the week before. Efforts were underway to find a replacement aircraft, but we would not be leaving as planned on July 3.

A BODY IN MOTION

Dan arranged a group outing to a secure park away from town as we spent another restless day in Timika. Whenever the team traveled somewhere, uniformed officers stationed at our hotel gates would stop traffic, and our motorcade of three dark vans would leave the compound at a running start. At some point, I realized that traffic lights and signs did not apply to us. We were someone going somewhere, and it was best to stay out of our way. I suspect this mode of operation was designed to avert hijacking or kidnapping, a body in motion being a less opportune target.

Ivan Ernesto Gomez Carrasco, the final member of our team, arrived that morning. After leaving his native Dominican Republic, Ivan was delayed in Hong Kong for almost a week with visa difficulties. We did not know much about Ivan at this point, but it soon became apparent that his family had connections. Chinese officials were contacted by the United Nations the night before, and all of Ivan's visa problems disappeared. A married man with a two-year-old son, Ivan had already summited four of the Seven Summits, including Everest, which he stood atop in 2011, becoming the first Dominican to do so.

THE OTHER SIDE OF NOWHERE

Our flight to Sugapa gave us our first good look at the topography we would be crossing over, a lush green series of steep ridges that stood on edge like dinner plates in a drying rack. Rivers gathered from myriad tributaries reaching up the valley walls. Elongated clouds passed beneath us at random intervals, wrapped across the hilltops like pulled taffy. Our twin-prop plane bounced and jolted as it labored to gain the seven thousand feet of altitude where Sugapa sat. Then I saw a spot of bare dirt stand out against the emerald jungle. The top of a steep mountain had been scraped flat. This was our landing strip, a dirt-and-gravel runway on the head of a pin. The plane made one pass, low and slow to warn off any villagers milling about the runway, then banked hard to line up our approach. I was looking out my window at the valley floor far below when our landing gear made abrupt contact with the landing strip. We lurched forward in our seats as the crew applied severe braking, then the plane turned back toward a point where a crowd of locals was already gathering. Steven, our local guide from Jakarta, leaned toward Carol and me. "Welcome to the other side of nowhere," he said.

A NIGHT NOT IN SUGAPA

The Moni tribe occupied the village of Sugapa. Few wore shoes, their feet displaying a width half again that of our own, thick and powerful like the hands of a boxer. Some wore Western clothes, gym shorts, or T-shirts endorsing sports teams they could not possibly have understood. Others were nearly naked. A few men wore the traditional penis gourd, a long, narrow, hollowed-out gourd that rests over the genitalia on one end and is fastened to stand upright by a string tied at the waist. The penis gourd combines the simplicity of the fig leaf with the pride of Trojan battle armor, resulting in a gift to fashion that somehow implies the present to be larger than the package it came in.

MONA CHIEF WEARING A PENIS GOURD. PHOTO BY DAVE MAURO.

Several men and women sat atop a hill just inside the crude wooden fence that defined the bare dirt yard of the "hotel" we walked to from the airstrip. They stared at us, commenting to one another in their native language. Sometimes they smiled at us, so we smiled back, having been encouraged by Jason to be extra friendly. Jemmy, who cooked for our team and coordinated the porters, negotiated wages with those looking to join our expedition.

Jemmy, like Steven and our assistant cook Raymond, was from Jakarta. He spoke several local dialects, as well as excellent English. Though we would come to know Jemmy by his ready smile, the careful balance of power he sought to establish with the locals did not allow him to appear friendly while bartering for their services. His expression was stoic and unflinching as Moni men stood before Jemmy shouting angrily when they were not selected. This was understandable given the stakes at hand. In a place where the average daily wage was just a dollar, each porter for our expedition could expect to take home a hundred dollars at the end of twelve days. A man could work two expeditions a year and nearly support his family on that alone. In return, each would carry a load of thirty-seven pounds, weighed each morning before it was shouldered. In a few cases, where the skills required also matched up with the complex social order of the tribe, women were hired. Other women in the crowd cheered for them, shouting, "Aieeeeeeee!" as Jemmy handed each their first day's wages and a rain poncho.

It was a chaotic scene filled with chatter, shouting, and waving arms. The Smick family walked among the tiny Moni, towering over them like giraffes at a petting zoo. I stood at the far perimeter with Pal and Deni, taking pictures and trying to follow the storyline. Then Jemmy said something to the large Papuan chief who had been negotiating on his people's behalf, and he in turn shouted one brief sentence to the crowd. With this, they all dispersed quietly. The hiring was over.

Evening was coming on, and the shadow play of low-angle light cast sinister tones to the stratus of smoke gathering above the village as dinner fires burned within the huts. I noticed Jason, Dan, Steven, and Jemmy holding a hushed consult in a far corner of the dirt yard. Jason displayed a look of grave concern. Then the four disbanded, with Jason and Dan walking back toward our shack.

"Hey, Dave, come inside. We have an announcement," Jason said.

Jason explained that Jemmy and Steven had heard and seen certain things since arriving in Sugapa that made them nervous. He said the decision had been made to break camp immediately and press on to the next village, Sunama. When asked what they had seen, Jason declined to cite specifics, still walking the guide's fine line between urgency and enjoyment. I knew Sugapa was one of the villages where rebels had taken climbing groups hostage and suspected these rebels were our unnamed concern, but I chose not to share this with anyone. The rumor mill can be a destructive thing to climbing teams, and I didn't want to feed it with my theories.

The only vehicles in Sugapa were motor scooters, largely concentrated in the hands of young local men who went out of their way to throw poses of dashing mystique while hiring themselves out as taxis for people clutching live chickens. Steven hired a tight-knit group we called the Motorcycle Boys to give each of us a ride nine miles down the village's only dirt road, thus expediting our departure. It was kind of exciting. I imagined a band of rebels hunkered down on a hilltop outside of town, waiting for nightfall and their chance to come rushing in, bristling with weaponry, and rob us. But now they could only watch as we buzzed away on speedy scooters like beetles flying out of a rotten log.

As team members arrived at the trailhead, two Dawa natives emerged, posting themselves as sentries. As expected, they too demanded compensation for entering their land. Jemmy set about negotiations, and soon our numbers swelled with the addition of fifteen more porters. Because the tribes of Western New Guinea raid one another with some regularity, the porters weren't willing to leave their families behind unprotected. So they brought their families along. A man might have three wives. He brought them all, along with all his children and any grandparents capable of making the journey. It was hard to tell what our total headcount was, being strung out along the jungle trail, but it seemed conceivable we were already nearing a hundred people at this point.

My first concern was that one of the locals might slow us down, which turned out to be a laughable notion. The slowest native was quicker than the fastest of our team. My second concern was how we would feed all of these people.

This too would prove a nonissue, as the locals were quite proficient at gathering their meals as we walked down the trail; they harvested tender fern shoots, wild yams, sugar cane, and an assortment of strange fruits without breaking stride. Finally, I worried about how easy it would be for the armed militias to find us. But this, it seemed, was the point of the matter: to gather a large enough body that attacking it would be impractical. Sure, the rebels might have guns where our escorts carried spears, but outnumbered ten to one, they would stand no chance.

The rains came as nightfall set in. We donned waterproof layers and head lamps then continued up the trail through dense jungle. Our path traversed steep hillsides, descending occasionally to cross a river. Our pace was fast, the trail narrow. We fumbled to keep up with one another in our clunky rubber boots. A few team members fell off the trail and had to scramble on hands and feet back up to it. The air was so saturated with humidity that my breath clouded in the light of my head lamp like steam from an engine. Our pace seemed unnecessarily rushed. It felt like we were being herded. Between the warmth of the air and the heat my body was generating, I became far too hot inside my rain shell. Realizing I was as wet with sweat inside my rain suit as I was wet from rain outside, I removed the coat, stuffed it into my pack, and just let the rain soak me, reasoning that if I was going to be wet, I might as well be cool and comfortable.

After three hours, we arrived at the village of Sunama, a tiny collection of huts on a hillside. We were led into a thirteen-by-thirteen wooden shack, shelter that night for all fourteen of us. Don was last to arrive, already stiffening up from injuries incurred when his motor scooter crashed en route to the trailhead. He immediately stretched out his sizable person on the floor and commenced groaning in pain.

Team members changed into dry layers as our duffels arrived. They set up their inflatable cushions and sleeping bags, and hung wet clothing from ceiling beams. My duffel did not arrive. Jemmy made inquires with the other porters and learned that the porter carrying my duffel had called it a night at the village just before Sunama. Jason and assistant guide Dan Zokaites seemed busy enough dealing with Don, so I said, "No problem. I'll just put on an extra layer from the gear in my pack." One of the Smick boys offered me his sleeping bag, feeling he would be warm enough packed tightly among his brothers. But Jason insisted I take his bag, and Dan gave me his mattress. The two shared a mattress and sleeping bag.

LESS TWO

It was a restless night of sleep as we bumped and nudged one another in the tight confines of the shack. The smell of wet, muddy clothing hanging from the ceiling crowded my senses, while a chorus of snoring tumbled forth. Still, I woke the next morning more excited than exhausted, glad to be in the jungle, underway in a strange new adventure that seemed full of possibility. Easing quietly out the door, I found my pack under the eaves, dug out a pair of flip-flops, and circled around to the rear of our shack to seek out the pit toilet. Our hillside perch fell away to a small terrace. Two grass privacy screens there shielded the open-air outhouse. Rough steps had been carved into the slick muddy hillside, but rounded off by rain and foot traffic, they were of little use. My flip-flops acted as miniature surfboards as I skidded and lurched down the hill, mud loading up between my toes as it washed over my feet. "Oh! Rat shit! Rat shit," I mumbled quietly as I lost control. Somehow I avoided falling. Carol had just finished using the pit. Gesturing with the slow wave of an arm, she welcomed me as a restroom attendant might do at a very high-end restaurant. I nodded with a slight bow at the waist, and we both laughed.

Other team members were moving about by the time I returned to the shack, rolling up their sleeping bags and air mattresses. We ate a hot breakfast of mung beans, chewy little dark beans swimming in a brown, sugary gravy. What the meal lacked in culinary grace it made up for in calories. This, of course, was the point, leading into a day that promised to burn many of them.

Don had experienced a particularly difficult night as his injuries from the motor scooter crash reported to him.

By morning, he had decided to leave the expedition, while Julie and their four boys stayed on. I felt bad for Don. Yet a part of me also believed his subtraction would improve our team. From the very start, he had struggled with following, establishing himself along the way as somewhat of a malcontent.

Roger also chose to turn back. Our nighttime trek through the jungle had shown him all he cared to see of Papua New Guinea. "Maybe I'm just a cold-weather climber," he speculated as a group of us saw him off. Roger left behind the lunch rations he had brought along, which turned out to be the best of anyone's. Dan and I would run out of trail food many days later and speak of Roger with admiration as we ate his cheese sticks and beef jerky.

Don and Roger left for Sugapa with Raymond, our camp cook. Our team of fourteen was now down to twelve.

We finally got underway after a two-hour delay, during which time Dani porters were hired then immediately went on strike along with the Moni and Dawa porters. This would be a daily occurrence. Once everyone was ready to leave camp, the porters would refuse to shoulder their loads, demanding still more money. Jemmy always dealt with this situation, meeting aggressive behavior with his trademark poker face. I don't believe he ever gave in to the demands for higher payment, but Jemmy did yield on load weight. With Don and Roger gone, we spread the burden thinner.

Lead by Jason, we each climbed over the pig fence that

circled the village perimeter and started down the muddy trail. I began sweating immediately as we traversed a steep hillside that had been clear-cut to build terrace gardens. Feeling I was capable of carrying more weight and wanting to take various extras along, I had ignored the advice of our guides to limit packs to fifteen pounds. Mine weighed in at thirty-one pounds. Now I was paying the price, and as the humidity soaked through my clothing, I could not think of one thing in my pack that justified its share of suffering.

We descended a steep hillside, slipping and sliding in our rubber boots, falling and flopping as we hung up in the low-hanging brush and vines, then crossed a beautiful clear stream at the bottom of the hill. I dipped my baseball cap in the water and replaced it on my head. A precious wave of relief glided down my body, chasing away the self-doubt that had already begun creeping in. Then we climbed up the steep opposing hillside, crested, and descended into the next valley.

Carstensz Pyramid is the lowest of the Seven Summits at 16,024 feet. As such, many climbers erroneously assume it's the easiest. Not so. On most mountains, a climber will gain two or three thousand vertical feet a day. It is hard work, but at least climbers know they are two thousand feet closer to their goal. However, the undulating topography approaching Carstensz is a complete game changer. While approaching the mountain, we typically ascended three to five thousand vertical feet a day. But we also descended two to four thousand feet a day, for a gain of perhaps a thousand feet. Of course, there was also the mountain itself to climb—and then the trek out across the same up/down topography. Climbers on the route we were taking could expect to ascend over forty thousand vertical feet by the time they concluded the expedition, easily exceeding the total elevation gain for most of the Seven Summits.

Three and a half hours into our trek, we descended another steep hillside. As we reached the bottom of the hill, I could see a large sheer rock rising up from a turbulent river below. A suspension bridge fashioned from trees fallen across the thirty-foot gap provided for the continuation of our trail. I stepped across two wooden planks that I assumed were bridging a muddy depression on the near side of the rock. Thick vegetation crowded up beneath the planks and around the sides. As I stepped off and onto the rock, I heard a loud crack and turned around. Julie Smick was crouched over, trying to arrest her fall as she slipped on the wet planks. She had grabbed the side of one board, which snapped off in her hands. This caused her to roll to the right as the weight of her pack took over. Then, Julie fell off the planks pack-first and disappeared through the vegetation.

For what seemed like a very long moment, there was no sound at all. My brain was trying to sort out the logical disconnect of how Julie had just been swallowed by the jungle. Then there was a huge, horrible splash. I realized at this point that the river was racing around *both* sides of the rock and that Julie had fallen twenty feet down into it. "We have one in the river!" I shouted, stripping off my pack. I ran to the edge of the rock, but there was no way to get down its sheer vertical face. I looked for Julie but could not see her. I ran to the downstream side of the rock to see if she was being washed away. There was no sign of her. Dan Zokaites arrived, then Pal, Ivan, Deni, and a few porters. We were all scrambling. Jered Smick began calling for his mother. The tone of his pleading voice was heartbreaking.

At one point, Dan turned to me and handed over his camera and GPS device. He said nothing, but the resigned look on his face conveyed an intent to jump into the river. He dropped down to his belly on the wooden planks and parted the thick vegetation, looking for a deep target in the water below. Just then, he spotted Julie, climbing out of the river on her hands and knees. Dan instructed Ivan, two porters, and me to form a human chain, which was then used to lower the lightest of the porters down the side of the sheer rock face. The Moni porter removed Julie's soaked pack and helped her to the place where our chain could pull her up the side. Blood ran down the back of Julie's head. So much blood. Jason arrived, opened up a first aid kit, and immediately started working on Julie. She was fortunate to be in such good company: Jason was a twenty-year EMT, Dan was trained in wilderness first aid, and Pal was a physician. They cut off most of Julie's long, beautiful hair, then cleaned and closed the gash in her head.

I took a seat next to Julie on the rock where she was being treated and put an arm around her. "God, you scared the hell out of me," I said with a trembling voice. Julie smiled and patted my leg, the wounded comforting the bystander.

After speaking with each team member, Jason called an impromptu meeting. He explained that the expedition would be turning back. As Julie had fallen from a height three times her own, this was considered a critical fall, and her head injury held the potential to develop into a much worse condition. Jason could accompany Julie back to safety by himself, but if she worsened and could not walk out of the jungle under her own power, he would not be able to carry her alone. In fact, it would take the considerable efforts of everyone on the team if we needed to carry Julie back over the brutal terrain we had already covered. Julie argued that she would surrender her own expedition but was not willing to cost everyone else their opportunity to climb. "It's not your call," Jason responded. All parties agreed that our first priority was getting Julie to safety. We shouldered our packs and began retracing the path back to Sunama.

Along the way, Ivan began venting his frustration at what appeared to be the end of our expedition. "This is not a camping trip," he declared angrily, implying that the

Smick family had grossly underestimated the demands of the expedition and that the rest of us were unfairly paying the price for that. The second time Ivan said this, we were standing near Bob and Nano Smick. I saw them look down in what appeared to be shame. "Let's just give it a rest," I said to Ivan. Though part of me shared his frustration, it seemed clear that we needed to focus on the rescue underway. Then we could worry about whether there would be a climb.

In fairness to Ivan, he was under pressures the rest of us were not burdened with. His entire expedition had been paid for by various sponsors, who very much wanted to see their corporate flag held up at the summit. Coming back empty-handed would mean not only explaining what had gone wrong, but also accepting the likelihood that he would enjoy little success gathering sponsors for future climbs.

We arrived in Sunama by early evening. Julie's dressing was changed. We all ate and turned in for the night. The team was wiped out. My attention drifted to the sounds of the jungle around us. The rains had rested, and in their place I heard birds of the darkness calling out. We were packed together, back in the same shack we had slept in the night before, strewn about like puppies in a pile—tired, fed, safe.

NOT READY TO QUIT

We woke the next morning and began packing our beds

up while Raymond and Jemmy cooked another batch of mung beans for breakfast. Very little joy is experienced in the consumption of mung beans, so we distracted ourselves by discussing the circumstance of our expedition. Jason and Dan were having a private consultation with Julie and the Smick boys out behind our shack, thus allowing the rest of us to speak candidly. Ivan, Pal, and Deni were keen to continue on. Carol preferred to defer to the judgment of Jason and Dan. I felt undecided. It had been very hard work trekking through the jungle. I was not sure I was up to many more days of the same. As well, owing to the delays of getting from Timika to Sugapa and our false start the day before, we would have no rest days if the team tried again. If the expedition set out for Carstensz, we would have to put in twelve straight nine-hour days under brutal conditions.

Jason called a team meeting after talking with the Smicks and informed us that, as expected, Julie would continue back to Sugapa, then Timika, and then Bali to a hospital where her injuries would be treated. Her boys were going with her. Jason said each of us would meet with him and Dan privately to discuss how we might like to proceed.

Carol approached me while Ivan was meeting with Jason and Dan. She was concerned that she would hold up the rest of us and perhaps jeopardize our summit chances. I assured Carol I had every confidence in her abilities as a climber and would welcome any moderation in pace so as to spare my ego from otherwise having to call for it myself. She nodded and walked off to meet with Jason and Dan. I was honored she had sought my counsel.

In the end, Carol decided to stay with the expedition, having at least one reason more than the rest of us for continuing on. At sixty-one, Carol had become the second-oldest woman to ever summit Mount Everest. Since that time, she had summited each of the remaining Seven Summits—except one. Now sixty-five, she was here in Papua New Guinea to claim that final summit. If she were successful, Carol would also claim a world record as the oldest woman ever to complete the Seven Summits.

Ivan pulled me aside to express his concern that Carol may not be able to complete the trek. At this stage, the failure of one team member would result in the failure of the entire expedition, such as it was. Though his point was valid and a rational person might have to agree, I felt in my heart that Carol could do it, that she was *meant* to do it, and that on some level I was on this expedition to make sure she did.

"I think she can pull it off," I said. "And if she needs some help here and there, I have it covered."

I told Ivan how the jungle trekking had been more difficult than I expected. Ivan told me he led jungle treks back home in the Dominican Republic. He said people always did much better after the first day as they learned how to move through the terrain. "Only use one trekking pole," he coached. "Easier to keep track of just one, and it will be out in front of you instead of getting caught up on the side. And one very important thing," he continued, "you must surrender to the jungle." I had to accept my reality, just as I would do in an improv scene. I needed to stop fighting vines that draped over me and just let them pass across my body like the uncertain hands of a new lover. I could no longer concern myself with whether I was covered in mud, bleeding, or stinking from the toes up. Falling down had to be expected, experienced, and then left behind without note. Though I could not hope to achieve the relationship our porters shared with the jungle, the answer to my problem lay in being more Moni and less American.

Jason and Dan called me over to talk. "I would like to continue on," I said immediately. I was surprised by the decisiveness in my voice. It felt like my statement came from somewhere deep inside me, not a place of considered thought, but a place of basic truth, the same source that had prodded me to sign up for this expedition in the first place. Jason explained that he would accompany Julie and the boys back, leaving us in the capable hands of Dan Zokaites, his assistant guide.

The two parties formed up, those turning back and those who would continue on. I walked over to the Smicks and offered a favorite Neil Young lyric. "Smick family," I said, "long may you run." Julie hugged me, and each of the boys shook my hand. I was sorry we had lost them. Our fourteen-person team had been winnowed down to six in just two days.

Dan led us out of Sunama on the same trail we had already seen twice. We scaled the pig fence and crossed the clear-cut, moving at a comfortable pace. There was no talk among team members as each of us redoubled our focus on good footing. Keenly aware of what was going on in the minds of his climbers, Dan shouted back to us, "You don't have to concentrate on every stretch of trail. You'll crap out mentally if you do. Focus on the tough parts, but then let your mind relax after that." It was sound advice. I cleared my thoughts and surrendered to the jungle.

THE TREK TO CAMP TWO

Having made a critical evaluation of my performance the prior day, I decided to fortify my water with Cytomax. It seemed plausible I was shedding electrolytes too rapidly to compensate by other means, thus exacerbating the fatigue. I began keeping my small eight-ounce water bottle in the left pocket of my climbing pants. This allowed me to hydrate without stopping. A profuse sweater, I was consuming half again the water of my team members. I pulled my REI quick-dry camp towel out of my duffel and kept it in my right pocket. The momentary relief that came with wiping the perspiration from my face was a comfort I would turn to every few minutes.

Lastly, I resolved to become better at walking in my

rubber boots. I focused on where I stepped, chose where to plant my trekking pole, and used my free hand to grab exposed roots or tree limbs (also a tip from Ivan). For the first time since the age of two, walking was complicated and challenging, offering risk and reward worthy of my best efforts. The dividends paid off immediately. I fell much less. I also did not waste precious energy flailing to arrest stumbles when traction quit me. The going was still difficult, but things were much better.

We passed over several steep hills, eventually descending down to the place where Julie had fallen the day before. The porters had already built a better bridge there, replete with handrails. It was a touching gesture that said more than could otherwise be communicated with the sparse words we shared.

I was glad to press on into new trail. There was redemption in it, and knowing Julie would be all right, our remaining group could focus on what lay ahead. Dan called for regular hydration stops each hour, and even though these were typically only five to ten minutes, the effect was meaningful. If we scaled a particularly steep hill, Dan would call for a three-minute breath at the top. The team was moving well, and as our confidence returned, a playful banter emerged. Ivan broke out in spontaneous verses of the Guns N' Roses song "Welcome to the Jungle." Carol would occasionally let out her silver fox howl. Pal told clever Norwegian jokes. Everything was once again possible.

We lunched at a place where the river had been partly diverted into a small pond used by natives for gathering salt deposits that leeched from the rocks next to it. The porters and their families were already there when we arrived. They were lounging about the rocky flowered terraces, eating strange fruits and a radish-like root they floated in the salt pond for flavor. A few of the children approached Pal for candies. Though he lived a demanding professional life back home, overseeing 150 physicians, Pal did not take himself too seriously. He could be clownish one moment and remarkably insightful the next. The children in our expedition had quickly sized Pal up for an easy mark, extracting regular sweets from his willing hands.

We arrived at camp two after nine hours of trekking. In total, we had ascended four thousand vertical feet and descended three thousand. Our pace had averaged less than a mile an hour, yet we felt victorious.

A DAMP SMOKY PLACE

Camp two was built on a sloping hillside next to a river. Many trees had been cut down to make room, but they lay where they had fallen, limbed out and scattered in a senseless hashtag of massive trunks. Aside from the small areas cleared for tents, the whole camp was a stumble-fest of branches and mud. The porters had constructed a semi-permanent longhouse for themselves at the lower end of the hill, built with logs and branches that were covered with thick layers of moss. Smoke rolled slow and dense out of each end while the low rumble of conversation hummed from within. Our tents had already been set up by Raymond and Jemmy, who had rushed ahead, arriving with enough time to also erect a skeleton frame of branches that they threw a large blue tarp over to form our cook tent. This was jungle camping, and it promised little.

We washed our socks in a small tributary, settled into our tents for a while, and then gathered in the cook tent for a dinner of curried rice and wild yams. Though exhausted, the excitement among us was palpable. This thing was real. We were many miles into one of the last primitive places on earth, wide-eyed and alive with an almost overwhelming sense of wonder.

I slept poorly that night and woke with spasms in my lower back, a condition that had dogged me off and on for years. Pal was now developing a hacking cough and cold-like symptoms. His struggle had kept me up much of the night. I took a dose of Advil and set about stretching my back out with some yoga positions. A crowd of porters and their children quickly gathered to watch. It was hard to ignore their presence as some crouched down to examine me more closely. The men commented quietly to one another, while a few of the boys tried to mimic my poses, laughing and falling over.

For some reason, I had chosen to squander precious ounces of gear weight by bringing along a small plastic battery-powered device left in my Christmas stocking by my sister Michelle. It had six buttons, each emitting a well-known Mr. T quote recorded by the man himself. I brought it to breakfast at camp two and addressed the team in a confessional tone. "You know," I began. "It was a hard day for me yesterday. I struggled. I fell, I thought about quitting and complained to myself bitterly. Then a voice came to me—a firm voice, a voice of inspiration, a voice of possibility. And it said"—at this point I pushed one of the buttons on the device—"Quit yo jibba jabba!" It would have been a comedic moment if not for the roar of the nearby camp stoves.

"What did it say?" Carol asked. I held it close to her ear and pushed the button again. It turned out she was not familiar with Mr. T. Carol nodded politely as Dan, who had taken my setup as genuine, started a discussion of the many trials of the trail.

"No. Wait a minute," I interrupted. I held the device near Pal and tried again. Apparently Mr. T was never big in Norway. I looked to Ivan then thought better of the notion. Deni was definitely out. Dan might know who Mr. T was, but too much time had passed. The comedic window had closed. I slipped the device back in my pocket and sat down, resolving to try again later with the better-known "I pity the fool!" button.

Raymond, who had doubled back to rejoin us after accompanying Don and Roger to the airstrip, had set up the kitchen in one half of our cook tent, a busy array of four white-gas camp stoves boiling water for drinking and simmering our next meal. A plastic foldout camp table was centered in the other half of the shelter. Jemmy kept an assortment of instant coffee, teas, Milo cocoa, and dry biscuits there for us. I had brought a handful of Starbucks instant coffee packets along, which I combined with a bit of Milo at each meal to make a mocha that represented my only remaining comfort from life back home.

Each team member had a small three-legged folding stool they brought to our low-slung table. Every few moments, one of us would suddenly heave to one side and tumble to the ground as a leg of their stool sunk into the soft soil. The natural reaction was to grasp at the nearest thing in an effort to arrest your fall. This was typically another team member, who then also fell over. After a while, we developed a kind of civil neglect, whereby one would override the temptation to grab the person seated next to them, and that person would override the impulse to help.

I had just fallen over and still lay sprawled across the branches that made up the floor of our group tent. A moment earlier, Dan asked if anyone had anything to report about their health or injuries. "I have a loose stool," I responded. It was one of those rare opportunities to be literal in two senses at the same time. The group laughed at my apparent pun. "I started a course of Cipro this morning," I added, picking myself up.

"Okay," Dan acknowledged, "I have the same thing going on. Let me know how that goes for you after a couple days of Cipro." Carol reported early symptoms of a reoccurring irritable bowel syndrome (IBS) condition she had fought periodically for years. Pal declared he was experiencing a full-blown head and chest cold. Deni and Ivan were fine. Discussion of each health issue was followed by a marshaling of relevant medications and a promise to report any worsening of condition.

MORE JUNGLE

We left camp immediately after the morning porter strike. It felt good to be underway again. Crossing a wide tumbling section of the river on another improvised bridge, we walked the slick wet bark of a fallen tree in our equally slick rubber boots. A vine had been stretched to form a handrail, but it was so slack that it would have served only to slow a climber's plunge into the rapids at best. Carol and Deni straddled the log, scooting across on their bottoms. Enjoying a good sense of balance, I walked across the log easily.

Soon the porters began slipping by us on the trail. Barefoot and sparsely clad, they quickstepped by, carrying duffels, provisions, and tarps. I was laboring up a steep muddy hillside when a native woman eased by me. She was carrying a basket of yams on her back, strapped to her forehead, and an infant riding her shoulders. She moved as casually as if she were pushing a shopping cart down the cereal aisle of a supermarket. "Makanay," she said, offering the customary greeting of the Dani people.

We lunched in a rare open meadow where the jungle allowed the light in. The porters ate yams retrieved from the ashes of the previous night's fire. A few of these were shared with us. They were sweet and rich, smooth and filling. One of the men climbed a tree with his machete and began hacking away at something. A strange spiny fruit the shape of a Rugby ball fell to the ground. A woman with another machete carved the spines off and quartered the fruit lengthwise. The children and the elderly made quick work of its contents. I was not offered any of this fruit, but one child did share his sugar cane with me in a bartered arrangement whereupon I also shared my gummy bears. At first he did not seem to know what to do with them. The rubbery candies bounced around in his mouth, popping out onto the ground. He looked confused. I took one from the packet and showed him how it yielded when clenched tight enough between my teeth. He then indicated that I was to do the same thing with the sugar cane. It had been split four ways lengthwise, offering easy access to its tender center. When I bore down on the cane, it gave off a surprising volume of sweet liquid, both tasty and refreshing.

Back on the trail, we began a series of steep climbs up minor creek beds and washouts that formed steps about four feet high. The mud collected deep at the base of each step as water trickled constantly down into it, but the forward lip was a gravel bed of clean stones. Those with enough stride and strength could launch themselves upward from the firm outer lip of each step. Tiny Carol was not so fortunate. I waited behind her as she struggled with one such step. Both her feet were sunk in mud up to the tops of her boots. As Carol lurched upward to gain the next shelf, her feet refused to come free. Her IBS had worsened by this time, and Carol had given up her pack to a porter's wife to conserve energy. It seemed senseless to me for her to squander what strength she had left, so after watching three fruitless attempts, I lowered my right shoulder behind her haunches and heaved upward. I suppose I expected the mud to hold on firmer or Carol to weigh more (she is but a bird), but she quite literally flew up onto the shelf, landing hard on the rocks with her hands and knees. Carol groaned in pain, pausing for a moment where she landed. I apologized again and again. She would have been in the right to curse me, but Carol just stood up, said, "Thanks for the lift," and headed up the creek.

We gained considerable altitude through the course of the afternoon, enjoying the cooler temperatures that came with it. The 95°F sauna of the low jungle gave way to the eighties. Still, we were working very hard, averaging less than a mile an hour.

It was late afternoon when we broke up out of the jungle and onto a rolling series of terraces covered with low scrub and prehistoric-looking sago palms. A single column of smoke could be seen rising in the distance. This was our signal fire, a palm set ablaze by the porters guiding us to our next camp.

We washed our muddy clothes, still wearing them, in a river near camp three. The water was very cold, but it felt good to be clean. I stripped down to red boxer briefs as I thrashed and soaked my shirt and pants. Several of the native girls stood by and watched us. I noticed them gesturing to me and laughing, amused by my red briefs. Later I returned to the river in trekking pants with my boxers in hand to wash them. A few of those same girls were still there, and they began chattering and pointing to my red boxers. After ringing them dry, I waved the shorts at the girls, who screamed and jumped back. With such a good reaction, I could not help playing further. I leaped at them with the red boxers stretched out in front of me like a fistful of toxic waste and roared. The girls scattered in the tall grass laughing as I chased them around, madly waving my crimson undergarment.

THE REASON PORTERS DISAPPEAR EACH DAY AT THREE

Our tent had been pitched at an incline that gathered my sleeping bag and me in a fetal position at the downhill wall several times during the night. Again I rose with a troubled lower back. I pulled on my rubber boots. They were cold, squishy, and wet. It felt like I was shoving my bare feet down the throats of carp. Then I trudged down to the cook tent, where Raymond had gathered our wet clothing the night before so the porters could dry them on a wooden rack over their fire. "Good morning, Mr. Dave," he said, offering up a broad smile. Like Jemmy, Raymond was vastly tattooed. Images of fish scales, spider webs, and vaguely ominous symbols shared space across his shoulders, back, and chest. When I ask about them, Raymond spoke of his misspent youth as a gang member on the mean streets of Jakarta. Remarkably, he had succeeded in breaking away from that life and was now studying to become a pastor with the Calvinist church. "Making up for past life," he explained with a tone of regret.

I gathered my stiff, smoky clothing and headed back to my tent with a hot mug of Starbucks and Milo—or *stilo*, as I had taken to calling it. After gobbling a handful of ibuprofen, I began the long process of stretching out my back. The sun had just risen, and warmth came with the first rays of light. It was a Zen-like moment. I imagined my yoga instructor, Loren, speaking soft words as I moved from pose to pose. Two boys from the tribe came to watch my odd contortions. I had come to know one by the name *Tatoosh*. He was twelve years old and liked to hang around me at the camps. Tatoosh and his friend could tell I was having difficulty, so they broke down the tent Pal and I had used and packaged it up neatly. As they resumed watching my yoga, I paused to demonstrate the Mr. T device. Much celebration resulted. I let them play with it as I finished stretching, the calming voice of my yoga instructor now replaced with repeated admonitions of "I pity the fool!"

Carol's IBS worsened. She did not carry her pack again during our move to camp four. Gone was her quick smile and booming joyous proclamations. At each rest stop, she would lie down in the mud and nap for a few minutes. We were all concerned for Carol, but nothing more could be done. If we halted the expedition where we were and her condition continued to deteriorate, we could neither carry her out nor arrange a helicopter rescue. To turn around would mean subjecting Carol to the most grueling part of the trek all over again and would take longer than pressing forward to Carstensz, where there existed a suitable spot for medevac extraction, should it be necessary.

The day's trail moved through a transitional zone above the jungle, but below the flattish grass savannah. Dwarf trees and woody scrub carpeted the rolling hills. We pulled into camp four, arriving a few minutes before the afternoon rains. The porters had constructed their own shelter next to our group tent on a small promontory overlooking the grassy savannah beyond. I noted there were no tribal members wandering about camp and asked Jemmy where they had gone. He exchanged shy glances with Steven and Raymond. "It three o'clock," he said. "They go inside to make some love." He gestured to the large common shelter next to us. We agreed that this might explain their eagerness to get to camp each day.

Dan surveyed the condition of each team member while we enjoyed a hot drink. Pal was worse than he was willing to admit. Carol could no longer keep food down. Ivan was strong and healthy. Deni, in a thick Quebecer accent, reported, "A tiny bit of sore in my throat. I don't know. Maybe it is nothing." Dan asked if the Cipro had helped me yet, adding that he had thusly tested his own condition at the cat hole a few moments earlier, describing the experience in terms suggesting it to have been much more than satisfactory.

I gathered an aside of Deni, Pal, and Ivan to suggest we reshuffle the tent occupancy. Noting that both Pal and Deni appeared ill on some level, I felt it obvious that they would tent together, leaving Ivan and me to partner up. But before I could suggest this orientation, Ivan and Pal chose one another and set about constructing their tent in the rain. This left Deni and me to share quarters, and though I knew he might possibly be sick, his symptoms appeared nowhere near as bad as Pal's. This seemed like an improvement to me. We grabbed our tent bundle and stepped out into the rain, making our shelter on a less muddy area of what was, for the most part, all mud.

BETTER

I woke feeling the best I had in days. Though my nine

hours of sleep were interrupted a few times by Deni coughing, the night had been peaceful in comparison to tenting with Pal. Jemmy and Raymond were busy in the kitchen tent making pancakes. They had probably sensed the team was at a low ebb and that it was time to put the mung beans aside. I ate five plate-size flapjacks and would have eaten more if not for the need to get underway with the day's miles. Pal was still fighting his lungs. He stood away from the dining tent, hacking and coughing for several minutes before joining us, hand sanitizer in tow. Carol observed the morning meal with dread. I had watched her consume an energy bar the night before, one tiny nibble after another. Each morsel was chewed so long it seemed clear Carol was stalling the point where she would swallow. In the course of force-feeding herself the energy bar, she also drank a liter of water. I have never seen anyone focus so intently on the process of nourishing their body, but Carol understood that no matter how unpleasant they may be, eating and drinking were not optional. Within minutes of finishing, she vomited it all up and went to bed. Things went a bit better at breakfast the following morning. Carol managed to consume some pancake and water fortified with electrolytes.

The porter strike was brief, so we were able to set out from camp four by seven thirty. A nearly cloudless sky stretched out above the open savannah before us. The trail was firm and unfettered by obstacles of any manner.

Though our sickly and battered band of trolls was struggling, the open landscape before us promised easier going and a sense that the whole enterprise was still somehow doable. Modest hills rolled away from us in pleasing folds that ran into sharp ridges in the far distance, silhouetted by the rising sun behind them.

We crossed through a river valley and began ascending the soggy hillside that would take us to the flat upper plain. Again we were slogging through mud, always looking for a rock or some piece of high ground to step upon. But our reward came as we crested the hill and threw down our packs next to a clear, slow stream meandering through the meadow above. Here the ground was firm and dry. We kicked off our boots and sprawled out in the tall brown grass. Steven said we had made good enough time to take a full one-hour lunch stop, a luxury we had not yet known. Several porter families were already picnicking on the other side of the stream. They welcomed us with waves and smiles.

We finished our lunch and napped in the warm sun. I woke after twenty minutes and decided to pass the remaining time standing stones on point like tiny statues around us. Several tribal members crossed the stream to study my standing rocks, looking all around the stones to see what trick I had used. In the end the rocks were all toppled by playful children throwing long blades of grass at them like spears.

We arrived at camp five by late afternoon. At 12,208

feet, the air was much cooler, so we all added warm hats and layers. Encouragingly, Carol seemed to have improved somewhat. Where she began the day pausing frequently to dry heave at trailside, Carol finished the day keeping pace with the rest of the team. I even saw her smile when I gave up the last few drinks of water in my bottle to her. By this point Carol's quest had become all of our quest, a source of strength and focus. We had come to admire her tenacity and spirit so deeply that any one of us would have gladly traded our own summit in exchange for seeing Carol succeed, knowing we had some part in helping this extraordinary woman take her place in history.

Deni's condition deteriorated rapidly into the same horrible respiratory affliction that had cursed Pal. All night long Deni blew his nose with a long trombone-like honk that seemed to know when I was just about to fall back to sleep. This was interspersed with coughing fits that shook the tent. Together, we suffered through the night.

Deni was a quiet man. Even at this stage, we had not gotten to know each other very well. He struggled with the English language, and this may have been part of the reason for his silence, but more so he seemed to be one of those thoughtful observers, more interested in listening than speaking.

I had just changed into dry clothes and was lying in our tent, missing Lin and my boys, when Deni crawled in the door and set about organizing his things. I asked him if he was married or had children. He said no to both then added, "Maybe when I am done mountain climbing." At forty-seven, Deni knew his first love was the mountains. He had spent the last two years saving for this expedition from his modest public employee's salary. He had planned for it, dreamed about it. It had been his constant companion, his mistress, his child.

Deni and I developed a cadence of communication where I would make short, simple statements to which Deni would say "Okay," indicating he understood me.

"I was married before," I said.

"Okay."

"I didn't climb mountains then."

"Okay."

"But I wanted to try."

"Okay."

"I was invited to climb Denali."

"Okay."

"But my wife said she didn't think I could do it."

"Okay." Pause. "Well, this is a problem," Deni said, shaking his head.

"Now I have a wonderful woman in my life."

"Okay."

"She believes in me."

"Okay." Pause. "This is good."

ARRIVING AT HIGH CAMP

The next morning we shuffled bleary-eyed through the mud to our kitchen tent. Deni apologized for keeping me up all night. I told him I knew it could not be helped. Jemmy and Raymond had prepared macaroni and cheese for breakfast. It seemed odd, but I was glad to not be eating mung beans. Carol seemed improved, and Pal was also doing better.

We trekked out the last high hem of the savannah, past a still lake surrounded on three sides by steep thousand-foot walls of rock and scrub. I recognized this place from *The Seeds of Singing*. It was here the extraordinarily attractive protagonists built a shack by the water and lived on their love for a year, safe from invading Japanese forces, hungry cannibals, and the jealous tyranny of a half sister bent on controlling the family rubber plantation. All of this played through my head, and I found myself smiling as we trekked along the lake's shoreline.

Our trail started up the far wall by way of narrow switchbacks and wedged logs put in place by the porters. The path was no more than a foot wide—and remarkably steep. Any wider part of the trail was a pool of mud.

We scaled bare limestone eroded to serrated edges by the steady forces of rain, crested the wall, trekked across a vast stony landscape, then scaled another steep hillside to the first of several mountain passes. Before us was a deep rock bowl with an iridescent green lake in its pit. I had seen photos of such a lake near Carstensz Base Camp, and for a moment I celebrated arrival. Then I realized this lake was not the right shape. We were simply passing down and through this caldera before marching up the opposite side to the next pass. Like the synchronous cradles of an egg carton, the topography formed an interconnected congress of many such rocky bowls.

The families of the porters stayed behind at camp five, gathered in the warmth of their smoky longhouses. Base camp was not a place any of them wanted to be. Lacking the means for building any form of shelter, the porters who carried our provisions to base camp would hole up there in a cave, wrapped in blankets while we went on to attempt the summit.

We descended 1,200 feet down a steep rocky face into base camp. The rain was coming down hard, and clouds obscured Carstensz. Steven, Jemmy, and Raymond had already built camp by the time we arrived. As the tents had all been assembled in the driving rain, a small pool of water occupied the interior of each. Deni crawled into our tent and began bailing water out the door while I carved a trench with my boot heel, directing any further runoff away from our dwelling. Chilled and tired, we eventually set up our beds and changed into dry clothing. The cooks made spaghetti for dinner, which we were strongly encouraged to eat as much of as possible. This was a carbo-load for our summit attempt. We had officially entered the game-on part of what we came here for.

A SYMPHONY IN THE NIGHT

We woke at three. I zipped open our tent and looked up into a night sky peppered with stars. The beauty of this might have been reason enough to celebrate, but to us it meant something much more practical—a dry rock face. The rains had been so persistent since arriving in the highlands that it had not even occurred to me that a dry climb was possible. "Damn!" I exclaimed.

"What is it?" Deni asked with concern.

"Take a look at that sky," I answered, smiling back into his head lamp.

Our gear had been carefully arranged the night before: harnesses, ropes, ascenders, hydration bottles, and the like. I had slept with my climbing clothes in the foot of my bag and, following a Houdini-like contortion, emerged fully dressed for the day ahead. We ate oatmeal for breakfast then set out on our two-hour trek to the foot of Carstensz.

A massive fissure ran down the lower half of the Carstensz rock face. This represented our best opportunity for climbing, as climbers could perform wedging techniques with their feet while taking advantage of the many ample handholds. The downside of this approach was that the fissure would turn into a river when the rains began. We would have to get up and down before that. This is why we started our climb at night. The rains typically got underway in the early afternoon, and we had calculated an eleven-hour round trip.

Another good reason for using this route was the many fixed lines left behind by prior expeditions. These came in various gauges and conditions, ranging from new to dangerous, but in any case they would save us time, effort, and exposure to falls. We brought along extra ropes to use when we did not trust the line we found, replacing a few of the worst and leaving ours behind for whomever may follow.

The first pitch required each climber to clip onto a rope while standing on a narrow ledge then swing out and around a massive orb-shaped stone face. It occurred to me that I had passed a point of no return as my body floated out into the darkness, a two hundred–foot drop somewhere beneath me. Then the rock face lit up in my head lamp as I swung back toward it. I could hear Dan's voice coming from a head lamp above me on the rock face. "Grab that handhold. Good. There's a ledge just above your right foot. That's it. Now follow the rope up this way." In short order, I was standing on the orb next to Dan, clipping into the next pitch.

We fell into a rhythm that required little conversation. The sounds of our carabiners clinked pleasantly in the darkness all up and down the rock face while the huff of our lungs set a base tone to the music. We were a living, breathing symphony in the night.

The pitches fell below us at a steady pace as we unleashed all the anticipation of our days leading up to the climb. This is really fun! We are flying up this hill, I thought. The six climbers who had persevered were all serious and accomplished mountaineers, and now we were finally free to do what we did best.

There is a sweetness to daybreak in the mountains. It comes first to the peak, slowly working its way downward. Sometimes I will shiver in the darkness below, counting the minutes until the promise of a new day wraps me in light and warmth. I pause then to give thanks and look down at a world still fast asleep. "Soon, my friends," I will say softly.

One by one, daybreak gathered us up as it slid down the steep rock face of Carstensz. Each climber switched off his head lamp and donned sunglasses. Now high enough to look out across the whole of Western New Guinea, I observed a full panorama of the rolling emerald jungles that tumbled seaward to the west.

We rested on a broad shelf a bit past midway up the face. Above us, the remaining thousand vertical feet of rock face reached still farther into the thinning air. Everyone was breathing harder now. Our bodies were well-conditioned to the thirteen thousand feet of base camp, but here at fifteen thousand, we struggled to take in enough oxygen.

The limestone surface felt solid and tacky beneath my tight leather climbing gloves. The flexible soles of my well-seasoned hiking boots held confidently to the coarse, dry surface. I exited the crack when it became too narrow, climbing the final forty feet on the open face. Raymond reached down toward me from the ridge, his familiar smile beaming. "Good climb, Mr. Dave," he said. I thanked him and found a place to sit atop the narrow ridge that defined the spine of Carstensz.

A few light clouds were moving in by the time the entire team had attained the ridge, a narrow catwalk that fell away three thousand feet on both sides. It was still a stellar day, but we knew there would only be more clouds, and very likely rain, as the day progressed, so we pressed on. At times the ridge was generously wide. At others it was a ledge perhaps half the width of a boot sole. The air was cool, and small tufts of snow lay in shaded depressions.

Twenty minutes up the ridge, we came to an eighty-foot gap where our route fell away several hundred feet below. The only means for crossing the gap was to hang from a cluster of lines strung across it and pull ourselves hand over hand over the breathless drop. Such an approach is known as a Tyrolean traverse, and Steven said about one in ten climbers choose to end their expedition at this point, never reaching the summit. It was easy to see why.

There were four ropes and a steel cable already in place, gifts from prior expeditions. Our guides inspected the condition of each line, as well as the anchors. Then Steven crossed first, followed by Dan. Together they inspected the ropes and anchors on the other side before signaling for the rest of the team to follow. When my turn came, Jemmy helped to clip a large locking carabiner through my waist harness and around all four ropes. He then clipped my safety leash around the steel cable. It was hard to imagine the failure of a system with so much redundancy, yet primal instincts screamed at me as I leaned back into the void. My harness took the weight reassuringly, and the ropes loaded into a shallow U shape. I could see team members waving encouragement from back on the rock, but heard nothing over the roar of my own breathing as I hung from a wire at sixteen thousand feet.

I looked over my shoulder at one point to view the world beneath me. Peering through wispy clouds below, I saw cascading terraces of limestone shaded blue-gray in the shadows of their rocky relief. My stomach leapt the way it does when driving fast over railroad tracks, but did not come back down. I felt a surge of adrenaline as I pulled hard to ascend the uphill end of the lines. Now I heard the reassuring voice of Dan. "Three more pulls and you're here," he said. And then I was. Dan transferred my safety leash to the next rope above the anchors while I clung to the wall like a squirrel. Then he removed my harness carabiner from the four ropes while I climbed up over the anchors and onto the ledge. Ivan greeted me there with an enthusiastic knuckle bump. We moved higher on the rope to make room for the next team member to cross.

THE TYROLEAN TRAVERSE. DAVE MAURO IN FOREGROUND.
PHOTO BY DENNIS VERRETTE.

It was Carol's turn. With a confident smile, she leaned back into the chasm, resting elongated, face skyward, in the cradle of her harness. Pulling hand over hand, Carol inched out into the middle, where the ropes hung low to form a belly. I had been surprised how much raw strength it took to pull myself uphill on the lines and reach the other side. Though Carol's health had recovered somewhat, I knew she was still weak from days of being unable to hold food down, and there was a good chance she had already used what strength she had climbing the three thousand–foot rock face. Carol gave four hard pulls then stopped to breathe. "C'mon," I said beneath my breath. "You can do it." She reached up and pulled four more times. It seemed to take every bit of strength in her upper body.

"C'mon Carol! Kick its ass," I shouted.

"You can do it," Ivan shouted. Carol took four more pulls. Pal, Deni, and Jemmy were shouting encouragement from the other side. Carol hung there panting for what seemed like a long time.

"Get to this side and you've got the summit," I shouted. "You'll own this thing!"

"You're almost there," Dan shouted.

Then something rose up inside of Carol. Her body went rigid as she grabbed the line with halting authority. She pulled hard with both arms, advancing jerk by jerk without stopping, pouring everything she had left into reaching the other side. I felt tears run down my face as an overwhelming joy rose up within me. We were all shouting, weaving a tapestry of belief shot through with profanity. At one point, I thought I heard Pal scream something in Norwegian. Carol kept pulling. She took one more brief rest then heaved three times, going limp as Dan snatched her by the coat, pulling Carol to the rock face.

Deni, Pal, Raymond, and Jemmy followed, then we all continued up the ridge. We were approaching the summit now, and Dan wanted us to arrive together. He called for those at the lead, Deni and myself, to let the team come together before taking the final pitch, so we hunkered down on a ledge and nibbled the dried coconut chips I had loaded in my pocket. I thought about all the months of training that had led up to this moment, the sacrifices, the planning, the money. I thought about the people who had supported me along the way: my boys, Lin, my sisters, my parents, and my friends. I looked over at Deni, seated beside me. We said nothing, just smiling at one another. Then Deni offered his hand in congratulations. We could see the summit from where we sat. It was no more than five minutes away. Just a bit more ridge then a steep scramble up about twenty feet. I could see colored flags draped over an ice ax wedged into the peak. This was it. We were going to summit.

Dan called out for us to continue as the last of the team came together. Deni and I stood and, with him in the lead, began picking our way along the remaining ridge, arriving a few minutes later at the base of the small rise leading to the summit. It was ten steps away now.

Deni stopped just then and turned back toward me. "Do you think we should let Carol summit first?" he asked.

"Absolutely," I answered. We each took a seat on the rocky incline, leaving an aisle between us. Without discussion, each subsequent team member likewise sat down until we had formed a path for Carol to walk up between us.

This would turn out to be the most rewarding moment of the expedition for me. Having gotten to know Carol quite well, I knew of the hardships she had endured in life: failed relationships, career obstacles, health issues, and an unceasing hunger "to do something remarkable." In the course of the trek, I had watched Carol fall to the ground countless times, always picking herself back up without complaint. I had seen her unable to hold down nourishment, unable to carry her pack. Yet Carol never quit. I do not recall even hearing the notion discussed. She was one masterstroke away from completing her life's work, and now the energy to do so seemed to come from moments and motivations far, far away.

Carol walked between us and up our path of honor, fist-bumping each team member along the way. Overcome with emotion, she broke down weeping a few steps short of the peak. Raymond stood then carefully guided Carol the remaining distance, helping her situate herself in a seated position upon the top of Carstensz Pyramid. From where I sat, the rising sun beamed clear and bright just above Carol as she howled with arms stretched wide.

We each took our turn standing on the summit for photos. I held up photos of my mom, Lin, and my boys. It was my way of sharing the moment with them, making sure they knew I was thinking of them. I had also gotten in the habit of bringing along a photo of someone I cared about who had recently passed. It was my way of honoring that person and seeking their strength while we took one last walk together. That person on this climb was Joe Luzzi, who had suddenly passed away earlier that year. Joe was always very interested in my climbing adventures. He asked insightful questions, offering equal portions of caution and encouragement. I had a summit photo taken of me holding Joe's picture, a print of which I later sent to his wife, Sue.

I then removed a small plastic bag from my coat and, holding it out above all of Oceania, released my brother, Danny, in a puff of gray dust.

THE NEXT CALLING

The team retraced its steps back down the ridge to the Tyrolean Traverse. Looking out across that chasm, our giddiness with summiting was replaced with the kind of sobriety normally reserved for coroners and TSA agents. More familiar with the routine, we crossed the gap in much less time than it had taken on our way up.

We then began down-climbing the rock face. This involved rappelling down the fixed lines we had used as safety during the ascent. There were nineteen such lines, each representing a variety of gauges, wetness, and disrepair. Thus, the more typical use of a mechanical Grigri device would not serve the task at hand. I clipped a steel figure eight apparatus into my waist harness and ran the line through it. Then, leaning back out over the rock face, I allowed the rope to feed through the figure eight, using my legs to push off and walk backward down the cliff.

My leather climbing gloves were already worn through at the fingertips from the ascent. The coarse limestone had chewed them off. Now it was a matter of making the leather palms last all the way to the bottom. At times the thicker line would load up instead of feed through the figure eight then suddenly release, leaving me to sprint backward as I crashed side to side off the rock. It was clumsy, but not awful. Occasionally, I would dodge a rock loosed by a climber above me. A few bounced off my helmet with a loud "clack." Then the rains came.

The lines refused to pass smoothly through the descender as they became increasingly soaked. A length would hang up then zip through. As I clenched the line back to slow, it would bite hard, leaving me bouncing like a squirrel on a bungee cord. The fissure we were working down became a creek of fast-moving water. The rocks grew slippery. I could see Dan working with Carol up above me. Deni was just below them, moving tentatively.

I paused on a tiny ledge as I finished rappelling one rope and prepared to start the next. Cold temperatures had come with the rain, and I felt chilled through. I stood there shivering for a moment with nothing on my mind except getting down the rock face. Then, out of nowhere, the thought of Mount Everest popped into my head, random and inorganic. In the same moment, a soothing warmth washed through my body as though I had just eased into a hot tub. The image of Everest came one more time as I stood there trying to figure out what was happening, and with it a voice in my head said, "It will be all right."

Back at camp, we hydrated while Jemmy pan-fried French toast for us. There was no syrup, which was just as well since it was not really French toast. The bread had been dipped in a mixture of reconstituted egg and powdered cheese mix from the boxes of Kraft dinner. But we were not inclined to be picky eaters. The sooner we ate something, the sooner we could collapse into our tents. I could feel a raw area at the back of my sinuses and desperately hoped I was not coming down with the cold. I crawled into our tent, removed my wet clothing, and climbed into my sleeping bag—warm, comfortable, and drained. The rain pummeled our tent, the sound reminding me of home in the Pacific Northwest. We were each headed to our respective homes now, and we would be taking with us what we had come here for. *We had done it!* I rolled to one side and reached an arm out the top of my sleeping bag.

"Congratulations," I said, giving Deni a pat.

"And to you," I heard him call back.

OUT

There was no question about it. I had the cold. The coughing fits began that night while we were still at base camp. Deni was improving, but he too still coughed and blew his nose all night. We were an even match with germs pitted against each other in the close quarters of our tent. I ached from both the sickness and the beating the rock face had dealt me the day before. As we shouldered our packs to leave camp the next morning, I looked at the cold wet stone rising up all about us. Rain clouds obscured Carstensz, and a chill went up my back. With better weather and health, this place might be beautiful in a raw way, but it offered nothing this morning. "Let's get the fuck outta here," I said to Ivan, who seemed to find joy in my frank appraisal.

A DIFFERENT KIND OF CATHOLICISM

We stayed that night at camp five then skipped camp four the following day, trekking all the way to camp three. The next morning I awoke to a chorus of native voices singing tunes I knew but words I did not. It was Sunday and the porters were conducting Mass. I asked Raymond, the pastor in training, about this, and he confirmed the Catholicism of these indigenous peoples. When I pointed out the problematic nature of their polygamy, Raymond simply said, "It is a different kind of Catholicism."

Dan and Pal checked on one of the porter's wives who had collapsed, lips blue, on the trail to camp the day before. Pal diagnosed pneumonia, and the team had all pitched in antibiotics from their dwindling med kits. She seemed to be marginally improved the next morning, but Pal insisted she should carry no load this day, and the tricky business of negotiating the cultural norms of the Dani people took some discussion before honor could be maintained in compliance with this wish.

Tatoosh and one of his friends appeared and broke down my tent without comment. "We could have someone carry your pack today if you want," Dan offered.

It sounded like a good idea, but my pride would not allow it. "I'd like to at least start off carrying it. Thanks," I said. He gave my shoulder a squeeze then left to check in with the rest of the team. Ivan gave me the last of his cold medications at breakfast. It was a noble gesture, the kind of thing done only by fools and saints. He was the one member of our team who had not been afflicted on some level. Such was his empathy that he surrendered his biologic lifeboat to me.

We set out on the trail and soon descended into the hothouse of damp flora, arriving at camp two by mid-afternoon and finding it empty. There should have been many porters with their families. This should have been where we stopped, where I rested and blew my nose, but it was a ghost camp. The message of this was clear, yet I campaigned against reality. "It's three o'clock," I complained. "Shouldn't they be here... in the longhouse... you know, making some love?"

Two hours down the trail, we caught up with the porters. They had built camp on a modest ledge above a river where a tiny meadow of ferns was clustered. The ferns were harvested for the evening meal, which cleared a space for our tents. We ate a dish consisting of rice covered in dark brown gravy then turned in. As Deni and I lay there listening to the muddled conversation of the porters, the air everywhere filled with the scent of cinnamon. The tribal members used whatever dry wood could be obtained for their longhouse fire each evening. This night, they burned a cinnamon tree. The smell was intoxicating, otherworldly. It permeated everything in camp—our sleeping bags and clothing, our hair and tents. It quashed the collective bouquet of our humanity, now ripened by effort and heat. With the weight of the climb behind me, I felt free to soak up the now, and in our cinnamon world, now was very, very good.

RETURN TO THE OTHER SIDE OF NOWHERE

We left early the next morning. The porters were excited to be returning to their villages, and the team relished the notion this would be our last day of trekking. Some hills brought back vivid memories of how miserable I had been during our trek in. I recalled seeking relief during those moments by focusing on positive thoughts.

One in particular I played over and over: It is a pleasant summer evening on Lopez Island. Lin is sitting by a beach fire. I am walking toward her with two glasses in one hand and a bottle of red wine in the other. She looks to me and smiles.

We passed Julie's bridge then into the series of steep hills we had already climbed three times prior. We were making excellent time, so Steven and Dan decided to give the team a rare one-hour break, resting in the shade of a tiny wooden schoolhouse built in the bosom of the jungle. We passed around fruit acquired along the trail: sugar cane, plantains, cooked yams, and a yellow citrus that contained sweet gelatinous globules that resembled tadpoles.

After a few hours more of trekking, we emerged from the jungle, moving easily now on the gravel road that led to Sugapa. We took up residence in the same wooden shack we had briefly stayed in after first arriving in Sugapa. I found my way to a tiny attached room with steel pipes for a floor. A drum full of rainwater sat in one corner with a ladle hanging from its rim. This was a Papuan shower. I retrieved a tiny bar of soap from my pack and my least filthy change of clothes. I wore the bar to a bare sliver, even washing my hair with it. Then I spooned the cold, clean rainwater over me as the sweat and blood and snot and mud all fell away from my flesh. It was the first time in two weeks I had been truly clean, and it felt marvelous.

Several porters milled around the outside of our shack, aware that we would be leaving some of our gear behind. We had been warned not to make gifts, as it would create jealous conflict among the porters. The chief would receive our combined offerings and distribute them as he saw fit. I left my rain shell, sleeping bag, rubber boots, fleece pants, and socks. All of these were still very usable, and normally I would have taken them home to clean up. But I had come to see that the value of these items to the porters would be many times the value to me. The rest of the team likewise gave generously.

GOING UPSTREAM

I woke at dawn the next morning as Ivan was going out

the front door. Deciding to join him, I walked out in my flip-flops and a pair of blue boxer briefs. Ivan was seated on a wooden chair in the chicken yard, concentrating on the rising sun. As I dragged a chair out next to him and sat down to enjoy the view, a man and woman appeared at the corner of our shack. They had come to watch the strange white people. The man gestured for Ivan to take a photo of him and his wife, all dressed up for something formal. I stopped Ivan long enough to position myself next to them in the frame. It was the only time I had worn less clothing than the natives, and the contrast was too good to pass up.

Voting in the presidential election was scheduled to begin that day in Sugapa, and we did not want to be around for it. Though it is customary for porters to throw a traditional feast with music and dance at the end of an expedition, we felt it was more important to leave Sugapa and caught the first flight out that morning.

I watched the rugged landscape of Western New Guinea pass below us—the tiny streams that fed into increasingly larger rivers, which themselves culminated and disgorged into the Arafura Sea.

The water is going home, I thought, just like us. But then what did it mean to go upstream? As you fork off into smaller and smaller tributaries, you give something up at each: the company of loved ones, familiar surroundings, and the ability to be comfortable, to be clean, to rest well, to eat as you wish. You keep going, up the trickling creeks surrendering common language, cultural relevance, and whatever paucity of control to which you still cling. Then, finally, you arrive at a bubbling spring. And whatever you find there is the reason you left home in the first place.

I thought a lot during the trek out about what I found at that spring. It had been something different with each expedition. This time, I found a reawakening to the joy of others, a realization that standing next to that joy and saying yes only makes it larger, and a sense that the joy a person creates is more valuable than that which he owns. Carol's summit, of course, was a watershed moment in this regard. But I enjoyed similar experiences watching Pal interact with the native children, seeing Dan rise up to lead the expedition, seeing Ivan weep as he put away his country's flag atop Carstensz, and watching satisfaction blossom on the face of Deni, a quiet man who had sacrificed so much. There were moments, too, among the porters and their families. I watched the look on a father's face as his young son tried to shoulder his load. I heard the women sing as they prepared a meal. A bright-eyed infant smiled at me from atop his mother's shoulders. So much joy. And it was this joy that pushed back against the hardships we endured. When I would tell the story of this experience in the weeks that followed, people had difficulty understanding why I did it. But they were missing the joy part, and the only way to truly get that is to go upstream.

BACK IN TIMIKA

"I want nice rooms and good security," I heard Dan say to the woman at the front desk. Our reservation at the Grand Tempaga had, through a miscommunication, been cancelled and there was no room for our team as we returned to Timika from the expedition. The apologetic staff was calling around town in an effort to secure alternate accommodations. Dan's emphasis on security reminded me that the postclimb ebullience we had enjoyed would need to be set aside while we lay low again.

Our vans took us to another part of the city, down alleyways of mismatched asphalt and wild-eyed roosters. We pulled into an ungated courtyard attended by a guard shack with two bare feet propped up in the window. Pal and I paid the front desk attendant 100,000 rupiah ($7.50 US) to find us some beers, to which our lone security guard was promptly dispatched on a Vespa. Dan asked that we not wander off the premises, promising we would dine together somewhere nice a few hours hence.

There had been a Sheraton near Timika at one point, on the outskirts of town upon a high and defendable hilltop. At various times of unrest the resort had proven sanctuary for Freeport executives and their families. Now it was owned by someone else, but still boasted both the grandness of a Sheraton and the fortifications of a Viking brothel. I suspect the room rate was beyond our allotted budget, and thus we hunkered down in town behind an army of one. But the fabulous restaurant at the resort was fair game. We drank. We ate. We toasted. I consumed a steak large enough to put me on the Hindu most wanted list.

The next day we flew out of New Guinea, over hastily sketched trees and slums, the reef, surf, and tiny islands with rocks arranged to spell SOS. We celebrated again that night in Denpasar, Bali. A restaurant on the beach took us into the comforts of a large padded booth facing postcard waters. The evening went on long enough for team members to slump over in the booth and sleep then wake and rejoin the party. I introduced the group to the merits of vodka and tonic with a lime squeeze. When the bills arrived, Pal was incredulous to see he had been charged for twenty-two of them. I pointed out that he had in fact only had eleven drinks, but they had all been doubles. Ivan and I saw Pal back to our hotel and I bade them good evening while I attended to details at the front desk. But voices beckoned me from the bar as I proceeded to my room. Pal had insisted on buying a round of whiskey for himself, Ivan, and me. Not wishing to offend, I joined them. When I finally got Pal to his room, he gave me a big happy, drunken hug. "You're my best friend," he declared.

LIN

I checked into the Grand Nikko Bali resort three days later. The warm, overemployed staff had just completed the busy season for Australian tourists and now drifted rudderless in the high vacancy tides of Ramadan. I was "Mr. Dave" the minute I arrived, and everyone somehow seemed to know it. The front desk attendant asked where I had come from. When I said I had just spent eighteen days in Western New Guinea, he commented "Ah. Papua. I think you go looking for trouble." I had not even mentioned the climbing part.

I approached the lobby concierge, explaining that I was going to meet my wife at the airport. "In my family we have a tradition of dressing up for such things," I explained.

"I see," he said with a warm smile. "And what do you wish to dress as?"

"Well. You," I answered.

He made a few calls, then a staff member appeared with a costume borrowed from their dinner show. They fitted me with a headscarf and colorful sarong wrapped tight at the waist then summoned a car to take me to the airport.

Lin scanned the crowd of taxi drivers and tour operators several times before picking me out like Waldo in a busy illustration. She smiled. I had not seen that smile in a month. I wanted to leap over the barricade but was certain my skirt would prevent it. Lin rushed over to me and we embraced, the barricade sandwiched between us as one of my new taxi driver friends slapped me on the back. Holding Lin tight, I felt closure to the expedition, as though I had arrived back home. It was over. I was safe now. We were together again, and life was good.

Back at the Nikko, we settled into our oceanfront room. The cabinets were made of a rich dark wood, the bedding a sugar-white set of fine linens. Plush robes hung at the ready in our spa-like master bath, and traditional Balinese music played softly on the stereo. I turned off the air conditioner and opened the doors to our balcony. Warm, moist air carried in off the sea, filling our sanctuary with a salty scent garnished delicately by the exotic plants and flowers of Bali. It seemed hard to imagine that this place was just a short plane ride away from the primitive desperation of Papua. I still felt better connected to that world, unsure whether this was owing to what I had left behind of myself or the part of Papua I would always carry within me. I suspected it was some of both.

The next morning, Lin and I made our way to the Nikko Club for breakfast. At the urging of others who commented on TripAdvisor, we had purchased a premium package that covered most of our food and drink, as well as access to the exclusive Nikko Club, a private rooftop retreat where a dedicated staff of four had only us to wait upon. They brought us chilled watermelon juice in martini glasses, fresh pastries, and delicate goat cheese omelets. Then we stretched out in one of the mattress-lined cabanas that stood on tiny legs over a shallow part of the private pool. The staff unfurled billowy muslin drapes on all sides except the one facing the sea. Periodically, they would slide a small plate of cucumber sandwiches through a break in the curtains, followed by regular provisions of Bintang, the local beer.

I slept most of that afternoon, stirring occasionally whenever an injury or bruise spoke to me. My body was dappled with the purple contusions of blunt force trauma, testimony to the many falls that had been a part of my expedition experience. Lin noticed them, asking if they hurt. "No," I lied. I didn't want her to feel sorry for me.

I spent long quiet hours just looking out at the sea, thinking about that moment on the side of Carstensz Pyramid, wondering: was it just postsummit euphoria? No. I knew that feeling, and it was definitely a high, but it always came the day *after* summiting. No doubt about it, I conceded. It was definitely a calling.

We walked the beach, listened to live music, dined on lobster, and spent many long wonderful moments holding hands in the peaceful last light of each day. But the invitation I felt Everest had made invaded my quiet moments. I had never regretted following a calling, but it felt just as hard to say yes to this one. Unlike that moment in my sister's guest room, when my life was at such a low place that I literally had nothing left to lose, I now had everything to lose. My relationships with Lin, my boys, my sisters, my mom and stepdad, and even my father were all solid and loving. I had shed the accumulated burdens of a lifetime and now experienced each day from a place of true joy. Yet I knew three things with absolute certainty: I had been called to Everest, I was capable of succeeding there, and if I never tried, I would always regret it.

Lin and I were relaxing in the sun on our fourth day as I silently combed through these thoughts, looking for an out that I knew was not there.

"I know you just came off the Carstensz climb and normally you won't think about a next climb until at least a month has gone by," Lin began, "but you must have some idea about Everest."

I paused for moment then said, "I would like to attempt it this coming May." I was surprised by the conviction in my voice and the decision to not take a year off. That would have given me a year and a half to prepare and save, but a strange sense of urgency seemed to be driving the process from within. Perhaps that urgency knew the following two years would see climbing on Everest canceled altogether as the worst tragedies in the mountain's history unfolded.

Lin was silent for a very long time. I imagined this was the moment she had most dreaded since meeting me. "Well, you better rest up," she said through both tears and a smile, "because you're going to have to start training as soon as you get home."

So that was it. That is how I decided I would attempt Mount Everest, and once that decision had been made, I knew a sense of peace. I liked my chances. As Ty was fond of pointing out, I had never failed on a major summit, having now gone six for six on continental high points. That doesn't happen. Most of those mountains require two, three, even four attempts before a climber reaches the top, assuming he ever does. I had learned a great deal about the physical and mental strengths needed to succeed in high-altitude climbing and, most of all, I had been called.

As I settled into the reality that I would be making an attempt on Everest, a mountain that kills more climbers each year than any other, I was comforted by the fact that, in all my climbing on some of the most lethal mountains in the world, I had never lost a teammate to death or, for that matter, known a moment where I believed I might be dying. Both these things would change on Everest.

EVEREST

FOR THE KIDS

AS I BEGAN THE PROCESS OF READYING MYSELF FOR Everest, I knew its name would draw a good deal of attention in the local community as a local boy set out to make good. It seemed to me this would be a great opportunity to raise money for an organization that helped kids, especially underprivileged kids, as I had been.

I arranged a meeting with the director of the local Boys & Girls Club and told her what I had in mind. I wanted to form a special fundraiser that would allow people to join my Everest team by making donations at different levels. For five dollars, a donor could be a member of base camp support, for fifty, they could be a guide, and for a hundred, a Sherpa. Contribution levels would scale all the way up to $10,000, a Mount Everest–level amount. I wanted to raise $29,035, a dollar for each vertical foot of Mount Everest, with 100 percent of the funds going to the Bellingham Boys & Girls Club.

The club embraced my idea, naming the fundraiser Climbing for Kids. They set up a special portal on their website so donors could contribute online with a credit card, made press releases, and had me in to speak with the kids and important donors. I knew there was no way of succeeding in this venture without a lot of publicity, and indeed I relished the notion of shared participation with as many people as possible, but I also felt nervous about all that this meant. On prior climbs, only my social circle and mostly anonymous blog readers knew my intentions. This time, I had proclaimed my intentions for all to hear. It felt audacious, like Babe Ruth pointing to a spot over the outfield wall where he promised to hit the next pitch. And what if I failed? It would be a very public failure. I may have raised the funds for the club, but that is not what I would be known for. I would be that fifty-year-old guy who was crazy enough to think he could summit Mount Everest.

I did it anyway. First, I seeded the fund with a thousand dollars of my own money. Then I waited for the donations to start coming in. First came modest amounts from people who knew me. Then donations started coming in from blog readers and former teammates all around the world. I spoke at service clubs and REI. I did interviews for the local newspaper. I made personal appeals to anyone I could corner. The Upfront Theatre kicked in a hundred dollars, as did the local pharmacy where I got all my vaccinations. Clients of my financial planning practice gave generously. Slowly my fear of failure was replaced with an immense gratitude for the support I was being shown, the good it would do the children, the belief so many people wished to express, and the collective spirit of possibility I felt within me.

A 29,035-FOOT-TALL DECISION

"I wouldn't even invite you if I didn't think you could do it," I said to Ty during a phone call a few weeks after returning from Bali. Recalling how these words from him had started me out on climbing seven years earlier, I could not pass up the opportunity to hand them back as I made the case for joining me on Everest.

"That's the big enchilada, Mr. Mauro," Ty said. "You've certainly got my attention. Boy. Two months away from the family and work, $50,000, and the best shape of your life."

"That's pretty much what this hill asks for," I agreed.

"Boy."

"Yeah, I know," I said. "But I can't see climbing this thing without you. Just think about it."

I checked back with Ty a few weeks later. "Your sister supports me doing the climb, but I don't know," he said. Ty decided he would first approach his employer, the Arctic Slope Regional Corporation. He was fairly sure they would decline his request for a two-month absence. This would end the whole idea of Everest, and he could just go back to his happy life. But they embraced Ty's dream.

As we spoke several more times in the days that followed, Ty sounded closer to declaring himself in. He said the entire cost would have to be financed through the family's savings and his 401(k). Ty said this felt like a selfish use of their resources. But Noelle still encouraged him. Like Lin, she had always felt this day would come. Noelle and Ty shared the belief that experiences in life mattered more than things. Noelle had supported Ty on various other climbs, and he in turn had supported her passion for marathon running, which took her to faraway places a few times each year.

Ty officially committed in the last days of October, securing the final spot on our team's roster of twenty-two climbers, then immediately launched his own fundraiser to benefit the Boys & Girls Clubs of Alaska, calling on corporate contacts he knew from his days as a news anchor.

VETTING

IMG required each team member to submit a resume of climbing accomplishments before being accepted into the expedition. But the vetting process continued even after each climber had been tentatively approved. I respected this and was happy to comply when IMG asked that a physician put me through specific tests then return the signed results to them.

Doctor Austin ordered a full workup on my blood, which later revealed an unacceptable cholesterol level. His nurse called to report this finding to me a few days later. "We recommend you go on a statin and begin a regular exercise routine," she counseled. I reminded her that I was already training to climb Mount Everest and asked if she thought I could actually get more exercise than that. She agreed, explaining this was the standard recommendation. In the end, I passed on the statin, feeling it made more sense to listen to the message my body was sending me and make some dietary changes. Subsequent tests showed solid improvement.

I was then referred to a cardiologist, who put me on a treadmill, advising that the test required me to get my heart rate up to 170 beats per minute (bpm). I cruised along comfortably, electrode wires flapping away, but my heart rate barely budged. He turned up the pace, but this just nudged me up to 110 bpm. He steepened the incline of the treadmill, which made almost no difference. This continued until the treadmill was pitched upward at its maximum 25 degrees and rolling along at a brisk runners pace. We eventually got to 170 bpm, and everything checked out fine.

162

One photo haunted me as I sat down to plan my training regimen. It had been taken by Ralf Dujmovits and published in an article for *Outside Magazine* earlier that year.

The past year, 2012, had been a freak year for weather on Everest. Instead of the six to eight days of good conditions that were typically scattered about the last half of May, there had been just one opportunity, May 26, for climbers to cash in the many weeks they had toiled to position themselves for a summit attempt. Over two hundred climbers forced their way into that single window, and four of them lost their lives. None were killed by the mountain. Rather, all four died of the compounding human errors that followed waits of up to two hours at critical bottlenecks in the route up Everest's south side. The photo that troubled me featured a long nose-to-tail line of over one hundred climbers traversing up the Lhotse Face. Delays like this one kept climbers in the "death zone," the area above twenty-five thousand feet, far too long. Those who died were taken out by exhaustion, altitude sickness, and a refusal to turn back when they reached critical way points too late in the day. Studying that photo and others like it for hours, I hoped to find some solution not discernible to the hypoxic brains of those who stood in the world's highest customer service line. I found just one.

It was obvious. The only way to avoid standing in those lines was to be out in front of them. The vast majority of Everest climbers employ a power strategy on the mountain. It is a slow and steady approach that conserves energy, maximizes the efficient use of oxygen, and incorporates heavier layers for the longer periods of exposure to the elements.

All in all, this is probably the smartest way to go—unless there are two hundred other climbers all doing it at the same time on the same section of the route. But a climber who used a speed strategy would be unencumbered by these delays and thus free to focus on the paper-thin margin of error that comes with a strategy intended to burn all of one's oxygen and energy in a concentrated period of time.

Though the weather anomalies of 2012 weren't likely to repeat themselves in 2013, I simply did not wish to accept the risk that they might. So from the very start, I bet everything on speed and planned accordingly. This carried substantial implications for how I would train over the six months leading up to the climb.

I knew the conditions on Everest would vary greatly. There might be a vertical ladder to climb in the icefall, followed by a scramble around broken seracs (massive chunks of calved glacier). Oxygen would become increasingly scarce as altitude increased. Temperatures would range from 95°F when the sun reflected off the glacier to –35°F at night up high. But the one constant would be my heart rate. A given level of beats per minute would need to be maintained for my speed strategy. Under some conditions, this would propel me forward at a solid rate. In others, I would barely advance. But this heart rate had to be the law of the land in everything I did, and it could not exceed my maximum aerobic threshold for more than a few seconds.

A fifty-year-old man with a resting heart rate of 64 bpm

should stay within 141–151 bpm. But I had been training and climbing hard for six straight years, the result of which was to lower my apparent age to thirty-five. At this age, a man's maximum aerobic threshold is 162. That became my number. I would train at 162, working to maintain it for longer and longer periods of time. Past that, it was only a matter of how efficiently I used those heartbeats.

TRAINING

I enlisted the help of professional trainer Mike Locke to design a system of workouts. Mike had worked for many years training first responders and athletes at the college, professional, and Olympic levels. He had also trained me for my Denali climb back in 2007.

I met with Mike in his small office next to the weight room at the Bellingham Athletic Club. "So, what's it gonna be this time?" he asked, leaning forward in his chair.

"I plan to attempt Mount Everest," I said.

Mike sat back and ran a hand over his head. At first I saw the flash of disbelief I had grown accustomed to seeing whenever I shared this news. Then Mike began to nod slowly as he looked off into space as though he was watching a film of me actually summiting. A beaming smile came over his face, then Mike looked back at me. "Okay," he said, "then we better get started."

We talked through the stages of the climb and the oxygen levels at each. If I would be carrying any weight, such as an O_2 system, that burden was noted. Then we divided responsibility between us, with Mike constructing the gym training and me choosing the outdoor training on steep trail systems in and about the nearby Chuckanut Mountains.

WHAT I WOULD GO BACK AND TELL MYSELF AS A CHILD

As my training hit full steam in January 2013, I came to love Thursdays and Sundays, my two days off. They were a chance to catch up with Lin, take care of things around the house, and heal from the minor injuries that came with the training. The Boys & Girls Club invited me to come speak with the kids on one of those rainy Thursdays, and I gladly accepted.

Not all kids who attend a Boys & Girls Club come from broken homes or poor economic circumstances. But from what I understood about the members of my local club, which is situated in the poorest part of town, this was largely the case. I felt an understanding, an empathy, for these kids. During the presentation I scrolled through slides from my prior climbs and talked about the importance of dreams. Fifty or so members crowded into the club's computer lab to listen. The staff had made a big deal out of it, and the kids sat wide-eyed throughout the whole thing. At one point I paused to ask if anyone had a dream of their own. Hands shot up all over the room.

There were aspiring rappers, dancers, painters, a few writers, a cop, and a few mountain climbers who I suspect were playing up to my topic.

I told the kids a bit about my own childhood, including the belief I once had that I could not dream the dreams of kids who came from better circumstances. "I now know that's not true," I told the audience. "You'll have to work harder than someone who has advantages you don't have, but you aren't afraid of hard work. What you are afraid of is failing to become everything you were born to be in this life."

HISTORY WORTH KNOWING

Mount Everest soon permeated every aspect of my life. When I wasn't training, I was researching the route, watching every piece of GoPro video I could find on You-Tube, and reading the personal accounts of those who had attempted the mountain. Unlike prior climbs, where I had intentionally left room for discovery, I wanted as few surprises as possible on Everest. Even when I took time away from these things, like when Lin and I watched TV together, I practiced manipulating my Jumar (ascender) with my thick lobster claw mittens on.

It wasn't just the here and now of Everest that interested me. I wanted to know its history, its people, and how it got to be the icon that it is. I learned that the Himalayas, where Everest is located, were formed by the collision of what were once the separate continents of Asia and India. This forced the sea floor up, not only creating the thirty-two tallest mountains on Earth, but also providing the vast deposits of sea salt that would bring humans to this area. Trans-Himalayan trading routes brought salt from Tibet to lower Nepal then linked up with the Silk Road, connecting Asia and the Middle East all the way to the Mediterranean Sea.

Mount Everest was officially recorded in 1841 by the surveyor general of India, George Everest, who named it "Peak B." Andrew Scott Waugh eventually replaced George Everest as surveyor general of India and renamed the mountain "Everest" in 1865 to honor his predecessor. George Everest declined the honor because his name could neither be pronounced by the natives of India nor written in Persian or Hindu. In spite of this, the Royal Geographic Society of London accepted the change, inking George Everest's place in history.

Long before George Everest came along, however, the mountain that bears his name already had a name of its own. The Nepalese called it *Sagarmatha*, meaning "Goddess of the Sky." Tibetans called it *Chomolungma*, or "Mother Goddess of the Universe."

Though Mount Everest captured the imaginations of mountain climbers the world round, it was not possible to attempt its peak until Tibet opened its borders to outsiders in 1921. A British exploratory expedition was launched that year, with a bona fide attempt following in 1922. George Mallory participated in both efforts and, though unsuccessful, he learned much in the course of these expeditions. Following a brief hiatus, the British mounted a third expedition to Everest in 1924. On June 8, 1924, team members George Mallory and Andrew Irvine disappeared while attempting the summit of Mount Everest from the north side (Tibet). They were last seen "going strong" for the top. To this day, speculation that the two succeeded swirls among the climbing community. Mallory's partially decomposed body was found in 1999, but no camera or other evidence to substantiate claims of a first summit was found with it.

Over the next thirty years, ten more expeditions tried and failed on Everest, with thirteen lives lost in the process. When the Chinese invaded Tibet in 1950, its borders were once again closed, putting an end to Everest attempts from the north. But Nepal relaxed its border restrictions about that same time, so in 1953, the British launched their ninth attempt, this time from the south side of Everest. On May 29, 1953, thirty-three-year-old team member Edmund Hillary, a beekeeper from New Zealand, and his climbing partner, Sherpa Tenzing Norgay, reached the highest point on earth and returned to proclaim, "We knocked the bastard off."

It would be hard to overstate the excitement this accomplishment generated around the world. Ten years after WWII, it was clear that humankind was capable of horrific things, but this achievement testified that it was also capable of greatness. Hillary was knighted. Tenzing Norgay was given a cash purse by the Nepalese government. Countries, universities, and various organizations scrambled to create honors for the sole purpose of lavishing the pair with them.

Sir Edmund Hillary, having seen the difficult life lived by the Sherpa people, used his celebrity throughout the remainder of his life to raise money that built schools throughout the Khumbu Valley. To this day, his memory is so beloved among the Sherpa that Hillary is typically the first name mentioned when they are asked about their heroes.

Others followed in the footsteps of Hillary and Norgay. At first they came in small numbers with limited success. Everest was summited in just seven of the first twenty-two years after Hillary and Norgay. But improvements in equipment, strategy, and technique gradually increased success to the point where Everest has now been summited every year since 1975. Further, where 33 percent of Everest climbers died during the first forty years of attempts on the mountain, by 1990 the death rate had declined to just 3 percent.

With this combination of greater success and lower mortality came larger numbers of climbers interested in taking a shot at the prize. By the time Jon Krakauer's *Into Thin Air* was published in 1997, about fifty ascents per year were being made on Mount Everest, a number the author seemed to feel was both dangerous and unsustainable.

Though one might have expected Krakauer's cautionary tale of horrific loss to have diminished attempts on Everest, it in fact did the opposite, igniting the imagination of thrill-seekers everywhere. By 2001, Everest was up to two hundred ascents per year. That number doubled to four hundred by 2006 then continued upward to a peak of 610 in 2007. The climber count has held at about five hundred a year since then.

People died along the way. Lots of people. As of 2017, approximately 304 people have died over the history of climbing on Everest. Many of these bodies could not be recovered, owing to the extreme altitude where the climbers perished.

Body removal comes down to manpower. First responder literature estimates a team of twenty-six is needed to carry an adult out of the wilderness at sea level. At twenty-six thousand feet, where a person is already struggling to move their own body, how many people would it take to carry a corpse down Everest? Would it take three or four times the number used at sea level? Now you are up to one hundred climbers needed to remove a single body and, statistically speaking, three of them will die in the process. So, the bodies are left there, frozen like statues at trailside, still reaching for whatever notion of hope last passed before them.

GARBAGE

Perished climbers do not pack up their camp and take it home. Their tents remain at the South Col, ripped by the jet stream to bare poles with tattered patches of material flapping in the breeze. Their sleeping bags, air mattresses, and other supplies likewise litter the landscape. But more typically, the garbage is left behind by the living. In short, when one is trying to stay alive, little thought is given to environmental stewardship.

Garbage at high camp is the most problematic. You are in the death zone, an altitude at which the human body is already shutting down. You might be dying quickly. You might be dying slowly. But by any definition, you are dying. Will you risk your life to carry a torn tent down the mountain?

Garbage has been a problem at lesser camps as well, and for lesser reasons. When I climbed Denali, a mountain that sees a very similar number of climbers each year as Everest, I found it to be remarkably clean. So why are conditions so different on Everest?

Part of the explanation is surely owed to changing attitudes. Long before the 1971 weeping Indian commercial brought social consciousness to the matter of littering in the United States, climbers were plying their passion on Everest. Their numbers were few and the landscape vast, so they probably gave little thought to what they left behind. The garbage pile started. It is probably not a stretch to suggest each of us is more likely to litter when we see garbage around us. Thus, garbage begets garbage. With increasing numbers of climbers and support personnel, the garbage grew faster still. This condition saw its worst moment in the early 1990s, when the total garbage on Everest was estimated at a horrific fifty tons.

Lastly, for most of the history of Everest climbing, there has been no attempt on the part of the Nepalese or Tibetan governments to manage or regulate refuse on the mountain. Contrast this to Denali, where national park rangers visit campsites to ensure strict compliance with the requirements for packing out trash and managing human waste. Climbing permits are revoked for any team that fails to comply. Climb over.

I have heard the cry that Everest should be closed to protect it. This is an understandable and well-intended reaction. After all, Everest is not just *a* mountain. It is *the* mountain, the high summit of our planet and deserving of special treatment. Everest is also a sacred place to the Buddhist people who live at its feet, a church they have allowed us to enter, a kindness we have repaid by littering that church with our trash.

However, closing Everest would be a blunt tool. It would fail to clean up the mountain, barring access to modern climbers, who are probably the best resource for any serious cleanup effort. Money also enters into the question. A vibrant economy of teahouses, inns, and eateries has sprung up to serve the thousands of trekkers and climbers who approach Everest on foot. These and the various support services to base camp are businesses that have brought an improved way of life to the people of this region, including education and health care. Take away Everest, and the people of the Khumbu will suffer.

There is cause for optimism. In 1992, the Nepalese government put various regulations in place requiring climbing teams to carry all of their waste back out of the Khumbu Valley, where it can be disposed of properly. Failure to do so results in hefty fines. Glass bottles were banned in the Khumbu Valley, and a financial reward was put in place for each spent oxygen canister a Sherpa brings down off the mountain. The major guiding companies have also gotten on board, organizing focused efforts to remove legacy waste from the mountain as they clear out at season's end. As well, a number of environmental expeditions have removed many tons of garbage from Everest. Progress is being made, yet some twenty tons of garbage still remain. Half of that is at high camp, so the rest of the cleanup will be considerably more difficult. But the climbers of today are committed to the environment, having come of age in the era of leave-no-trace. They respect the mountains they climb and want nothing more than to see them pristine. There is awareness of the problem, the will to address it, and the kind of personal stake that can move a mountain of garbage one piece at a time.

After five years of dating, Lin and I decided we would become engaged. We bought rings for each other and wrote our own vows before leaving to spend the Christmas holiday in Arizona. Then, on December 24, we stood in the Sonoran Desert beneath a clear night sky and promised our tomorrows to one another. We called it a "permanent engagement," agreeing that legal marriage was not something either one of us wanted to do again.

Lin and I spoke often of Everest from that day forward. It came up when I held out for a closer parking spot at Costco, when we shared what went on in our dreams, and when we planned the spring planting of the flower beds. It was always out there on our timeline, demanding that everything else come before or after the two months I would be away.

I sometimes thought about the people who served in the military, how their home lives had to go on without them for many months at a time. I have mad respect for these people. Yet for those of us doing the leaving, things are easier in some respects. We are busy with the task at hand. If we worry over a situation, it might be possible to do something about it. But the helpless worry carried into idle moments by loved ones is pernicious and the cumulative weight considerable.

These people are emotional Sherpas.

"There is angst in the not knowing," Lin said as we

talked about the climb in February 2013. "I don't climb. I don't know. But if anyone can make it to the top of that thing, you can!"

I asked my sister, Noelle, about her feelings on the climb. She would have both her brother and her husband on Everest. She told me that she and Ty talked often about Everest. At bedtime they tended to discuss "the gravity of the climb, how long he is going to be gone, what he knows about the route, are there parts that concern him." During the day they tended to discuss logistics. Noelle knew from Ty's journals of past climbs that he tended to miss the mundane things about life back home. "There are times I will make a lunch and think Ty is missing this," she said.

When I asked Noelle about managing her fears, she said, "Because our kids are so young, I do feel particularly vulnerable to this thing. It's not anything I take lightly, but it's just compartmentalized. I know Ty goes prepared and has a good team. If anything happens he is prepared. I don't think I have ever had a bad feeling when Ty has left climbing, but just whether he will stay healthy and make the summit or have a good time."

SORRY

Shortly after visiting my son Chase in March, I flew to Chicago to see his older brother, Trevor. I felt haunted in each case by the notion that this could be a last good-bye. Though we didn't want to acknowledge this possibility, it colored both visits in a way that made it impossible to pretend we were just hanging out together.

I had written a letter to my sons to be delivered to them if I did not return from Everest. It was the most difficult piece of writing I have ever produced. At first I felt like there was so much to say that the letter would be book-like. But in the end it was just one page. I told my sons I loved them, I was proud of them, and that part of me would live on within each of them. I said I believed my spirit would watch over them throughout their lives, cheering for them and sharing their sorrows. They would never be alone.

But there was something I needed to say in person before I left, and I felt it welling up inside of me as Trevor and I ate breakfast at a downtown diner. I don't recall how the door opened to the topic of my leaving his mother, but it did. At that point, I told Trevor that I did not regret divorcing Jenny, but I did regret the pain it caused to him, his brother, and his mom. "I am sorry," I said. We both wept, and in that moment I felt Trevor release a burden he had carried for years.

SENDOFFS AND SLIDESHOWS

I did my last slideshow five days before leaving for Everest. It was at Meridian Middle School, where Lin worked as a sign language interpreter. I also did a few newspaper interviews during my last days. One was featured on the front page of *The Bellingham Herald*'s Sunday edition. A good friend of mine immediately emailed his congratulations, writing, "You're the first person of my acquaintance who has made the front page of the *Herald* for something other than criminal activity." It was a nice piece that referenced my blog, creating a sudden spike in hits. But more importantly, the article featured information about my Climbing for Kids fundraiser at the Boys & Girls Club. Contributions began coming in at a brisk pace. By the time I left for Everest, the fund had grown to $19,235, including a $10,000 contribution from my employer, UBS Financial Services.

The Bellingham Boys & Girls Club threw a nice sendoff party for me, as did my neighborhood. I visited my mom and stepdad then drove to Anacortes to see my father. I wanted to make sure he understood why I would be absent for the next two months. We sat down in Don's dark living room, each holding a cup of decaf coffee, and I walked him through what I would be doing. I kept things pretty basic, never touching on the dangers of the climb. Don nodded in understanding occasionally, smiling simply as though I were describing someone's birthday party. He asked no questions, but interjected with, "That's nice," a few times. Then something happened as I finished talking. The father version of Don seemed to inhabit his body for a brief moment. He stiffened upright. His voice shifted to the low, strong timbre of a grown man, and he said, "You can do it! I believe in you!"

The next day Lin drove me to Seattle-Tacoma International Airport. She parked the car and helped me lug my massive gear duffels to the check-in desk. Lin joined me in the line for TSA screening until it came to the point where those without tickets could go no farther. Then she stood at the far perimeter of the crowd crying as she flashed the sign language symbol for "I love you." I looked back several times, hoping she had left, but Lin was always there, dodging about to find a clear shot where our eyes could meet through the crowd. My throat caught each time, but I held back the tears, for some reason feeling I needed to be brave. We exchanged the "I love you" sign one last time as I cleared security, then Lin and I both turned away.

I met Ty at the gate for our outbound flight from Seattle. His flight from Anchorage had arrived a few hours earlier. "Let's light this candle," he said with a big Alaskan smile. After a one-night layover in Dubai, we continued on to Kathmandu, arriving late the next night. A local representative of IMG met us at the airport with carnation necklaces then drove Ty and me to Hotel Tibet in the heart of Kathmandu.

Our portion of the team, wave three, gathered for the first time the next morning. The first two waves were already making their way up the Khumbu Valley, and our group, consisting of twelve climbers and trekkers, would meet up with the others at Everest Base Camp. All told, the 2013 IMG expedition would include twenty-two climbers.

Eight of the climbers paid $69,000 each for the Hybrid Climber package, which offered a separate dining tent and close attention by a Western guide. The remaining fourteen Classic Climbers (including Ty and myself) paid $44,000 each to IMG. Though this sum purchased a full range of services that rivaled those of all but a few of the expeditions on Everest, the Classic Climbers would come to see themselves as the working-class members of the team, taking pride in the self-sufficiency they believed this imbued upon them.

ARRIVING IN THE KHUMBU VALLEY

I woke the next morning at three. I had taken a few good pictures in Kathmandu, and I wanted to get them loaded onto my blog since, after leaving the city later that morning, I would not likely find the bandwidth to do so. I took my laptop to the hotel lobby and spent the next two hours building out my entry from the day before while sipping on a cup of instant coffee. Team members eventually began wandering in with their duffels. We ate breakfast, boarded a shuttle to the airport, and lifted off aboard a twin-prop commuter plane. I was amazed by the sprawling scale of Kathmandu as we climbed up and away. It reached outward from the city center for what seemed like miles, consuming tiny rolling hills then larger valleys until abruptly coming up against the Himalayas. The dry brown cast of dirt and brick suddenly yielded to lush green ridges that rose aggressively then plunged downward to cradle a white, tumbling river. The plane climbed higher and higher, its engines growling noisily as they struggled to chew up the big bites of sky being carved off by their propellers. Out the window to my left, I could see the Himalayas, jagged and white, punching holes up into the jet stream. Every one of these peaks looked formidable, yet Everest was not among them. It lay farther up the Himalayan range to the east, where it was surrounded by mountains that would make what I saw look puny.

After forty minutes, the nose of the plane dropped as it took aim at the Tenzing-Hillary Airport. Located at the village of Lukla, this single-strip airfield features an abbreviated tarmac cut into a cliff at 9,383 feet. The strip is perpendicular to the cliff, thus eliminating the option of aborting any landing attempt. This creates an incentive to set the plane down as early as possible—though too early is just as problematic as too late.

For a moment we all went silent, watching the cockpit window fill with cliffside, then runway, then cliffside. My breath grew short. I felt my arms and legs tense. Then the wheels chirped, and we all lurched forward as every aspect of the airframe, from brakes to prop pitch, was immediately repurposed for the sole objective of stopping before the runway ended at the cliff face. Still moving quickly, the plane turned a hard right just short of the cliff and came to a full stop next to a modest terminal. I watched for the pilot's expression as we exited, wondering if we had just experienced some kind of close call. He looked pleasant and relaxed. This was business as usual at what is officially the world's most dangerous airport.

LUKLA

Our team settled into the sunny courtyard of a nearby cafe while we waited for our gear to arrive on the next plane. There I ran into my good friend Guy Manning, who had been a member of my Vinson Massif team in Antarctica. Like myself, he had come to attempt Everest. Guy, a British expat now living in the Cayman Islands, had signed on with the British outfitter Jagged Globe as part of their Everest 2013 team. We caught up with each other over a cup of tea. It was nice to see a familiar face in such an exotic and unfamiliar land.

It was noon when our IMG wave three guides Max Bunce and Jenni Fogle started us out on our trek. We eased down the cobblestone road that ran through Lukla, passing a counterfeit Starbucks and a McDonalds knock-off named YakDonalds along the way. Crowded tightly among donkey trains loaded with supplies, trekkers, climbers, and the residents of Lukla, we shuffled slowly by T-shirt shops and purveyors of keepsakes both genuine and less so. There were no motorized vehicles, not even a scooter. The Khumbu is simply too rugged to accommodate them. For the same reason, there were no bicycles or carts. Everything that moves in the Khumbu moves on legs: donkeys, cows, horses, yaks, and humans. Any supplies needed by the villages and expeditions up-valley must be carried there.

We passed out of Lukla and onto a narrow stone path traversing a hillside of wild rhododendron and magnolia trees in full bloom. I was comfortable in short sleeves, taking in a perfect spring day as I trekked through tiny villages, past stone walls and terraced gardens. Sad-faced old women turned the soil with wooden hand tools, and children played hopscotch on grids scratched in the dirt. Most of the men were gone, off to work for the expeditions or some other role supporting tourism through the coming season.

Our team spread out along the path as members settled into their own pace. I would find myself walking next to someone and strike up a conversation. We would chat for a bit until one of us stopped to take a photo and the other continued on. In this casual manner, we formed a meandering river of trekkers, replete with back-eddies and faster water. At times, I listened to music. Other times, I listened to the babbling brook of varied dialects around me.

We arrived at the Sherpa Farmhouse Inn in Phakding (8,691 feet) in the late afternoon. The dining room at the inn did a fine job of turning out dinner for the team. I enjoyed a yak steak and Sherpa salad, as well as an assortment of quartered onions, cucumbers, and tomatoes.

MANY BRIDGES TO CROSS

We left Phakding at eight thirty the following morning. Blessed with clear skies and kind temperatures, we soon found ourselves zipping off pant legs and skinning down to T-shirts. The valley narrowed a few miles into our trek. Our trail scaled steep switchbacks, gaining several hundred feet and then cashing it in as the route descended low to a suspension bridge. Over and over, we found ourselves climbing, descending, then crossing the river. Our team spread out quite a bit as each person dealt with the hills at their own pace. At times, I was alone on the path. I felt excited by these moments. Though I knew at least one guide was always behind us, sweeping stragglers along, I could kid myself that I was treading hallowed ground as a pilgrim on his solitary quest.

The trail crossed a high suspension bridge 150 feet long. The river below crashed over massive boulders while the tattered remains of silk prayer scarves reached out in the hundreds, suspended horizontal by the powerful wind passing through the canyon. Each of the scarves had been blessed by the Lama Geshe as visitors called upon him at Panboche. These visitors then tied their scarves to the bridge so the Lama Geshe's blessings could be carried off on the wind, gracing all it touched.

The final four hours to Namche Bazaar (11,350 feet) required two thousand vertical feet of tight switchbacks. We took it slow, knowing our bodies were already pressed by the day's altitude gain. This unhurried pace, combined with stunning views of Ama Dablam, passed the hours pleasantly. Soon we walked past women scrubbing laundry by a stream and up into the horseshoe-shaped caldera, where Namche rests among steep hillside terraces. Namche Bazaar, population 1,700, enjoys the fruits of a hydroelectric facility built several years ago by the Austrian government. This enabled the proliferation of guest houses, tea houses, internet cafes, pubs, and myriad other services aimed at the needs of trekkers and climbers.

We took our rooms at the Khumbu Lodge, a three-story structure built mostly of stone. The top floor was a restaurant, with the lower two levels broken up into guest rooms divided by plywood walls so thin I could literally feel it when someone on the other side rolled over in bed. Ty and I unfurled our sleeping bags atop the two twin beds that filled our room.

Each floor had one shared toilet that was easily overwhelmed as guests succumbed to intestinal illnesses, which in all likelihood were contracted by contaminated food from the restaurant upstairs. One of our team members woke that first night with an urgent need to empty his bowels and ran down the unlit hallway to our toilet. He did not see the strangely low doorway header and thusly knocked himself unconscious and fell to the floor—where he then soiled himself.

WHAT IS A SHERPA?

We should begin answering this question by understanding that "Sherpa" is not a job description. It is a people. About 153,000 Sherpa live in Nepal today. The Tibetan term Sherpa translates to eastern (shar) people (pa). Originally a nomadic people on the plains of India, the Sherpa transitioned to agriculture and livestock farming after arriving in Nepal in the 1500s.

Most of us would never have heard of the Sherpa people were it not for their invaluable contribution to climbing endeavors in the Himalayas. Sherpa men were hired by early expeditions as guides. Their keen knowledge of the complex valleys and peaks of the Himalayas proved essential to the first climbers, explorers, and cartographers to venture into the region. Soon the Sherpa were likewise recognized for their extraordinary ability to function at high altitudes, and expeditions began hiring them in great numbers to carry supplies. This practice continues today as Everest expeditions benefit greatly from the remarkable load-packing ability of the Sherpa. Anyone who has climbed with a Sherpa probably recognized there was something quite different about that Sherpa's ability to function in a low-oxygen environment.

Dr. Kenneth Kamler, in his excellent book Surviving the Extremes: A Doctor's Journey to the Limits of Human Endurance, discusses the physiological adaptations of humans to high altitude. Sherpas are specifically addressed in one part of his book. Doctor Kamler identifies several fascinating differences between Sherpas and us mere mortals:

1. Sherpa lungs have a high idling speed, which is to say they have a high sensitivity to low-oxygen environments and will maintain an increased rate of breathing, even at rest. Most climbers take a drug called Diamox to accomplish this.

2. A Sherpa's heart muscle can take in glucose. Glucose burns 50 percent more efficiently than fat (the fuel used by a typical heart) in a low-oxygen environment. The net result is the same cardiac output with much less work.

3. Sherpa blood has something extra. The capacity of a Sherpa's blood to transport oxygen is greatly increased by special enzymes that ride along with the hemoglobin to speed up the capture and release of oxygen.

4. Sherpas' lungs produce more vasodilators, which in this case translates to twice the nitric oxide as almost everyone else. Nitric oxide acts as a vasodilator, opening up constricted vessels in the lungs. This may be why Sherpas are virtually immune to pulmonary edema.

5. Sherpas working at maximum capacity produce less lactic acid than the rest of us, a condition known as the lactic acid paradox. The probable explanation is that Sherpas don't need to form lactic acid because they can maintain high fuel-burning efficiency, even

in low oxygen, by using enzymes researchers still have not identified.

All of this combines to make the Sherpa people, and thus the Sherpa climber, extraordinary human beings when it comes to functioning at high altitude. There have been a few female Sherpa climbers, though tragedy has dogged them. Pasang Lhamu Sherpa was the first Nepali female climber to reach the summit of Everest. However, she died during the descent when harsh weather suddenly hit the mountain. The great female Sherpa, Pemba Doma Sherpa, summited Everest two times before she died in a fall from Lhotse on May 22, 2007.

About five thousand Sherpa live in the United States as of this writing. Half of these reside in the peaceful hamlet of New York City. Go figure.

A REST DAY IN NAMCHE

I woke at five, feeling rested and restless. I love mornings, and the thought of wandering the empty stone alleys of Namche was just too tempting, so I pulled on some clothes and slipped out of our room. I had noticed a sign in the lobby the day before informing guests that the doors would be locked at ten every night. "So don't come back later than ten," it counseled. I understood how literal this was when I came upon a large timber thrown across metal brackets on the inside of the hotel doors. I removed the timber and let myself out.

A soft hue of predawn light was settled upon the snowy peaks above. The shops were shuttered. A lone black yak stared me down from the other end of the alley. Nobody moved about. Just a few windows showed light. I climbed higher up the terraces, taking the uphill fork whenever the path split, past gardens, pastures, one-room homes, and brightly painted prayer wheels.

Though acclimatization required us to stay in Namche that day and the next, we nevertheless planned to tease our physiology with day hikes. After a breakfast of apple and banana pancakes, the team set out for the Everest View Lodge, approximately 1,200 feet above Namche. The Everest View Lodge offered stunning views of the Himalayas, including our first sighting of Mount Everest. From so far away, it did not look much taller than the other mountains around it, but I knew that would change as we drew closer. I did not want to look at Everest up close. Sure, it would be magnificent and beautiful, but that image, once inside my head, could be all it took to crush my will on a hard day. I had seen this happen to climbers, and so resolved to take all the pictures I liked of Everest on my way home.

SECOND REST DAY IN NAMCHE

It is common to encounter intestinal bugs on expeditions. As well, any cold or flu one member picks up is all but assured to be passed to other team members. Knowing this, we all washed our hands compulsively and used hand sanitizer at each meal. It was a fight worth fighting, even though we had been told 90 percent of us would become sick at some point during the expedition anyway. IMG maintained its own base camp operations at Everest and was purported to do an excellent job of controlling food and water cleanliness there. The company also maintained a lower base camp at Lobuche, where it had enjoyed similar hygienic success. But there was little that could be done, aside from the handwashing, to manage the exposure of expedition members to sickness while trekking through the villages of the Khumbu Valley. Ty was up much of our second night in Namche with fever and nausea. I brought breakfast back to our room for him, but he was unable to hold anything down. Mostly he just shivered in his sleeping bag. Max and Jenni, diagnosing a GI infection, started Ty on antibiotics. As beautiful as the villages of the Khumbu were, it seemed we were running something of a bacterial gauntlet.

BETTER

Ty woke the next day with improved health. He was able to eat half the donut I brought him from a village bakery. Later he came to breakfast and managed some scrambled eggs. But his strength was not sufficient to continue on with our team to Deboche that day as planned. It was decided

Ty would spend another night in Namche, and I elected to hang back to look after him. We were not alone. The night before, two more members of the team also came down with symptoms much like what Ty had.

Four of us set out from Namche Bazaar the following day, accompanied by one of our team's local guides, Pasang Sherpa. We settled into a methodic pace under sunny skies, glad to be moving on. The first hour of trekking took us up a long, high hillside through rhododendron forests. Here at the higher elevations, the first pink buds were just starting to open. We walked beside white pines, juniper, and prickly barberry shrubs, the scent of each garnishing the air. I listened to an album of Native American cedar flute music on my iPod, just soaking it up.

Much of the path through this section was hand-placed stone. When the terrain became steep, there were typically stairs made of stone. Such even, reliable footing felt like an immense luxury. The path was wide enough for trekkers and pack animals to pass comfortably, and an amazing array of retention walls had been built to maintain what was the only highway up the Khumbu Valley. As well, the trail was remarkably clean. Garbage and recycling bins certainly helped to make this so, but more important still was the sense of stewardship that seemed to be shared by the people of the Khumbu Valley and those who visited it. I did not see even the smallest bit of trailside litter. Breathtaking peaks rose up all around us like nature's cathedrals. Every step was a pure joy.

We gained two thousand feet of elevation, arriving at the Tengboche Monastery, a fort-like feature looking out over the entire valley. Its entryway was flanked by prayer wheels so large that at one point four of us were working on the same wheel. The ornate facades of the building were contrasted by stone walls made from tablets carved with sacred Buddhist teachings. We rested for a bit on the front steps before moving on, silenced in reverence.

TREK TO PHERICHE

We stayed that night in Deboche. The lodge prepared a fine breakfast for us the next morning. Sherpa bread, a round flattish baked good, had become popular among team members. Fresh-baked and adorned with honey, the bread couldn't have offered a more satisfying start to the day.

The trail narrowed a few miles out of Deboche, and the stone paths of earlier miles turned to dirt. A cool wind greeted us as we rose above the tree line. We paused at the village of Pangboche for the customary Buddhist blessing of our expedition. Lama Geshe draped each of us with a silk scarf, or *khata*. He prayed for each team member then lightly bumped his forehead to theirs in a traditional sign of love.

We arrived at Pheriche (14,000 feet) around two o'clock. The clean stone structures of this village stood defiant of the barren landscape around them. The wind blew. The dust flew. It was like living in a David Lynch film. Piles of yak manure were heaped against each building. The principal source of fuel this far up the Khumbu Valley, yak dung was spread out to dry in the sun each day. The flat round patties were then stacked in entryways to be burned for heat and cooking. The gathering room at our lodge, the Himalayan Hotel, was warm and inviting, heated by a yak-dung stove in the center. Measuring twenty by forty feet, the perimeter of the room was furnished with carpeted benches facing inward. Teams from Norway, Germany, Argentina, and Saudi Arabia lounged about the tables. Electricity here was expensive, so most hallways remained unlit. Even the dining room enjoyed the illumination of just a few bare incandescent bulbs fighting against a thin haze of dung smoke. But the cheerful banter of occupants hailing from varied and distant lands weaved a colorful auditory tapestry.

By morning, it was cold enough in our room that Ty and I released steam-engine plumes of frozen breath from our sleeping bags. I grabbed my laptop and headed down to the common room, knowing the stove would already be cranking out heat and hopeful I could post a blog entry before the hotel's modest Wi-Fi was overwhelmed.

I met up there with a seven-person subgroup of our team comprised of active-duty Air Force members, the same Seven Summits team I had met in Antarctica. Collectively, their various members had topped out on six of the Seven

Summits. Like myself, they were here to see if they could touch 'em all. If successful, they would be the first US Air Force team to do so. Several members were pilots, flying everything from F-16s to Hercules cargo jets. Others were special ops members. Two were medics, and a few others were involved in operations.

THE NEXT SEVERAL DAYS

We arrived at Lobuche Base Camp (15,800 feet) around one o'clock the next day. Our advance Sherpa team had already set up the tents, kitchen, dining tent, and drop toilets. The kitchen staff brought us warm moist towels scented with menthol to clean up before lunch then served hot dogs on fresh baked buns, baked beans, and cucumber and beet salad. There were thermoses of hot tea, coffee, and citrus drink. It was the kind of pampering almost never associated with tent camping.

After moving into our tents, we spent the remainder of the day socializing and getting to know the trails around camp. A low-rolling hillside formed a protective cul-de-sac around our perimeter. Just beyond that rose Mount Lobuche, powerful and bare-chested, into the Nepalese sky. Free-range yaks grazed on the dry grass, their bells clanging softly.

Snow started to fall in heavy wet flakes as we finished dinner. The temperature dropped to the midtwenties as I burrowed into my big down sleeping bag and journaled the day's events by the light of my head lamp.

Aside from a brief acclimation hike, I spent the next day journaling too. A few team members practiced free-climbing a massive boulder at the center of camp, while others relaxed with a book in one of the folding chairs scattered about.

Our first case of the Khumbu cough surfaced during our second day at Lobuche. This is an incessant cough brought on by exertion in the dry cold air of higher altitudes. We were told our best defense was to breathe through a buff (a tube-shaped garment worn about the neck), especially at night, and avoid overly strenuous pacing when on the move. That said, it was likely 70 percent of us would contract Khumbu cough over the next two weeks and not be rid of it until returning home from Everest.

TREK TO EVEREST BASE CAMP

We left Lobuche Base Camp (LBC) early the morning of April 13. The seven-hour trek to Everest Base Camp (EBC) took us through the dusty and unremarkable villages of Lobuche and Gorak Shep, following the Dhudh Khosi (Milk River) as it tumbled by, thick and brown, carrying chunks of the Khumbu Icefall with it. I could see snow in scattered patches along the shady side of the valley as our trail traversed the sunny side through pasture lands, smelling of summer as the day's warmth awakened the low-cropped grasses.

We wandered through a vast glacial moraine to the

place staked out by IMG for its EBC, a broad area gathered around a melt pond, providing a ready source of clean water. IMG Team Chief Greg Vernovage greeted us while lunch was served in our group dining tent. A tall, affable man with a quick smile, Greg was a veteran of Everest expeditions and sported the kind of physique that testified to his year-round climbing lifestyle. You could bounce a quarter off his chest and it would ring all the way to the ground. Never without his radio, Greg was interrupted several times as he spoke. Various parties seeking the final word on some aspect of our sprawling operation all turned to Greg. Each Everest camp had such a person, a "big boss," as the Sherpas called them.

By the time a person gets to the altitude of Everest Base Camp (17,500 feet) some 40 percent of sea-level oxygen is already missing. Greg looked us over, slumping in our chairs and dizzy with fatigue. "You probably want to crash in your tents right about now," he said with a lively smile. "But that's about the worst thing you could do. Eat something. Drink a lot of fluids. Don't move around much, but try to stay awake and do some breathing."

We each had our own two-man tent, a vital piece of personal space to call home over the next many weeks. The Sherpas had set them up around the perimeter of the melt pond. Ty moved into the tent on one side of me, while John Beede, a motivational speaker from Las Vegas, Nevada, occupied the other side. I set up my air mattress and sleeping bag, hung pictures of family on the tent walls, and drank a liter of water.

The relative comfort of a sunny afternoon was quickly replaced with 20°F temperatures as evening came. We all arrived at dinner wearing down coats and pants. Conversation was sparse as we sat along three folding tables placed end-to-end, clouds of breath rising in mismatched sequence like Morse code. The kitchen served tomato soup, followed by curried yak meat and fried potato wedges.

Several large icefalls in the surrounding hills woke the camp that night as spring inched a bit closer. Each sounded like a train derailment. I lay awake after one avalanche woke me at three then decided to pull on my down clothes and step out into the night. The brilliance of the stars easily challenged a thin crescent moon and the pale yellow light it cast on Everest. Our puja monument in the center of camp crackled with the fire of juniper bows as prayer flags reached out from it in every direction. I am here, I thought. Having spent so much time thinking about this climb and the experiences it would bring, the moment felt surreal and pleasing.

We gathered before the climbing Sherpas the next afternoon for the process of pairing into teams of two. It bears noting that IMG is the oldest, best organized, and most successful organization on the Everest south side route. They pay their Sherpas well, train them thoroughly, provide them with health care, and treat them with respect.

For any Sherpa lucky enough to rise to the elite ranks of guiding climbers, there are probably three teams he would most like to work for. IMG is one of those. Every climbing Sherpa (as opposed to those who pack loads or cook) on the IMG team had already summited Everest multiple times.

Each IMG team member was paired with a Sherpa they would work closely with whenever they climbed. Jangbu, our head of logistics, had studied the vetting file for each climber and chosen the Sherpa he believed to be the best match. Through this process, I somehow won the Sherpa lottery. Jangbu paired me with Mingma Chhring Sherpa, ten-time Everest summiter. Remarkably, Mingma had never failed to reach the summit of Everest, having gone ten for ten. He greeted me shyly then stood for a photo of the two of us. I threw an arm across Mingma's tiny shoulders and beamed into the camera. He looked about half my size. Mingma was a senior Sherpa and quite often seemed to be the guy other Sherpas came to for help.

SHERPA WISDOM

We left EBC, backtracking to LBC two days later, to climb Mount Lobuche. By the time we arrived there, I felt chilled through. I immediately set up my sleeping kit—a foam mat, inflatable air mattress, and sleeping bag. But before crawling in, I decided to take a dose of cold medication to ward off what felt like a bug coming on. I grabbed my folding knife to open the tin foil packaging, but my cold, numb hands fumbled it once the blade was opened, and it fell point down, piercing my air mattress. "Shit!" I exclaimed. With weeks still of sleeping on ice and rocks ahead of me, that mattress had promised one of the few comforts I would know.

The next morning, I drug my miserable air mattress out of the tent and examined its wound. Mingma, ever attentive, came over to wish me a good morning. I told him the story of what had happened to the mattress. He studied the mattress then looked at me. He studied the puncture then looked at me again. Mingma's face displayed a quiet wisdom, as though some deeper truth was emerging in his thoughts. I imagined he was about to share a time-tested Sherpa saying, some understanding that spoke to the human condition. Then Mingma looked at me and said, "Shit."

CLIMB MOUNT LOBUCHE:
ELEVATION 20,161 FEET

We climbed the lower flank of Mount Lobuche the following day and established a high camp at seventeen thousand feet. This was the first of several rotations designed to prepare our bodies for summiting Mount Everest. The next morning, we woke at three and geared up for a push to the summit. I dressed in my layers, harness, and climbing boots then joined the others in forming a head lamp circle around our cook in the open area at the center of camp.

He had prepared porridge, cheese omelets, and hot coffee. I hastily ate a bit of each then returned to our tent. There was more to do, more to fret over before leaving for the summit, and I was determined not to be the last one ready.

I was the last one ready. Our guide, Max, made the rounds, checking on each climber. "You're gonna sweat like a pig," he said after examining my many warm layers of clothing.

I had made the same rookie mistake that defined my first day of climbing on Denali. Of course I would heat up once I started climbing. What had I been thinking? C'mon, Dave. You know better. Get your head in the game, I thought. Max recommended a combination of clothes so scant I might have easily worn more when flying a kite. But I accepted his guidance and began stripping down as the rest of my team left camp. Mingma stayed behind with me while I reoutfitted, then the two of us set out, a full ten minutes behind.

We caught up with the team after thirty minutes and settled in as the last few head lamps in a line of twenty-five climbers and Sherpas. I passed a few team members here and there, eventually catching up with Ty. We climbed together the remainder of the night. Shortly after dawn, Ty told me to move on past him, so I did. I did not intend to set an aggressive pace, but it felt so good to finally be climbing that I just kept going. My crampons bit into the steep ice face with satisfying purchase. Settling into 162 beats per minute, I passed climber after climber until I found myself leading the climb with three members of the Air Force team. I should point out that this was not a race—and indeed there were downsides to climbing quickly. But I had held back from using my 162 and just needed to let it run to assure myself I still had it.

I ate lunch on the summit, traded photos with the Air Force guys, and then started down, passing Ty as he finished his ascent. "Hey, big dogger," I said. "You're almost there." Ty nodded as he braced his hands against one knee, sucking in deep gulps of oxygen.

Back at LBC that night, as Ty and I settled into our sleeping bags, he said, "That was a good bit of climbing, Mr. Mauro. I'm proud of you."

There it was again, just like during our Aconcagua climb. I snaked an arm out the top of my sleeping bag and gave him a pat. "Thanks, man," I said. "You too. One rotation done. More to go."

The team left for EBC the next morning. I took a long last look at Lobuche Base Camp as we wended the traverse away to the west. This had been a good camp, a clean camp. I studied the massive rock face that stood over it, its stratified layers standing on end with snow capping each. "She would be scary as hell if she weren't so beautiful," I commented aloud to myself then smiled as I recalled saying pretty much the same thing about a sorority girl I tried to date in college. Even then, it seemed, beauty always came with danger. I turned away and started up the path toward Gorak Shep, EBC, and Everest, the most beautiful mountain in the world.

NEXT DAYS

I woke early the following morning to the sound of snow sliding off my tent. I peeked outside at our whitened camp, illuminated with the blue light of dawn. It felt peaceful and renewed. A gas cooker was already hissing in the cook's tent, so I pulled on some clothes and walked over to see if I could find a cup of coffee. Llama, the cook's assistant, cleared a place for me to sit on a bench next to the burners then brought me a steaming cup of water and some instant coffee. We talked as they cooked bacon on a huge flat grill. Soon the first rays of direct sunlight reached over the shoulder of Everest and touched down beside our dining tent. I drug a chair out into the light and soaked up its gentle warmth as I finished a second cup of coffee.

Fraser McKenzie, the Australian member of our team, wandered over from his tent and joined me. This climb was a trial run for Fraser. He planned to go only as far as camp four, the South Col. If all went well, he would return to attempt Everest's summit the following year. Boisterous and animated, like most Aussies, Fraser was typically the guy leading any mealtime conversation worth listening to.

The first helicopter of the day arrived shortly after breakfast. Though the improvised landing pad was a full hundred yards away, the rotors kicked up enough fresh snow to blanket our camp all over again. Two men helped an injured climber into the helicopter, which then lifted off and disappeared. Helicopters came and went several times each day at EBC, typically removing the sick, wounded, or deceased. Everest had already claimed the season's first fatality nine days earlier when a Sherpa working in the icefall plunged down into a deep crevasse.

As I passed the green communications tent, little bursts of radio talk emerged from it. It sounded like some Sherpas were moving up to higher camps. I continued back to my tent and dug out an inflatable palm tree I had brought from home. It had been easy to imagine this whole venture getting very serious, and I wanted to make sure a little room was left for mirth and the random moments that make life interesting. I was pleased to see that others had conjured the same thought. Frasier had tethered an inflatable kangaroo to his tent, while flags representing the origins of other team members decorated their shelters.

Our planned foray into the icefall was cancelled the next day when Greg Vernovage judged the conditions unsafe. It had snowed heavily again all night long, and that new load would need to settle before we got anywhere near it. "Hey, Dave," Greg called from outside my tent around two thirty. "I'm calling off the climb for today, so get some sleep." Then he shook my tent to relieve the heavy accumulation of snow, commenting, "Nice palm tree."

I checked out a radio from the com tent after breakfast and set out on the four-mile trek down-valley to Gorak Shep. A biting wind swept up the valley, stinging my face as I squinted through watery eyes. Over the next hour, I dodged around yak trains, offering the occasional word of encouragement to fatigued trekkers slumped over trailside. The path then entered the windblown dusty valley where Gorak Shep huddled apologetically. I pulled my buff up over my nose and mouth then started across, a lone traveler, a random nomad, a monk descended from the church of thin air.

A loose association of eight stone buildings forms the tiny village of Gorak Shep. Each rents out unheated rooms to trekkers. Some also house small restaurants featuring various dishes that had once been freeze-dried. This far up the Khumbu Valley, nothing is grown, gathered, or harvested. Nothing. It all has to be carried here, so weight counts—and the menu says so. I settled into a restaurant and ordered a bowl of ramen noodles. It was cold still, so the other patrons and I all wore our down coats as we ate. Then I bought an hour of internet time and a steaming pot of tea, and began uploading the blog entries I had written during my days at EBC.

I used the last twenty minutes of internet time reading the comments on my blog and Facebook page. Family, friends, past teammates, and complete strangers all around world were following my climb, checking for new posts each morning, then pouring forth with encouragement and affirmations of belief. My cousin, Sasha, wrote, "You are amazing! My mom and I were talking the other day about how you inspire us to live our lives more mindfully." Others likewise shared how my experience was impacting their lives. The only time I could recall having such an immediate influence on the lives of so many was when my sixty-nine Chevy Nova died during rush hour traffic in Seattle.

It truly felt as though we were all climbing Everest together. And while I was the legs and lungs, in some respects I owned no greater part than the reader who penned, "We are cheering you on from flat, warm, and watery Venice." We had all chosen to believe in this thing, this adventure into a world most of us had never seen and the uncertain prospect that the guy taking us there might just go all the way.

INTO THE ICEFALL

We finished breakfast at three thirty the next morning and began shuffling over to the Sherpa group tent. I was once again the last climber to arrive. Mingma looked concerned but did not ask me to explain my tardiness. This was fortunate, as I had no good excuse aside from the general malaise that comes with being up and active at such an hour. Under Mingma's lead, he and I immediately began passing other climbers, sometimes leapfrogging four at a time. I would have asked him to slow down, except this pace solved a different problem I had. I had only dressed in thermals and a shell layer, anticipating hard work ahead, and presently felt quite chilled. Soon I was generating enough body heat to be comfortable as we navigated the blue ice statues standing sentry at the start of the icefall.

By far, the greatest number of fatalities on Everest occurs in the icefall, a frozen gauntlet of ice chunks that have calved off the upper glacier. These pieces, comparatively ranging in size from mailboxes to office buildings, are all melting, toppling in slow motion, and advancing about six feet a day as gravity and warm spring temperatures work on them. Occasionally that movement is not slow. Several climbers have been killed by blocks of ice that suddenly fell over on them. The icefall is also littered with crevasses, yawning fissures sometimes hundreds of feet deep. These can open or close without warning while a climber walks one of the aluminum ladders laid crosswise to bridge them. Finally, the icefall is susceptible to regular snow and ice avalanches sweeping down off the west shoulder of Everest. One such avalanche would kill sixteen Sherpas as they climbed the icefall a year later. However, even that number was eclipsed in 2015 when the Nepal earthquake triggered avalanches that killed twenty-two people—the greatest tragedy in the history of Everest climbing.

The air grew stingy as we began the two thousand–foot ascent. I felt winded, but was getting along all right until we had to climb something vertical or speed through an avalanche chute. "I need to breathe," I shouted to Mingma, barely able to stand. Each time he paused for about forty seconds, but not much more. Though some parts of the icefall are more dangerous than others, there are no safe places, and the best way to manage risk there is to get in and out as fast as possible. We pushed so hard that I felt my heart rate race well above 162. Mingma started clipping my safety leash around anchor points for me so I could conserve energy and gasp for a moment longer. This brutal pace went on and on. I would burn everything I had to climb the face of some massive ice block, promising myself the reward of a long rest at the top, only to find we were standing beneath another still larger block when we got there.

As we paused for another short break, I heard Mingma's radio come to life. Mingma said Big Boss had just turned everyone around. We had already crossed most of the ladders and were only ten minutes from our objective, the Football Field, an open expanse about two thirds of the way up the icefall where climbers typically rested. Exhausted as I was, I still wanted to finish what we had started. Mingma got on the radio and received permission for us to finish out. In the end, I made it up, along with two of the Air Force climbers, Rob and Drew. I felt good about this, but was also spent after four hours of hard climbing. We arrived back in EBC a bit after nine, and I slept until lunch.

Big Boss, Max, and one of our team members, Cesar, interrupted lunch that day to make an announcement. Cesar had decided to end his bid. The altitude was causing severe blurring of his vision. Feeling it unsafe to continue, he had decided to leave EBC by helicopter in a few hours, returning to Kathmandu where his eyes could be examined by a specialist. Cesar was tearful as he talked about how hard it had been to make this decision. We tried to console him, assure him he was making the smart choice, but really, what words can numb the pain of a severed dream? I walked with Cesar to the helicopter pad and kept him company while we waited for his bird to arrive. It was hard watching Cesar tear up as he pawed through the crushed remains of his life's ambition, but I wanted to bear witness with him, even if all I could say was, "I understand."

CAMP ONE

We left EBC two days later for camp one (19,685 feet). Having promised Mingma I would not be late again, I set my alarm for one thirty. Mingma seemed pleased to see me arrive with the rest of my teammates. I assumed my reward would be a more comfortable starting pace, but Mingma took off like a branded mustang, running me straight to 162 as we passed climber after climber on the trail to the icefall. In all fairness, this was our plan, to train for speed so we would have it on summit day, but a bit of warm-up would have been welcome.

After passing several camps by the light of our head lamps, Mingma and I trekked over an area of small melt ponds and broken ice. A few team members were already changing into their crampons when we arrived at Crampon Point. The sound of heavy breathing mingled with the clink of metal crampons in the darkness. I caught the face of Kyle Martin in the light of my head lamp. He reached over and swatted the back of my shoulder. Mingma was already waiting next to me as I cinched the last crampon strap down hard. Without exchanging a word, we clipped into the fixed line that would guide us through the icefall's frozen labyrinth and set out into the night. Our first experience with the icefall had been by the light of day, but all subsequent passages would occur at night, when chill temperatures limited the movement of the ice.

We scaled a twelve-foot vertical face with footholds carved into it then dropped down the other side into a room-sized cavern that glowed cobalt blue by the light of our lamps. Then Mingma and I climbed a ladder up through the room's ceiling and onto an ice ledge. I remembered feeling half dead already at this point during our first trip into the falls, but this time was not so bad. I had acclimated. We crossed the first series of ladders, one of which was buckling within the closing crevasse it spanned, then up around and over many more broken seracs. A loud rumble high above us signaled an approaching avalanche just as we navigated the Popcorn Field, the part of the icefall where most avalanches land as they come off the west shoulder of Everest. So much force impacted there with such regularity that everything was pulverized to the size of popcorn. "Hurry! Hurry!" Mingma shouted to me as we ran for cover. But no avalanche came. The tumbling ice had found some other path. I panted hard for the next five minutes, trying to recover from the combination of adrenaline and my redlined heart rate. Mingma stood beside me, breathing normally, with a sympathetic hand on my back.

Five hours after entering the icefall, Mingma and I popped up out the top of it. By this time, I was so completely spent that the remaining gradual trek to camp one took a full hour—with many rests along the way. I wondered, If I'm having this much trouble with the icefall, how am I ever going to make it up the Lhotse Face? Then the lesson of prior climbs came to me, saying, "Your problem right now is not the Lhotse Face. Your problem is the icefall. There will be plenty of time to dread the Lhotse Face when you get to it. But for now, you need to focus on getting better at this part of the route."

Ty arrived at our tent at camp one an hour later. We spent the rest of that day napping, eating, and laying out in the warm sun that reflected down on us from the flanks of Everest, Lhotse, and Nuptse.

REST DAY AT CAMP ONE

We ate breakfast in our tents the next morning. The Sherpas brought us hot water for tea and oatmeal. Then we set out in light gear on the path to camp two. We had no intention of covering the entire distance, but merely wished to keep our legs from stiffening up after the difficulty of the prior day.

We turned back at the halfway point, returning to camp just prior to the onset of a sub-zero storm. Ty and I ate MREs (meal-ready entrees) while hiding in our thick down sleeping bags then rested for the move to camp two (21,300 feet) the following day.

I peeked out of my sleeping bag looking for my journal and noticed a wayward butterfly had come into our tent seeking shelter. This was one very lost butterfly, having wandered a full vertical mile higher than he was intended to roam. When we woke the next morning, the butterfly had perished and lay frozen atop Ty's sleeping bag. We asked Ty's Sherpa, Lakpa, what symbolism this might hold. "This is good luck," he said. The butterfly had given his life to protect ours.

We left camp one at six in the soft light of dawn. Though the altitude gain to camp two is modest, the long, exposed path up the glacier turns into a convection oven by noon each day as the white faces of the three giants all reflect down upon it. It was a strict no-no to get caught out in the valley during the heat of the day, when the 10°F of morning quickly shot up into the midnineties. Ty and Lakpa climbed beside Mingma and me that morning, enjoying a casual pace that delivered us to camp two just as the first direct rays touched its tents.

I dreamed of Lin and my boys that night, odd pedestrian dreams where I followed them around through their day-to-day doings. I watched Lin fold an entire basket of clothes and Chase eat a sandwich. Trevor rode his fat-tired cruiser bike all around the Illinois Tech campus while I hovered over him.

Wanting to stack the deck in favor of my thorough acclimation, I took a dose of Diamox that night before bed. Though I had never taken it before, Diamox was commonly used by climbers to ward off Cheyne-Stokes episodes at night and aid in acclimation. Diamox is not a narcotic and has no addictive qualities. The side effects of Diamox include increased urination (about two liters a night in my case) and a tingly sensation at the extremities, which can be especially distracting in the man zone.

SHERPA "RIOT"

We spent the next day resting at camp two while an elite team of sixteen Sherpas, comprised of the best from several expeditions, began setting fixed lines up the Lhotse Face. These lines would provide protection from falls as teams moved up toward camp three. But the fact that those who set the lines would not enjoy that same protection made for a very dangerous job. It was agreed among the climbers that no one else would venture onto Lhotse while work was underway.

But three European climbers ignored this understanding. Swiss climber Ueli Steck, Italian Simone Moro, and their British photographer, Jon Griffin, approached the base of Lhotse as the Sherpa team prepared to fix the route. The Sherpas asked them to wait until the following day when they would be welcome to use their fixed line, but Moro, Steck, and Griffin started up anyway, telling the Sherpas, "We will do as we please." The three later traversed above the Sherpas, crossing the fixed line en route to their site at camp three, and knocking ice down on them. The lead Sherpa then rappelled down from his position above the Europeans, confronting the men. Moro says at this point the Sherpa threatened him with an ice ax. The Sherpa claims Steck grabbed him by the coat. Words were exchanged. Simone Moro called the Sherpa a motherfucker, the absolute worst of insults in Nepali culture. The ensuing scuffle broke off almost as soon as it started, with the lead Sherpa descending and calling off rope fixing for the day. That should have been the end of it. It wasn't.

Several people I spoke with said that Moro, who already had a reputation for being a hothead and general jackwagon, then got on his radio, on an open channel, and peppered the Sherpas with racial epithets. For bonus points, he did so in Nepalese, a language he had acquired through years of running one of the helicopter services operating in and out of EBC. It is alleged that Moro concluded his broadcast by promising to kick someone's ass once he got back down to the base of Lhotse. Normally a highly passive people, the Sherpas may have seemed like an easy target to bully. Not this time.

Approximately one hundred Sherpas, who had all heard the radio transmission, were waiting when Moro, Steck, and Griffin arrived at their camp two tents. I noticed members of my team running toward the crowd, so I joined chase, curious what was going on. An angry mob of Sherpas was gathered and shouting in front of two tents. I saw one man (I believe Simone Moro) emerge from a tent to confront the Sherpa who seemed to be leading the demonstration. I could not hear what was said, but the Sherpa slapped the man's face hard. Then the man took refuge in his tent as a hail of stones pelted it. Ueli Steck broke from cover at this point, running off into a cluster of boulders near the foot of Mount Nuptse.[2] He shed his jacket then walked back to the scene casually, as though no one would recognize him. They did, and Steck again retreated to his tent. (The practice of shedding a layer came to be known as "a Ueli" among my team members henceforth). At this point, IMG Guide Max Bunce, Big Boss Greg Vernovage, and Sirdar Phanuru joined Western climber Melissa Arnot in form-

---

2   Ueli Steck would die four years later near this very spot when he fell from Nuptse during a solo attempt.

ing a protective barrier between the tents of Steck, Moro, and Griffin and the crowd of Sherpas. A temporary truce was negotiated under the condition the three men leave camp two within the hour. They did so, in what came to be called "The Walk of Shame."

As both Steck and Moro were highly sponsored climbers, enjoying the support of equipment manufacturers Mountain Hardware and The North Face, neither could allow this incident to color their public persona in a way that might cost them these lucrative endorsements. The two immediately reached out to their publicists, who coordinated a laughable portrayal of the incident. Steck and Moro were victims, attacked by a group of people synonymous with the very notion of peace. The media gobbled it up. Like any other story attached to the name Everest, this one sold lots of magazines and newspapers—despite being complete nonsense. Not a single Sherpa was interviewed.

RETURN TO EBC

We left for EBC on April 28 at five o'clock. Mingma and I hustled along, enjoying the downhill momentum, anxious to get through the falls before direct sun set them to grinding. From time to time, my concentration was summoned as we crossed another aluminum ladder, but otherwise I felt free to be with my thoughts.

These were my thoughts:

1. On the 1960s sitcom Bewitched, it was unfair of Darrin to demand Samantha not use her powers. She should have turned him into a newt.

2. The only track I can recall John Entwistle, bass player of The Who, singing lead on is "My Wife." This lyrical indictment paints his wife as being a maniacal shrew for not understanding how he might have "had a bit too much to drink," taken a wrong turn, and thus been AWOL the last four days. True or not, this song could not have been good for his marriage.

3. Mingma declined my invitation to make barnyard noises. Is it possible he is ashamed of his cow noise?

4. I wonder how much weight I've lost.

Mingma and I spent the rest of that day at EBC leveling my tent platform. The glacial moraine we lived on was more ice than rock, and it was slowly melting as spring arrived in the upper Khumbu. My tent and everything in it had sagged tragically to one side while I was away on the last acclimation rotation, so we removed it and set about rebuilding a flat, stable platform. Without the demands of climbing, Mingma was more talkative than usual, so I indulged in asking him a few questions.

"Hey, Mingma, how old are you?" I queried. He just shrugged his shoulders then explained that Sherpa culture places no importance on such things, so he did not know what year he was born. Though birthdays are not celebrated in the Sherpa culture, Mingma believed his was May 5, which would have had to also be a Tuesday since male Sherpas are named for the day of the week they are born. The name Mingma is Sherpa for Tuesday. That said, Mingma was most likely born in 1981.

Born in the village of Phortse, Mingma grew up with eight brothers and one sister. Two of his brothers died from disease as children, and one was killed while leading a climb on the notoriously dangerous Annapurna. Mingma did not attend school until joining the Tengboche Monastery in 1996, where he studied to become a monk. At that time, each student was required to pay a thousand dollars a year. After five years of study, Mingma was no longer able to raise the tuition, so he returned home to Phortse.

Mingma was then hired by International Mountain Guides as a load-carrying Sherpa in 2001, taking part in expeditions on Everest, Ama Dablam, Manaslu, and Cho Oyu. He worked hard to learn English and distinguished himself as tireless at high altitude. Attending the Khumbu Climbing School the following January, Mingma returned as a guiding Sherpa in 2002 and summited Everest for the first time. With the exception of 2005, when he tried working as an electrician in his home village, Mingma had successfully led an IMG Everest client to the world's highest summit each year.

Though he liked guiding, Mingma also knew it was a

dangerous occupation. His sons would talk about following in their father's footsteps, but Mingma forbid it. "This is a danger job," he told them, "and I want you to become doctor or engineer." Mingma hoped his sons would go to America to start their careers. "They can be comfortable there, have a car and some money and same freedoms as here in Nepal," he said. Mingma and his wife, who ran their small vegetable farm in Phortse, paid a yearly tuition of $1,500 US for each boy to attend a boarding school in Kathmandu, where they studied English, Nepali, Tibetan, math, history, and science.

THE FINAL ROTATION

The next several days were spent recovering from our trip to camp two then waiting for good enough weather to launch our final rotation, which would take us to camp three before returning back to EBC. It was frustrating to think of making it that far up Everest then coming all the way back down, but I understood the mandate of altitude climbing. Above nineteen thousand feet, a human cannot recover from exertion or injuries. If we did not descend below this level after tickling our physiologies higher, the acclimation we sought would not take place. Quite the opposite. The human body begins shutting down above nineteen thousand feet. By any medical definition, the climber is dying. The whole strategy behind high-altitude climbing is built around the objective of dying slowly enough that a person can summit and return to base camp before that process concludes.

Conditions came together on May 3. There was a nervous energy to the team as we all rushed about in the two-thirty darkness. Conversation was limited to requests for items spread out along the table we sat down to for breakfast, while each of us studied the day ahead in our minds.

Things went according to script as we got underway. But two hours into the climb, as Mingma and I entered the Popcorn Field, the shoulder of Everest released an avalanche of boulders and ice. I heard a concise snap, like the sound of a broomstick being broken, then the rumble of a locomotive coming our way. Mingma and I scrambled frantically to climb clear of it, running up a long, straight ledge. More afraid of the avalanche than accidental falls, we didn't even bother to clip into the fixed line. My legs were burning as I willed them to keep going until the effort reduced me to crawling. We took cover behind a tall ice formation and listened as the break of the fall line carried the debris beneath us. I could hear Mingma chanting Buddhist prayers beside me as a smaller avalanche then passed just above us. Then Mingma's radio leaped to life as Sherpas checked in with Big Boss from points throughout the falls. I listened carefully, still on all fours and breathing hard. Remarkably, no one had been hurt.

We continued to press hard through the remainder of

the icefall, arriving at camp one four hours after leaving EBC. This was much faster than the six hours normally needed. I was spent and nerve-wracked as I collapsed into a vacant tent. One by one, other team members arrived, likewise knackered. The wind was blowing hard in the pre-dawn chill, bringing the temperature down to 8°F as I tried to consume the contents of my packed lunch: frozen juice box, frozen salmon spread, frozen cheese square, and frozen dessert pastry. After twenty minutes of futile gnawing, Air Force flight instructor Marshall Klitzke and I abandoned our lunches and set out with our Sherpas for camp two.

By this time, I could see direct sunlight slowly working its way down the side of Nuptse, staging a soft landing on the valley floor. The tents of camp two, an hour and a half up the valley, had to be reached before the sunlight hit them, but now the overexertion of the icefall came to collect payment. I stopped in the trail and breathed hard for twenty chest-fulls. Feeling marginally better, I motioned to Mingma to continue on. A hundred steps later, I had to stop and breathe again. "I'm sorry, Mingma," I apologized. "I just can't catch my breath."

"It's okay," he offered. "We go slow." I continued to deteriorate, only able to go eighty steps, then sixty, and so on before needing to rest. We straggled into camp two a couple hours after leaving camp one. Remaining team members staggered in over the next four hours. Our stories were very similar: the fear and adrenaline of the icefall had overtaxed our resources, and from there on, the will to place one foot in front of the other had gotten us to camp two. We slept until dinner then logged another twelve hours to breakfast.

We rested for a day at camp two then set out for our next objective the morning of May 5. Camp three sat at twenty-four thousand feet, carved into the side of the Lhotse Face by the mean trade of ice axes. Ten tents clung there, an outpost of the most minimal accommodations for climbers en route to Everest's high camp, the South Col. Our original plan for this rotation was to have each team member spend a night (without supplemental oxygen) at camp three to establish the high threshold for his acclimation. Our first team of three climbers had thus spent the night of May 4 there.

By the next morning, the weather forecasts had changed to severe wind and cold up high, so our group was instructed to climb to camp three, spend a few hours acclimating, then return that same day to camp two. Mingma and I left camp two at four o'clock in our down suits and warmest gloves, arriving at the Lhotse Face an hour later. I looked up the icy incline, only able to see as far as my head lamp threw light. The surface of the Lhotse Face was a lumpy sheet of ice, polished to a smooth luster by daily thawing and freezing. Its vertical gain was so severe I could reach out and touch the ground while standing plumb vertical. I kicked a crampon point into the mountain and it barely penetrated the bulletproof ice. Okay, this is the real shit, I thought as we clipped into the fixed line.

We were only twenty minutes up the face when Mingma stopped to listen to his radio. "Sherpa sick," he said. One of our teammates, a Sherpa above us at camp three, had gotten up, dressed, and eaten some breakfast, but then started to feel dizzy. The Sherpa vomited then went to lie down in his tent. A camp physician was patched onto the line, and I could hear her instructing the people at camp three to administer nifedipine and place the sick Sherpa on bottled oxygen. We continued our climb upward.

Mingma stopped again twenty minutes later and turned to me. "Sherpa died," he said pointing at his radio. He then told me this Sherpa was his brother-in-law, DaRita Sherpa. We would later learn that two team members, Dan Meyer and Mike Chambers, had worked frantically to save the man's life, later descending, traumatized by what had happened. DaRita Sherpa was a longtime veteran of IMG and had spent a lot of time higher than camp three on Everest, so his sudden death was a mystery. I told Mingma how sorry I was for his loss and suggested we turn around and go back to camp two, but he insisted on continuing up. Mingma felt an obligation to get to the body as soon as possible so he could make sure certain proper Buddhist traditions were observed.

I unclipped from the fixed line and joined a group of team members on an ice ledge just below camp three. We ate our lunches and hydrated while looking out over the most breathtaking panorama I had ever seen. Yet I could not enjoy it. Like everyone else on that ledge, I'd had the joy of the moment kicked out of me by the news of DaRita's death.

Then a snap and rumble above us suddenly announced another avalanche coming.

"Quickly!" one Sherpa called out as he motioned us toward the fixed line. The first bits of snow were already coming over the break above us as I knee-skidded to the rope and snapped my carabiner in place. We all curled into snail-like balls, our toe spikes and fingers gripping as much hillside as possible, and waited for the wash of force that might be the last thing any of us knew. It's odd what a person's mind chooses to think about in moments like that. I flashed to a time when I was six. My mother, still bruised from my father's latest beating, held my hands in hers and said, "David, you are a very special boy." Then the freight train of snow raced by, twenty yards to our right.

A team of Sherpas lowered the body of DaRita Sherpa down the Lhotse Face, where a helicopter picked up Mingma and the body of his deceased brother-in-law, transporting them to their home village of Phortse. IMG located the man's parents in another village and had a helicopter take them to Phortse as well.

HEALING AND WAITING

I called Lin. As she had been throughout this whole strange journey, Lin was supportive, inspiring, and spoke from a place of love. We discussed the days ahead and my plans for the upcoming summit attempt, agreeing that focus on each step would be the key—and that staying present would be essential. I said nothing about DaRita's death or my own close calls with avalanches. No good could come of doing so.

That night, the climbers invited the Sherpas to join them for a movie in the group tent after dinner. Swaddled in down layers, we watched Anchorman with Will Ferrell. The humor did not always translate well, but the Sherpas definitely thought the fight scene was funny. This group movie became a nightly ritual as we drew closer in grief, closer in hope.

At this point, the team had completed all phases of preparation for a summit bid of Everest and now we stalked a summit date. The key to that date was the movement of the jet stream. As the monsoon season approaches, the jet stream moves from the south to the north side of Everest. This creates a slack tide in the killer winds that strafe the peak, allowing summit attempts for a few days each year.

These were simple days. If I could come up with and complete one task that gave purpose to my life, I then freed myself to nap and eat chocolate bars with impunity. I leveled my tent, shaved, washed socks, and trekked several times to Gorak Shep to post blog entries. I journaled and built stone sculptures, threw rocks at our frozen pond, and listened to the happy/sad voices coming from neighboring tents as teammates called home one last time.

Many expeditions' members used this lull to mingle with other camps. Russell Brice, the renowned leader of Himex, eased into our cook tent early one morning and had a cup of coffee with the kitchen crew and me. He was about the nicest guy you could ever meet. Cason Crane, the first openly gay Everest climber, hung out with our team. Marty Schmidt, legendary climber/guide, joined us for lunch, spinning story upon story from his twenty-five years of adventures.[3] I visited the Adventure Consultants camp and coffeed with guides Mike Roberts and Ang Dorje, who had guided me on Elbrus and Kilimanjaro respectively.

Mingma returned from Phortse on our second rest day. He was eager to get on with the tasks of day-to-day living at EBC. We sharpened our crampons and examined our gear without speaking of DaRita Sherpa. This was also part of the Sherpa culture: to mourn the lost then move on, honoring them through the service of good and useful pursuits.

When the forecast for two days of light wind at the summit proved correct, the rope fixing team pounced on the opportunity, placing anchors and lines all the way from the South Col to the summit. The fix was in, and Everest was now climbable.

The next day Greg Vernovage held our instruction session on how to use the oxygen bottles and masks. I did not

---

3   Tragically, Marty and his son Denali would both die in an avalanche on K2 just
    three months later.

expect to feel any different breathing the denser air, given the many weeks we had acclimated to base camp and higher. But the instant clarity that came to my head as I took in the first breath of bottled oxygen left me wondering how I had managed to feed and cloth myself up to this point. In addition to helping me climb higher into thinner air, I knew this supplemental oxygen would also keep me feeling warmer. Like a wood stove with its damper thrown open, the calories in my furnace would burn much hotter with the benefit of more O_2. This, in turn, would reduce the threat of frostbite.

I decided to visit my Antarctica teammate, Guy Manning, at the Jagged Globe camp on the other side of EBC. Along the way, I found my progress bogged down by a film crew, which in turn was bogged down by an elderly man making slow progress just ahead of them. I told myself to just accept the pace and enjoy the sunny morning, but the man in front was going so slow that I just had to pass. Easing onto a narrow shoulder of the trail, I skipped past the crew, offering various greetings and apologies. But the trail narrowed just as I was about to overtake the man. Leaping awkwardly, I managed to get in front of him while only modestly cutting the man off. At this point, I heard a voice shout, "Cut!" and I looked back to recognize David Breashears in the film crew and Reinhold Messner as the man I had just cut off.

No one talked much about the Reinhold Messner

filming. He had long ago insulted most of us by stating, "Climbing Everest with the aid of anything more than aspirin is cheating." In other words, no bottled oxygen. Our catlike indifference toward him was an expression of our contempt, which climbers maintained until such time that Messner actually walked into their camp and its occupants set about bootlicking shamelessly.

By May 14, the weather window we had been targeting for a May 20 summit took shape as the jet stream migrated to the north of Everest. The summit was expected to see very low winds for the period of May 17–24.

A plan was formed for three successive waves of IMG climbers to make summit attempts. The first of these would be the Hybrid Group of eight climbers, plus four of the strongest Classic Climbers. This team was dispatched immediately. The second wave, consisting entirely of Classic Climbers, included Ty and me. The third wave, finishing out the Classic Climbers, would follow a day behind us.

Mingma and I visited the puja altar before leaving EBC the morning of May 16. This was something we had done before entering the icefall on prior rotations and, given the protection it had brought us, we were both keen to maintain the tradition. I left the chanting to Mingma. It was my job to toss rice on cue. He chanted through several verses, paused, looked at me, and nodded. I scattered a handful of rice across the altar, then Mingma began the next set of chants. The air was thick with the scent of smoldering juniper, while the clumsy rumble of passing climbers reached out from the darkness.

Daily temperatures had warmed enough in the time since arriving at EBC to meaningfully increase movement within the fall. Ladders used in the last rotation were crushed miserably between fallen seracs. Parts of the route had been completely redirected to avoid the fields of refrigerator-size ice blocks now piled on the path we had once trod. Open sky directed our attention to the now-missing "ice cream cone" landmark that had dominated one section of the route. Where had it fallen? There was no sign of it. Probably it had tipped over and been consumed by the crevasses working their jaws tirelessly at its base.

Mingma and I completed the icefall in three hours then, following a brief rest, continued on up the valley to camp two. That same day, wave one of our team advanced to camp four, the South Col. They left that night in very windy conditions. The forecast suggested these winds would abate as the night went on, but they did not. All climbers were turned back short of the Balcony, a small flat notch almost two thousand feet above the South Col. Several of them returned with frostbite injuries.

Two of the Classic Climbers descended to camp two, as they no longer had enough bottled oxygen to attempt the summit. One of these climbers, Dan Meyer, a thirty-four-year-old FedEx courier from Highlands Ranch, Colorado, was not ready to accept defeat. Dan made arrangements to

obtain a new supply of oxygen and persuaded Greg Vernovage to insert him into wave three of the IMG climbers.
The two Classic Climbers who remained at the South Col,
Paul Niel of Austria and Knut Heggland of Norway, had
each purchased an extra bottle of oxygen in advance and
so had the means to make a second attempt the evening
of May 17. Both prevailed, scoring the first summits for
our IMG team.

DIZZY ON THE LHOTSE FACE

Wave two left for camp three the morning of May 18.
Some troublesome GI problems interrupted the first stages
of my ascent up the Lhotse Face, but I thought little of it,
as such occurrences come and go with frequency at high
altitude. Mingma and I settled into our regular pace, carving
out the first two thousand feet of gain up the steep blue
ice and then stopping on a small ledge to rest and hydrate.
Nick "Gibby" Gibson, one of the Air Force climbers, soon
joined us on the ledge. Trained as a pararescueman, or PJ,
Gibby would jump from airplanes and provide medical
aid to wounded soldiers on the ground. He was a kind
and generous man who had, again and again, engaged his
skills to help team members who fell injured or ill in the
course of our expedition. Gibby and I were both clipped
into anchored protection as we stood there looking out
across the vastness of the Himalayas when suddenly I began
feeling dizzy.

"Gibby, there's something wrong with me," I said. Gibby sat me down on the ledge, asking questions as he held me steady. I did not know what was happening with me, but I did know it closely mirrored the symptoms of whatever had killed DaRita Sherpa in almost the same spot two weeks earlier. My vision narrowed for a moment. "Shit. Gibby. I almost passed out just then," I said.

"Just keep breathing," Gibby said, "and try to sip some water."

I had been in many dangerous situations in the course of my climbing career, but none so precarious. And the sudden onset of whatever had come over me felt powerful, lethal. This might be it, I thought. I might be dying.

HAPE and HACE were quickly ruled out. A new bug had hit camp two a few days earlier, afflicting Fraser McKenzie and one of the Sherpas. Though more severe, owing to altitude, my symptoms matched theirs. Jangbu, at camp two, searched out Fraser to see how he was feeling. Fraser confirmed experiencing dizziness, which passed quickly, and said he was now back at 100 percent. As descending would take more time than moving up to a wider ledge, we agreed that I would continue higher to a flat shelf where I could lie down. If I did not improve, I would have to go back down to camp two, ending my Everest climb.

We climbed for another thirty minutes to the shelf, where Mingma found a generous space for me to stretch out. Gibby sat next to me, watchful. A few other team members joined us for a rest as they ascended the face. All had been monitoring our earlier radio transmissions and asked how I was doing. I ate most of my lunch and swallowed another liter of energy drink. By the time Ty joined us, I was feeling much improved. Gibby consulted with EBC, receiving approval for me to continue up to camp three, where my condition would be closely monitored. Hey, I thought, maybe I'm not out of this thing after all. It would be hard to say how many steps come between "I'm dying" and "I want to continue climbing," but I had somehow skipped all of them.

I felt better as we resumed the climb, making decent time the remaining thousand feet to our tents. Another sick climber, D. G. Rogers, an attorney from Raleigh, North Carolina, and I were quarantined in a tent by ourselves. As camp three was the point where climbers began using bottled oxygen, we strapped on our masks, got them flowing at one liter per minute, and relaxed in the luxuriance of breathing.

DAVE MAURO AND D.G. ROGERS. PHOTO BY DAVE MAURO.

There's a process altitude climbers go through involving the tearing down of everything not essential to their reaching the summit. They might leave gear behind or burn off excess body weight. They will surrender basic hygiene, comfort, and the ability to rest well. Their appetites will wane, and even their sense of smell may cease as they move higher, the air eventually thinning to a point where their ability to hold and process complex thoughts is compromised. What's left is a basic desire and, hopefully, enough physical and mental strength to see them through. These climbers have become whatever animal that mountain requires. I thought about this as D. G. and I lay silent in our tent. I believed something about what had happened to me that day fit within the context of becoming my animal. I had to believe this or quit. But I also knew no guarantees came with it. We like to speak of mountains as though they are people, with intent, judgment, and mercy. We like to imagine our virtue as being part of the mix. But mountains don't give a shit. They will kill you the same as anyone else, regardless of your faith or fitness, experience or effort. Mountains don't care that you have a young family counting on your return or that you are raising money for charity. They will tear you down to your most basic components then invite you to go for broke.

ON THE WINGS OF BOTTLED OXYGEN

Virtually all of camp three overslept. Even the Sherpas. We had worked so hard moving up the Lhotse Face the previous day and rested so deep with the aid of bottled air that our slumber was impervious to alarms of all manner.

The O2 masks tended to gather condensation then purge it through a valve at the base. This moisture had spilled out onto my down suit and sleeping bag all night long, creating a sheen of frozen drool. I snapped it off in large chunks, tossing them out the tent door. The dry air had long ago worn bare the lining of my sinuses so they partially filled with blood each night. The first order of any day was to clear this. But the rush for time left me unwilling to seek out appropriate means and thus the right sleeve of my thermal shirt was employed, giving me the appearance of an extra from a slasher movie.

It took a surprising amount of time to do ordinary things. The short leash to my oxygen tank required constant accommodations as I put away my sleeping bag and put on boots. A Sherpa ducked his head into our tent to see if we needed hot water for tea or breakfast. A short while later, he returned with my bowl of instant cream of wheat half filled with cold water. Unable to find my spoon, I gave it three quick stirs with my index finger and drank it down. Breakfast over.

Still weakened from my illness, I struggled to find our rhythm once Mingma and I started climbing. Other climbers passed us by, and I felt my ego growl. Mingma, sensing my frustration, asked me what was wrong.

"My oxygen bottle is leaning to one side," I said.

"Mine too."

"I am moving slow."

"We have plenty of time."

"I don't feel strong."

"I will turn up your oxygen."

He did so, and the effect was immediate. When depleted muscles receive oxygen, a tingling sensation accompanies it. I could feel this move down my legs like tiny ice crystals tumbling through a pachinko machine.

From a distance, the Yellow Band appeared as a lightly colored stripe in the otherwise dark composites that made up Everest. It was quite steep and thus held almost no snow. This meant climbing the bare rock with the points of my steel crampons as they screeched and skidded unnervingly. There were fixed lines for protection from falls, but little else was available to suggest the means by which climbers should ascend. I witnessed several methods of dubious construct being employed, the result being an exhausted climber hanging like a tuna in a net.

A complete mental shift was required for this obstacle. The linear approach of mountain climbing had to be shed. I am now a rock climber, I told myself. Instead of relying on the rope, I looked for handholds in the rocks. Instead of toe-pointing the tiny ledges before me, I reached out sideways to form opposing compression. I thought of my rock climbing coach, David Hutchinson, and the calm voice he used to shout advice up to me from below. "See if you can get a few fingers around that rock above and to the right," I heard him say. "Use the legs, not your arms."

We continued upward on a rising traverse toward the Geneva Spur then rested for ten minutes at its base. The Geneva Spur forms a rocky shoulder that sticks out from one side of the South Col. We climbed the backside of the spur and continued up its spine to high camp. I looked around and recognized much of what I saw from stories I had read: the steep drop-off at either side, the wind-strafed rocks, the abandoned campsites, and the demoralizing face of Everest looking down from above.

I was shown to my tent by Phanuru, IMG camp chief for the South Col. Mingma returned regularly to bring more water and check on my condition. He took an MRE packet from me then returned a short while later, having boiled it in water. I forced myself to eat the chili entree, hopeful for the strength it might give me and grateful to Air Force member Andrew Ackles for offering it from his rations when my own did not arrive. These first few hours were critical in seeing if I would recover or break down in the 26,300-foot elevation of the South Col. I lay still for ninety minutes breathing bottled oxygen. As my strength returned, I began to feel restless. Recalling how I had packed my inflatable palm tree on a lark, I dug it out, inflated it, and tied the toy down beside the entrance to my tent. Then I stood back and watched the confused reaction of exhausted climbers as their hypoxic brains tried to sort out the existence of a palm tree at 26,300 feet. It was my statement of whimsy in the midst of some very serious business, my moment of daily joy.

Ty arrived a bit later and was shown to our tent. It was the most tired I had ever seen him. We sprawled on the floor inside, sharing a half-spent oxygen bottle, speaking little during the nervous hours that followed.

THE DRAGON CHASE

The IMG game plan for summit day had been articulated to each of us ahead of time.

Climbers would leave the South Col in three waves: seven o'clock, eight o'clock, and nine o'clock on the night they arrived at high camp. Central to this staging was the intent to avoid any large crowds, especially the "Indian Army"—a very large team composed of personnel from the Indian military. They climbed together in a large, slow pack that was often impossible to pass. Though they were polite mountaineers and willingly allowed themselves to be overtaken by faster climbers, circumstances rarely afforded a stretch long enough to do so safely. The IMG seven o'clock team was composed of the slower Classic Climbers. It was hoped this would get them out ahead of the Indian Army, which was believed to be leaving later in the evening. The eight o'clock group was the solid core of the Classic Climbers, and the nine o'clock Classic launch was a select group of the four fastest IMG climbers: Drew, Kyle, Colin, and Marshall of the Air Force team.

Each climber would leave the South Col with a fresh bottle of oxygen and exchange it for another fresh bottle at the Balcony. Those, like myself, who had opted to purchase an additional bottle would change out again at the South Summit. We were to each climb at our own pace, accompanied by our Sherpa, as our ability, health, and oxygen permitted.

Most stories about Everest end at the summit. It is a convenient point of closure. Yet it is widely understood that most accidents and deaths occur during the descent. Fatigue unquestionably plays a huge role in this. Mental acuity also suffers during descent as a climber relaxes, having accomplished their goal. But more serious still is the fact that a climber, by reaching into the altitude of Everest's death zone, awakens a physiological dragon within. This dragon, breathing the fatal threats of HACE, HAPE, and other sudden illnesses, will then chase that climber all the way down to camp one. It was for this reason IMG insisted that a climber returning from the death zone rest at the South Col for no more than ninety minutes before continuing to descend. In spite of everything a climber has been through, they must continue all the way down to camp two that same day.

Consider Roger Snyder. One of the strongest Classic Climbers on our team, Roger arrived at EBC having taken three months off to do nothing but climb and live at high altitude prior to our expedition. Confident and fit, he evoked images of Robert Duvall's character in Apocalypse Now. After successfully summiting Everest with our eight o'clock wave of Classic Climbers, Roger returned to the South Col feeling tired but healthy. In the ninety minutes that followed he contracted HAPE and his lungs began to fill with fluid. As the staff there treated him, he lapsed into HACE with fluid starting to fill his brain. In a matter of moments, he went from being a strong, healthy man who had never taken anything stronger than aspirin to someone desperately forcing down niphedipine, dexamethesone, and Diamox in order to survive. He continued descending with help, yet still had to be medevacked out by helicopter a few days later. The Dragon had caught him.

THE GRAND WAGER

From the moment a climber wagers they can stand atop Everest, they are required to make certain payments to keep that bet alive. First comes the money. Depending on the guide company and various other options, this might be $50,000 to $100,000, all paid in advance with no hope of refund under any circumstances. The bet is on. They next make numerous physical payments in the form of training for hours each day, six days a week. There are payments involving the purchase of expensive equipment, lost wages, forgone vacation time, evacuation insurance, and costly vaccines. There are psychological payments, taking the form of mental fatigue, the doubts of third parties, and the painful two-month absence from loved ones. None of these are negotiable.

But the final payment a climber must lay on the table is their life. To think one could leave the South Col without doing so would be delusional. If they wish to wager that they can stand on top of the world, a climber must go all in, betting all their tomorrows. This is an easy notion to view in the abstract as one prepares for a climb many months away, but the weight becomes awesome as the last few minutes pass prior to leaving the South Col. I watched Ty closely during those minutes.

The wind was blowing harder than the forecast had suggested. If it persisted, there would be no making the summit, and lives would likely be lost. But we were going. It was 6:50, and Ty's Sherpa, Lakpa, had stuck his head into our tent several times already, trying to keep Ty moving along. I could see the nerves winding up through the expression on Ty's face. There was a sense of resignation. Ty was making that final payment.

"We can do this," I told him. "Twenty-four hours from now, we will be down at camp two with an Everest summit under our belts. We just need to keep clear heads and execute," I said. Ty nodded in agreement, but his mind was clearly elsewhere. I could almost see him staring at the mountain of chips he had just slid out onto the table. We hugged, then he slipped out the tent door into the darkness.

The next hour passed quickly, and soon I too was making the Grand Wager. I was nervous, but felt at peace with the decision. I was prepared, had a game plan, and had tested both with success through the course of the rotations, though it was unclear how much the sickness had taken out of me. I looked one last time at the photos in my pocket: Lin, my sons Chase and Trevor, my mother, and a recently deceased friend. I examined a small plastic bag with my brother's ashes in it then returned these items to the pocket. Pulling the oxygen mask over my face, I stepped out into the night.

A string of sixty or more head lamps was already reaching up the side of Everest. The Indian Army had gotten out ahead of us. We would have to deal with this through the night. Mingma introduced me to the young Sherpa, Pasang Sona, who would be carrying my extra bottle of oxygen up to the South Summit. We would climb as a trio, spelling one another in the lead as we clawed upward.

My Khumbu cough had gotten bad enough to bring on back spasms. I launched into an episode as we prepared to leave. Mingma and Pasang waited patiently then helped me on with my pack. It was going to be a slow start for me. I could feel it. At fifty, I was no longer able to bounce up and hit it. My body needed to be put on notice, reminded, and then coaxed along for the first hour.

We started off easy, passing a few climbers here and there as we gradually worked up to our rhythm. The half-moon set a light glow to the snow. The stars were brilliant and vast. Soon the wind fell off to almost nothing, and the only sounds were those of our respirators and the bite of crampons into ice. We caught up to a slow line of eight climbers and left the fixed line protection to pass them. A while later, we eased out around another ten climbers as the route entered a particularly steep section of the Triangular Face. Each time the three of us left the fixed line to free-climb past someone, we clipped our safety leashes to each other, a contract of sorts that assured we all would be fine or we all would not.

Lin would tell me later how she spent the many nervous hours of my summit attempt. She burned her cellular minutes well into overage, called my mother and Noelle, and took calls from others seeking some kind of update on Ty and me. Then, as a sense of helplessness overtook her, Lin realized there was one thing she could do to protect me while half a world away. Adhering to the random belief that the disposition of one's toilet paper roll has bearing on whether that person will come into money, Lin set about reversing every roll in our house. Aware that considerable life insurance proceeds would come her way if I perished, Lin sought to block such financial providence by making sure each roll fed from the bottom.

Halfway up the Triangular Face, we threaded into a narrow seam in the rocks about two feet wide and four feet deep. A dozen or more climbers had formed a slow logjam there, and we had to wait them out. I felt Mingma turn down my flow rate to conserve oxygen while we shuffled slowly in the line of climbers. I would take a step, breathe four times, and then the man in front of me would advance enough so that I could take another step. I felt a tension rising inside me, winding like a steel coil as our slowed pace held back a force that had been building for months, a momentum that would not relent. As soon as the three of us cleared the rock seam, Mingma reached over and, with one quick motion, removed our safety leashes and clipped them together. I felt Pasang clip his own leash to the back of my harness in the same instant. We skirted past the line of climbers then continued on, free-climbing the open face. We were cooking now. My legs were solid, and the rest of my body seemed to have come to the party. We passed a trio of climbers, a group of four, and two down-climbers who had given up. I felt a strength I had never known, and yet I was moving at the same 162 bpm that had been my gold standard for months. It was magical. It just kept coming, passing through me like an electric current. I was the man holding a high-voltage wire. We passed groups of four, groups of eight, and a few pairs. Somewhere in the night, we passed Ty, though I was not aware of it at the time.

We reached the Balcony (27,600 feet) a short while after a large team had also arrived. It was about ten thirty, and the moon had swung around the other side of Everest. The mountain's silhouette against the stars was the only way I could tell what kind of climb remained above. It looked astoundingly tall and steep. We changed oxygen tanks quickly, getting back out on the route ahead of the large group, then settled in behind a solo climber working his way up the long demanding pitch to the South Summit. He fatigued after forty minutes and, leaning on his ice ax, waved us by. We carried on for another ten minutes before I rotated to the lead, plowing upward through hip-deep snow so fine it barely put up a fight. At some point I wondered, where are the tracks from the other climbers? I looked up the mountain. There were no head lamps above us. Not a single one. We were alone, the highest humans on the planet, leading the attempt on Everest. Something inside me relaxed for the first time that night. I knew success was within our grasp. As we paused before a rock face, I looked up at the stars. I could almost feel their light touching me. "Wow," I wondered aloud.

In spite of the bottled oxygen, the effects of altitude started to creep in as we labored higher. My right foot was going numb with cold, so I turned up the electric foot warmer for that boot. Our pace became more difficult to maintain. I was stopping to breathe hard now, unable to keep a continuous cadence. The South Summit had disappeared somewhere in the stars and seemed to be running away from us. You're kidding, I thought. People actually climb this thing?!

There are four deceased members of our family that Lin and I refer to as our angels. We believe each spends time by my side during critical moments of any climb. I paused for a rest and touched on each of them: first my brother Danny, and then Lin's father Bob, brother Greg, and stepfather Chuck. The doubts slipped away. An hour later, we crawled up over a rock ledge, and Mingma announced, "This is South Summit."

We took off our packs to rest, and I got out my thermos of hot tea to share with Mingma and Pasang as they changed my oxygen tank. This was the point of return for Pasang Sona Sherpa, having fulfilled his mission. But back at high camp, Mingma and I had discussed the possibility of allowing Pasang to continue on with us to the summit if he performed well up to this point. Mingma said it would be my call.

Every Sherpa boy grows up dreaming of one day being a guiding Sherpa. They are the rock stars of their culture, thoroughbreds who use their unique abilities to do things other people cannot—and they are paid well for it. After gratuities, Sherpas who guide clients to the summit of Everest typically make more money in the course of a single Everest season than their average countryman will make in ten years. But a Sherpa must typically have an Everest summit before he can be permitted to guide others. This represents a catch-22, given that they lack the financial means to buy their way onto a team. Rare opportunities like this one are a Sherpa's best bet for breaking through that barrier and into a life of financial security.

Mingma approached me while Pasang finished hooking up my fresh oxygen tank. "Will Sherpa go to summit?" he asked. I stepped over next to Pasang and threw an arm over his shoulders. Mingma nodded happily then turned to put on his pack.

By the light of my head lamp, I recognized we were on the Cornice Traverse, long, graceful, and dangerous as it curled over into oblivion. I flicked a tuft of snow with my ice ax and watched it disappear down into the blackness. Trying to recall the order of what landmark came next, my thoughts swirled and faded in a hypoxic ghost-work, so I abandoned the effort. "We are working on this project all night," I told myself, trying to release the urge to measure our progress and instead simply exist in the moment. An hour later, Mingma stopped before a large boulder and, gesturing like a tour guide, said, "This is Hillary Step. Very famous."[4]

Mingma then scampered up and over the landmark with the agility of a Romanian gymnast. I stood there a moment, remembering where he had placed his feet, how he had used his hands. "You can't just muscle this thing," I told myself. "You'll blow out your arms and never see the summit." This was rock climbing again, and I needed to think that way. I started up the massive boulder the same way I had seen Mingma scale it. My crampons wanted to screech down the surface of the icy, round boulder, so I created a wedge-like force with one hand and foot-braced out to the side against an ice face. I took my time with each placement, testing for surety before weighting it, while Mingma looked down from above.

I had read about a rock halfway up the step that climbers must straddle to get over. There is a crack to the right

---

4   In 2015, a massive earthquake rocked Everest hard enough to dislodge the boulders forming Hillary Step. They tumbled down into Tibet, leaving what is now the Hillary Slope, a much tamer conclusion to one of climbing's greatest adventures.

that looks like an inviting alternative for foot placement, but a climber will almost always find his boot wedged in it. This is quickly followed by flailing and exhaustion. When I came to this rock, I knew what I had to do. To straddle it, I would have to commit fully with a belly flop onto the rock and hope I did not slide off into Tibet. I sprang at it like a desperate starfish, arms and legs open wide, and landed with a force that knocked the wind out of me. Gasping for a moment as my hands sought out holds, I pulled myself up to a cowboy position then flipped my downhill leg up over the rock and shuffled around a narrow ledge. I looked up to see Mingma waving a rope that hung down in front of me. There were several ropes, some of which had probably been there for years. These were not to be trusted. I clipped into the line Mingma had indicated and started up the steep snow and rock face constituting the upper half of the Hillary Step's forty-foot vertical rise.

Bottled oxygen does not equate to sea-level breathing. Providing oxygen at three liters a minute, the tanks pause a climber's physiology at twenty-three thousand feet, a level at which only 43 percent of normal oxygen supply exists. This buys a climber some time, but even with a continuous flow, he will eventually come to experience the full brunt of the death zone. I reached that point while scaling the upper step. It took longer for my legs to recharge after each step. I leaned into the hillside, breathing for protracted periods of time. My mind wandered randomly, with flashes of birthday parties and the voices of family chattering excitedly in my head. Then I reached up to prepare for the next step and felt Mingma take my hand. He pulled while I threw what was left of my legs into the effort, and I emerged at the top of the Hillary Step.

I remembered my good friend, Phil Drowley, telling me how he began laughing when he got past the step. He knew he would summit at that point. I began to sob. My goggles had frozen over several hours earlier, so I was climbing without eye protection. The tears froze immediately to my face and eyelids, leaving my left eye partially frozen shut.

We climbed for another twenty minutes up a gradual snow slope. Then, in the light of our head lamps, I saw a pile of prayer flags at the point where planet Earth ended. I have nothing left to climb, I thought—as much figuratively as literally. I was all out of mountain. Followed by Pasang, Mingma and I took the last ten steps together, like Hillary and Norgay, then I sat down upon Everest's snowy peak.

"This is summit," Mingma announced warmly. It was 3:43 a.m. on May 20, 2013. The sun would not come up for another hour, and by then the summit would be crowded with other climbers. But for now, we had the pinnacle to ourselves. I looked off into the darkness at the stars, wrapped like a bowl all around us. The lowest stars sat beneath us on the horizon, where the curvature of the earth confirmed our rarified altitude.

DAVE MAURO. PHOTO BY MINGMA CCHRING SHERPA.

We took several photos of Pasang to verify his first Everest summit. Then Mingma snapped some pictures of me as I held up images of family members and a banner for The Boys & Girls Club. I released a small quantity of my brother's ashes and watched them carry away in the jet stream. In all, we spent forty minutes alone on the summit, and while I did feel the weight of the moment, I could not sense its measure. I was simply too exhausted. It was like being paid in a currency you do not understand; only when it is spent completely will you know its full worth.

I stood up and looked one last time into the darkness. I thought about the last six years and the epic journey that had taken me from the lowest point in my life to the highest. There was so much about that journey I still did not understand, but one thing seemed clear, and in that moment I heard myself say, "Thank you."

CHASE ON

Air Force member Kyle Martin was the first ascending climber I passed on my way down. He was only a few minutes from the top. We exchanged congratulations then continued on our separate ways.

Pasang and Mingma each rappelled off the top of the Hillary Step. I paused for a few minutes to give them time to clear out of the landing spot on the narrow ledge below then clipped into the rope and kicked backward off the top. An ascending climber was already standing on the ledge as I came to rest. I had nearly landed on top of him. Realizing we were going to have to pass one another, he backed up against the rock face. I unclipped from the safety line then swung out around him with one arm and leg. But halfway through this process, another ascending climber popped up to occupy the spot on which I'd intended to land. So I paused there, straddling the first climber, my arms holding him in a tight bear hug. I looked down to see thousands of feet of sky falling away beneath me. Then I looked back at the second climber. He had reversed direction to clear space for me.

It was impossible to know who was who with all the gear we were wearing, but I noticed that the climber I was holding close had sponsorship patches all over his down suit. I knew Guy Manning was highly sponsored for his Everest climb and wondered what the chances might be that this was the man I now held so close that our faces touched.

"Guy?" I asked at point blank range.

"Yeah."

"Guy Manning," I confirmed, still disbelieving the odds that would have us meet up in such a way at such a place.

"Yeah."

"Dave Mauro," I said.

"Oh! Congratulations, Dave," Guy offered. "Very nicely done with your summit!"

"Same to you," I said. "You're almost there. Kick its ass!"

"Righto," he agreed, then we went our separate ways.

I would later learn that, after summiting, Guy had frostbitten several toes and had to be helivacked out from camp two to Kathmandu.

I paused a few minutes below the Hillary Step. A long line of climbers extended back to form what already looked like an hour-long wait to get up the step. Nine places down the queue, I spotted Ty.

"Hey, little brother," I said, slapping his shoulder.

"Hey."

"Howzit goin'?" I asked. Ty just nodded. I realized that Lakpa had probably turned Ty's oxygen flow down to conserve it while they waited in line. That meant he was breathing one liter a minute, which was not much more than what it takes to remain conscious at twenty-nine thousand feet. "Congratulations," I said. "The step is fun!" Ty nodded. It seemed clear conversation just wasn't an option. "Well... see ya," I said then continued my descent.

The sun was coming up now, so Mingma, Pasang, and I paused to take a few photos and put on our glacier glasses. The rappel down to the Balcony went surprisingly quick. We continued descending toward high camp, taking breaks to drink and breathe, arriving at the South Col around seven.

Phanuru congratulated me as we walked to my tent. "I give you until eight thirty to drink, rest, eat. Then you go down," he said, more an order than request.

"Okay," I agreed, not liking it but having accepted these terms many days in advance. The next ninety minutes passed quickly. Mingma helped me into my gear and set the oxygen flowing at a generous four liters per minute. I felt myself spring to life as though an IV drip of caffeine had just been opened wide. The heat was coming on, and temperatures began to soar as the sun rose, making my down suit a sweatbox. I opened leg and chest zippers to let some air in, but this seemed to make little difference.

Various items shot past us down the Lhotse Face as we rappelled: a helmet, a water bottle, an oxygen canister. The careless handling of these things spoke to the level of exhaustion suffered by all climbers. I was past running on fumes. Even the supplemental oxygen (which we were encouraged to keep breathing all the way to camp two) seemed to have no effect now. I had devolved into a troglodyte, a stumbling, drooling beast incapable of higher thought.

I staggered into camp two about two in the afternoon, wanting only to drink a liter of water and collapse. But something I overheard on Mingma's radio changed that. Ty was just then arriving back at the South Col.

I made several inquires with IMG guides and expedition leadership and was told Ty had encountered difficulties descending. He had been administered acetazolamide, nifedipine, and dexamethasone, the hardest-hitting pharmacological cocktail available to altitude climbers—the dragon slayer.

Though Ty seemed to be in stable condition, a complete "nose to toes" examination was conducted on him at the South Col. "I've looked at all the findings," Big Boss Greg Vernovage said, "and to me Ty just looks like a tired climber. Nothing more." It was decided Ty could safely stay the night at camp four with the benefit of the meds he had already taken plus an enhanced O2 level. IMG Guide Aaron Mainer slept next to him that night, keeping a close eye on his condition.

I should have checked on Ty before leaving the South Col. I could have had Mingma raise Lakpa on the radio. Then I would have known something was wrong. That said, there was nothing I could have done about it. At that point,

I no longer had the oxygen or strength to go back up. My own dragon chase was on, so I could not have even waited there for him. Still, I wished I had checked.

DONE

At the insistence of team leadership, I descended to EBC the next day while Ty made his way down to camp two. I called Lin and Noelle, assuring both that Ty and I were fine. Wanting only to sleep, I continued on toward my tent, but Paul Niel intercepted me with a can of beer, steering us toward other teammates celebrating near the com tent. The combination of two months' sobriety, altitude, and exhaustion combined to deliver me into a state of almost immediate intoxication. I fell asleep in a folding chair still holding what remained of that first beer.

I woke a short while later and shuffled off to my tent. Stretched out on my soft, comfortable air mattress (repaired from my earlier mishap), I looked into the warm yellow glow of the tent's rainfly and relived the climb. It did not seem real. Not yet. Any satisfaction for having summited Everest was pushed back by a greater force. My immediate sensations were flooded with a deep gratitude that I had won the right to live the rest of my life. I would get to see my children marry and have children of their own. I would get to grow old with Lin, holding hands like each day was a prom date. I could fish for crab, mountain bike, perform improv, and write. I could return to the work I loved as a financial planner. I would see summer and cheeseburgers, candles, and campfires. I had not realized how completely these things had been set aside. Nothing was on my calendar post-Everest, but now I was free to fill it up with the pile of chips being slid back across the table toward me.

The camp cook's assistant, Llama, made money on the side doing laundry for climbers. For two thousand rupees (about sixteen dollars), he would wash, dry, and fold a garbage bag of dirty clothes. I sorted out the worst of my garments and delivered them to him with a Hershey bar meant more as an apology than a gratuity. Llama loaned me a tiny mirror from his kit so I could shave, then he filled the water cistern for my shower.

The on-demand water heater popped to life as propane and spark came together within. A satisfying warmth fell upon me as steam filled the tented walls. Large flat stones had been placed to make a shower floor. Their texture felt pleasing against my bare feet. I stood beneath the water, sensing something close to comfort while examining the ravages of altitude upon my naked body. There were bruises, cuts, a swollen knee. All of the muscle mass I had spent months building was gone, consumed by my body through weeks of burning more calories than I could eat. In all, I had lost thirty pounds.

I walked out of camp the next morning to meet Ty and Lakpa as they exited the icefall. Spring had arrived, so even at seventeen thousand feet, the morning temperature was warm enough to sit out in short sleeves. I perched on a boulder tall enough to afford a clear view of the trail and waited. Ty and Lakpa appeared an hour later, looking tired but happy.

"Gimme that pack," I said to Ty.

"No. I gotta finish this thing," he answered with a prideful smile.

We walked back to EBC together, talking over our summit bids and what we missed most about home.

LEAVING THE KHUMBU

Our trek back through the Khumbu Valley descended into summer. Dirt patches we had passed next to village homes at the onset of our journey now flourished with rich green vegetables. Yak herders struggled to keep their trains moving as an abundance of trailside temptations lured the beasts to graze. Many cottage entryways had baskets of flowers set out to dry for tea. These were the milk-and-honey days for a people who endured a hard life the rest of the year. Soon the men would be returning from the expeditions they had worked on various Himalayan peaks. Husbands, fathers, brothers, sons. A fortunate few would have made enough money to support their families clear through to the next climbing season. They would tend their gardens, play with their children, and remember those who would never be coming home.

Mingma was one such Sherpa. As a premier climbing

Sherpa, he was paid well by IMG. It is common for clients to tip their Sherpas. I did so for Mingma, and he seemed pleased with the level of my gratitude. I also gave him my −40°F Marmot down sleeping bag and the portable DVD player we had shared during my stay at EBC. I asked Mingma about his post-Everest plans as we sat next to my tent saying our good-byes. He said he would probably guide some other climbs after the monsoon season. In a culture where most men made three dollars a day carrying freight on their backs, Mingma could collect several hundred dollars for a month of guiding. But May would be the month I'd worry most for Mingma as he returned each year to Everest. I will remember our time together at the top of the world, how he shook my hand then abandoned the gesture for a full-out hug. We shared something timeless as partners in the Grand Wager, and we will forever be connected in the Ozone Brotherhood.[5]

Jangbu assigned a young Sherpa to escort Ty and me as far as the airstrip at Lukla. We ordered fried chicken for lunch at a teahouse then waited while the cook harvested a bird that never saw it coming. We took time to snap photos and spin every prayer wheel we passed. At one point, an old Sherpa woman approached me while I rested

---

5   Mingma's home was destroyed in the same 2015 earthquake that destroyed the Hillary Step. Upon discovering this, I raised the funds and work party to rebuild it, and we traveled to his village of Phortse in October of that same year to begin construction. Mingma and his family moved into their new home in January of 2016.

on her stone wall, curious about the iPod I was fidgeting with. I placed a speaker bud in her left ear and selected "The Longer I Run," by Peter Bradley Adams. She smiled broadly, painting a horizontal stripe in the space above us with her open hand. To her, the music was suddenly everywhere. A moment later, the Sherpa woman directed my attention to a small goat standing next to her home. A trade was being offered. I smiled, nodding no. Then I removed the ear bud and patted her weathered hand. She took my hand and bowed to meet her forehead with the back of it, a deeply personal gesture in the Sherpa culture.

The Air Force climbers had left EBC the day before. Four of the six had summited Everest. Collectively, the team had now summited each of The Seven Summits in honor of the servicepeople who had fallen since September 11, 2001. They had struggled through the entire epic adventure to find the funds and support for each mountain—in some cases taking out second mortgages. At times met with indifference by commanding officers, they were now going home heroes. They represented all that was remarkable about the kind of person who served in the United States Air Force, and they had already been invited both to the Pentagon and to make various television appearances.

We shuffled into Lukla after three days more of trekking. That evening, we ran into Llama. He was wearing a soccer uniform and very intoxicated. "I have been playing the football, and now I am drunk to watch the football," he announced gleefully, gesturing toward the television at one end of our hotel dining room. Llama had worried about us each time we left EBC for the icefall. He liked to hug each climber, affixing what he saw as a protective shield. Seeing him finally relax and cut loose that night impressed upon me just how great a stress the past weeks had been for Llama. It had not just been the climbers or their families and friends. Everyone had lived this thing. Everyone. And now it was over.

We boarded our flight out of Lukla the next day. As it sped down the runway, I prepared myself for the drop off the cliff. I had read that aircraft here typically go into free-fall until the thickening air and airspeed combine to support proper flight. One last thrill. But we lifted off in orderly fashion with a few feet of runway in reserve. In an instant we were already cruising nine thousand feet above the lush green hills that tumbled down toward Kathmandu. I reached out to the seat in front of me and slapped Ty's shoulder. He just nodded without turning around. We both knew.

THE EVEREST LEDGER

Three days passed before our gear duffels arrived in Kathmandu from Lukla. In that time, Ty and I allowed ourselves the consumption of whatever food and drink seemed even mildly amusing. The French Open was underway, so we passed many hours watching it on the television in our room. Ty is a huge tennis fan, waking at three in the morning to see certain matches broadcast live. I watched mostly so I could entertain myself, floating fictional red herrings about each player.

"I understand Federer was recently photographed kicking a dog," I offered casually during his match.

"Sharapova has a dwarf named Juan Pedro in her entourage," I said as she took the court. "Always carries a loaded crossbow."

I frequented the hotel spa for massages, had my first shave with a straight razor, and caught up with my blog. The activity board in our hotel lobby offered various adventures ranging from zip line rides to river rafting. Ty and I passed on all of them. We were done. We just wanted to go home.

The four-hour flight from Kathmandu to Dubai delivered Ty and me into a world of modern amenities that hummed with vibrancy, even at one in the morning. Through some stroke of good fortune, Emirates Airline upgraded Ty and me to business class. I ordered a bloody mary as soon as the jet lifted off. The flight attendant brought us warm towels, shaving kits, slippers, and eyeshades. After breakfast, she made each seat into a fully prone bed with sheets and pillows. I settled in to sleep off as much of the fourteen-hour flight as possible, but my mind would not quiet. I needed to make a final accounting of things before critical information was lost in the comforts of the life I would return to.

Our team suffered the tragic loss of DaRita Sherpa. This sadness would be with us the rest of our lives. Frostbite injuries claimed a few toes and fingers. Pulmonary edema afflicted two team members, necessitating helicopter evacuation. One Hybrid Climber, a woman from China, suffered some manner of mental breakdown after descending from her failed summit bid. She had to be carried to the helicopter pad, despondent and limp. In exchange, twelve of twenty-three IMG climbers realized a personal dream, summiting Mount Everest. A fair bargain? Certainly not. How could it be? That said, most everyone involved would choose to do it all over again. Indeed, several later would. This is perhaps the greatest mystery of Everest.

But the costs of an Everest expedition cannot be viewed in sum any more than the benefits. Both reside on the personal ledgers of the individuals who chose to take part. For all the talk of "team," Everest remains very much an individual endeavor, with rewards differing climber by climber. Still the question remains as to what precisely those rewards are.

I have read the opinions of those who believe it is all done for bragging rights or status. This is pure nonsense. No ego is large enough to get a climber to the summit of Everest. Period. I will stand by that the rest of my days. One might show up with such designs, but Everest will quickly slap them to the ground. Better they should lie, say they climbed the mountain, and save the money.

Ironically, I found most Everest climbers, at least ostensibly, were climbing for someone else: a cause, a charity, a fallen friend. In as much as such rewards are derived, they probably take the form of quiet satisfaction. Admirable, but still not enough to balance the costs.

When I press climbers to explain themselves, the rewards are elusive, like sand passing through their fingers. George Mallory once put it this way:

People ask me, "What is the use of climbing Mount Everest?" and my answer must at once be, "It is of no use." There is not the slightest prospect of any gain whatsoever. Oh, we may learn a little about the behavior of the human body at high altitudes, and possibly medical men may turn our observation to some account for the purposes of aviation. But otherwise nothing will come of it. We shall not bring back a single bit of gold or silver, not a gem, nor any coal or iron... If you cannot understand that there is something in man which responds to the challenge of this mountain and goes out to meet it, that the struggle is the struggle of life itself upward and forever upward, then you won't see why we go. What we get from this adventure is just sheer joy. And joy is, after all, the end of life. We do not live to eat and make money. We eat and make money to be able to live. That is what life means and what life is for.[6]

---

6   Though this quote is widely attributed to George Mallory we were unable to identify the original source. It was most probably taken from a speech given in 1922 following Mallory's early reconnaissance of Everest.

For me, Everest was one of seven inflection points on my personal path. Along the way, I learned that a person does not come to believe in himself by climbing mountains, but by facing his problems. I learned that the only way to truly experience love is to risk your heart completely. I was shown the courage to live genuinely and the power of forgiveness. My path taught me to listen, trust, and act; to place the success of others before my own; and to value the potential for making a difference in the life of a child. But most of all I learned that every big mountain is really just a lot of little mountains, and they can only be climbed one at a time. What's more, your ability to climb today's mountain is largely dependent on whether you found joy in climbing yesterday's. I believe my summit of Everest was a reward for everything that preceded it, and somewhere along the way, I came to believe in myself again.

THIS IS HOW IT ENDS

Our flight landed in Seattle at 1:35 in the afternoon. Ty and I claimed our duffels in the international baggage terminal and accompanied them through customs. As he was connecting to another flight and I was not, we parted company at this point. It caught me by surprise that this was good-bye. I felt like I should have had something memorable to say, but my sleep-induced stupor left me as groggy and confused as Ty had looked when we met below the Hillary Step.

"Let's get together again some time and not do this," he said.

"Yeah."

We hugged and turned our separate ways.

I was riding the escalator up from the satellite tram when it occurred to me Lin would almost certainly be waiting at the top. I felt my senses lurch to life. I had spent so many hours imagining this moment, hoping it would not be diminished by the baggage of failure, and now I was seconds away from seeing Lin's sweet smile. I tried to improve the horrific state of my hair, but my hand trembled too much to accomplish anything. She would be in costume, as had been our custom. What would it be? A yak? The stairs began curling over at the top, and I could see the faces of the first few people. Then, straight ahead, a few feet back, I saw Lin draped in pink veils and exotic shawls. It was her own interpretation of a Sherpa woman, and though it looked more "genie in a bottle," I could not have been more taken. Lin held a sign announcing my accomplishment, our accomplishment. I gathered her up in my arms while the people next to us speculated aloud as to what "seven summits" stood for, and in that instant, all we had risked and any rewards that might follow did not matter. We were together and safe and done.

There were homecoming parties and speaking events. Another surge of donations came into my Climbing for Kids fundraiser, pushing the total past $33,000. My name appeared in the official registry of Everest summiters as David Jon Mauro, USA. Though not an ax-throwing Olympian, I had finally come to represent my country proudly. People wanted to know why I had done it, what the experience was like, and what I would do different. But most of all, people wanted to know what came next.

A year earlier, before I had even left to climb Carstensz Pyramid, Lin and I were gathered around a fire with several of the teachers from her school at a summertime potluck. A dog was chasing his tail on the lawn next to us, and it became so entertaining that our conversation stopped while we all watched. He chased it and chased it, stopping to catch his breath momentarily, then resuming the chase. I was feeling a little melancholy and commented, "I hope he never catches it. Life will be so disappointing after that."

There was a pause as this notion was considered, then one of the teachers asked, "So how about it, Dave? What about after you summit Everest?"

"I don't know," I said, having never even considered the notion. Then I realized the dog already knew the answer to this question. He had probably caught his tail many times, only to rest for a few moments then set about chasing it again. Because it wasn't the catching that drove him so much as the chasing. When the dog chased his tail, he was alive, engaged, and part of the great possibility that drives all of us "upward, and forever upward," as George Mallory said. And the joy that comes from the climb far eclipses the joy of standing on any summit. "I suppose I will chase my tail," I said with a smile.

So that is my answer. I will chase my tail the remainder of my days, listening for the call and seeking what lesson it holds. I will share these experiences and exist within their moments, always grasping for some basic truth.

Hope comes next.

Possibility comes next.

In the meantime, I will dream the dreams of a chubby kid, throwing an ax at a stump and eating crackers smeared with mayonnaise.

ACKNOWLEDGMENTS

I CHANGED THE NAMES OF THOSE CHARACTERS WHO exhibited unflattering attributes in the course of this story. In cases where I was not granted permission to use a person's actual name I likewise changed it...even though they may be perfectly lovely human beings who just don't respond to repeated emails and phone messages.

Were it not for Ty Hardt I would never have climbed mountains. Were it not for my third grade teacher, Mrs Morgan, I would never have become a writer. Both saw something in me that I did not, a switch they could reach out and flip, the result of which is the book you now hold in your hands. I thank them both and apologize to Mrs Morgan for eating classroom paste and vomiting on her desk.

Several brave souls accepted my invitation to act as readers for the painful early drafts of this book. John Hanrahan championed the personal tale that is woven throughout the book, while Marian Alexander could be counted on for the plain unvarnished truth. Dr David Netboy worked tirelessly to winnow away any clutter that diminished the core story, and Sue Luzzi showered me with encouragement when I felt like giving up. Susan Syferd Moore, my high school senior prom date, and her husband Bob took on the delicate task of coaching the manuscript away from bitter moments that weren't worth hanging onto. Dr Bruce Bowden, who followed my blogs through each climb, cared so deeply about this project that he slid the first draft of the final 10 pages back across the table at me, saying "It's not good enough. We (readers) deserve better." He was right. My longtime assistant, Sonia Alexis, listened while I talked through critical elements of the plot. I thank each of these people and promise to return the favor should any of them ever climb the seven summits and write a book about it.

The readers of my blogs were a tremendous source of energy throughout the climbs. I could see them checking in by the hundreds each day, voicing their encouragement and concern in the comments field. As these entries were posted in real time, neither the readers or myself knew what was coming next. I truly feel we climbed all these mountains together. So to those of you from Germany, China, Russia, the United States and Australia, to those of you from the Isle of Mann and Cayman Island, I say thank you. It was great having you on my rope team.

I am grateful for the sound counsel of my Editors, Chas

Hoppe and Amanda Martin Hoppe. Chas, who is too wise to be fifteen years my junior, sports a fuller beard than I could ever grow. I call him The Bearded Wonder (but never to his face). Amanda brought an important female perspective to the story offering keen insights into my character's development. As this is a self-published work I have no Agent to thank, but my best friend Chuck Blair often pretended to be my agent, suggesting I "work a vampire into the plot" or maybe some "gun play". Thanks, Chuck.

It is a certainty I would not have reached any of the continental summits without the superb climbers I teamed with. They were remarkable individuals who found room for kindness beside courage and intelligence within grit. They inspired me, fueling the journals that became this book and forming a club I call The Ozone Brotherhood; John Harris, Sam Satothite, Mark Anderson, Ty Hardt, Brian Burkholder, Dr. Richard Birkill, Ang Dorjee Chhuldim Sherpa, Zuwadi Martin Nguma, Mike Roberts, Phil Drowley, Guy Manning, Steven Novick, Carol Jean Masheter, Dennis "Deni" Verrette, Dan Zokaites, Dr Pal Morten Tande, Ivan E Gomez Carrasco, Rob Marshall, Andrew Ackles, Nick Ryan, Colin Merrin, Marshal Klitzke, D.G. Rogers, Kyle Martin, John Beede, Knut Heggland, Dan Meyer, Fraser McKenzie, Mingma Chhring Sherpa, Roger Snyder, Mike Chambers, Paul Niel, Greg Vernovage, Aaron Mainer, Max Bunce.

Thank you to the staff at Adventure Consultants and

International Mountain Guides. You showed an incredible ability to move people and supplies into areas so remote they are defined by the impossibility of doing so. There is no one better at what you do.

My mother opposed my climbing at first, then came to accept it, but never stopped worrying. She would stay up all night praying while I reached for a summit on the other side of the planet. Also a writer, she later pushed me to turn out a manuscript worthy of all that worry. Thanks, Mom.

I am grateful for my step-father, Jack, who supported my mother while I put her through hell. His keen insights to climbing showed in his questions. His calming effect showed in my mother.

My sisters, Michelle Cushman and Noelle Hardt, are as essential to this story as the existence of Everest. There were times I had no one else to turn to and they gathered me up in their arms. I thank them for accepting my madness and believing in my path.

I carried the ashes of my deceased brother, Danny, to the summits of the last six mountains. A tiny portion remains on each. It is possible Danny taught me more posthumously than he did during his lifetime; the fragility of life, the puniness of fear, and the rhythm of truth. Danny's spirit was always with me as I climbed and I leaned on it often. Thank you, Danny.

Whenever possible I called my sons, Trevor and Chase, from the summit. They waited for these calls through the tiny hours of the night and still keep the voicemails I left in those instances when we did not connect. Their love gave me strength. Thank you, boys. In my mind we stood together on every peak.

Linda Lehn believed in me long before I believed in myself. Her love, patience and understanding lifted me up out of the darkness and into the light of a new day upon peaks both literal and figurative. She is my climbing companion, though she does not climb, my most enthusiastic reader, though I read the pages to her aloud. Like my mountain climbs, Lin championed this book from start to finish. So to her I say thank you, my sexy stack of pancakes. I love you.

PHOTOS

Denali: https://photos.app.goo.gl/CKbe7NmoMkWi45FA2

Kilimanjaro: https://photos.app.goo.gl/0fS7dmeMJsi0pn512

Elbrus: https://photos.app.goo.gl/3DKqnUrc5GXaJJsm2

Aconcagua: https://photos.app.goo.gl/ZhhaL16VOHZLn8ai2

Vinson Massif: https://photos.app.goo.gl/hZmCk1xFO3zICmJC2

Carstensz Pyramid: https://photos.app.goo.gl/8xWzgMzOJBEwSli02

Everest: https://photos.app.goo.gl/5Mitfg2W2UHX0EP62

Improv and acting: https://photos.app.goo.gl/nlG89XfaUDt1PLC42

Website: davidjmauro.com

ABOUT THE AUTHOR

DAVID J. MAURO is a Certified Financial Planner®
who also writes for *Adventures NW* magazine and blogs
extensively on topics ranging from mountain climbing to
why sardines are safe. In addition, he is an actor who has
appeared in television, radio, and internet commercials and
in print advertising, and he's an improv alumnus of The
Upfront Theatre. David is the father of two grown sons,
Trevor and Chase, and he currently lives in Bellingham,
Washington, with Lin Lehn, to whom he is permanently
engaged.